T0364914

Harvard University
Center for Jewish Studies

THE PRIDE OF JACOB
Essays on Jacob Katz and His Work

edited by

Jay M. Harris

Distributed by
Harvard University Press
Cambridge, Massachusetts and London, England
2002

Library of Congress Cataloging-in-Publication

Pride of Jacob : essays on Jacob Katz and his work / edited by Jay M. Harris.
   p. cm.
   Includes bibliographical references and index.
   ISBN 0-674-00846-4 (cloth)—ISBN 0-674-00847-2 (paper)
   1. Katz, Jacob, 1904–1998. 2. Jews—Historiography. I. Harris, Jay Michael,
   1956–
DS115.9.K37 P75 2002
909'.04924—dc21   2001058195

Cover design by Duy-Khuong Van.
Book production and design by CDL Press, POB 34454, Bethesda, MD 20827.

Publisher: Harvard University Center for Jewish Studies.

IN MEMORIAM
JACOB KATZ (1904–1998)
PSALMS 47:5

TABLE OF CONTENTS

6 TABLE OF CONTENTS

PREFACE

In May, 1998, the world of Jewish scholarship lost one of its last giants, Professor Jacob Katz. The Center for Jewish Studies at Harvard University joined the rest of the academic world in mourning the loss of our frequent guest and teacher. Never again would this wonderful mind (and engaging raconteur) grace our lecture halls or enliven our conferences. The loss was great and keenly felt. A commemoration was in order.

As Professor Katz's *yorzeit* approached, we began plans for a conference to coincide with his second, devoted to a review of his multi-faceted corpus. It is indicative of the esteem in which Professor Katz was held that putting together this conference was an unusually easy task. Although scholars are sometimes loath to be distracted from their work, in this case the many scholars whose work appears in these pages—most of whom had never written on Katz before—jumped at the chance to participate in this conference. And each in turn produced an incisive treatment of his or her chosen topic. As a result of their gracious efforts, Katz's remarkable range and versatility became readily apparent to all; even those familiar with his work could only marvel when confronted with the near full menu of Katz's interests over a short time.[1]

I will eschew the common practice of editors and refrain from describing each paper in a paragraph. Such descriptions as I could produce would scarcely do justice to the richness that is in store for the reader. I wish to note only that, in the pages that follow, Katz's work is subjected to its fair share of criticism. Although some might deem this improper in a volume such as this,

---

1. The one major area of interest not discussed at the conference and not represented fully in these pages is Katz's work on Jewish nationalism. As our plans were coalescing, Katz's student, Yosef Salmon, published a paper on that very subject, and another treatment so soon after seemed superfluous. See Yosef Salmon, "The Historical Imagination of Jacob Katz: On the Origins of Jewish Nationalism," *Jewish Social Studies* 5/3 (1999): 161–79.

I am convinced that Professor Katz himself would not be among them. Katz was blessed to have had critics who engaged his work with the utmost seriousness and respect (with occasional exceptions among his peer group at Hebrew University), and his work was the better for it. Although his pen has been stilled, and no improvements will result from the discussions that follow in these pages, the readers' understanding of Katz's accomplishments will achieve greater clarity, precisely as they are set against the backdrop of the space he left to others to distinguish themselves.

I would like to thank all the friends and colleagues whose work appears here; I especially wish to thank Professor Israel Ta-Shma for all his help in planning the conference. Thanks as well to Dr. Michael Silber, who agreed to gather the photos that grace the cover. Special thanks to the Katz family for sharing these precious mementos with us. I would also like to thank Rachel Rockenmacher and Judith Bloomstein of the Center for Jewish Studies for all their work in making the conference a success.

I would like to close on a personal note. I came to know Professor Katz only in the last ten years of his life. Yet I will never forget how he generously opened his home to me whenever I was in Jerusalem. I will always treasure our leisurely talks over tea and cookies. His hospitality was exceeded by his generosity in sharing with me his insights into Jewish history and much more. For me, he was not only the model scholar and mentor, he was the quintessential *mentsh*.

Jay M. Harris
November 20, 2001

Rebel in Frankfurt:
The Scholarly Origins of Jacob Katz

David N. Myers
University of California at Los Angeles

Jacob Katz's stature as a towering figure of contemporary Jewish historiography was belied by his unimposing physical presence, elfin physique and small, high-pitched voice. But it was also belied by a set of qualities not usually associated with a scholar of his reputation—an uncommon modesty, a ceaseless curiosity, and a sweeping generosity extended to young student and distinguished colleague alike. Perhaps this rare combination of virtues can be traced back to his humble origins in Magyargencs, the small village in western Hungary where Katz, along with six other Jewish families, lived amidst the thousand or so Christian inhabitants.[1] Or perhaps these qualities were ingrained in Katz through his youthful travails as a foreign student seeking admission to a German university or his more well-known difficulties in gaining a professorial appointment in an Israeli university. Although there is something poignant in Katz's educational and professional struggles, there are few traces of self-pity in the man. In a retrospective moment, Katz demonstrated little regard for the fact that he was first granted a place on the faculty of the Hebrew University at the age of forty-five. Explaining his lack of bitterness, Katz simply averred: "Academic age is one thing, biological age another."[2]

Such magnanimity is not merely the product of a gracious man, but of a supremely confident man. Indeed, behind the placid façade of the undeniably humble Jacob Katz lay a fierce, and often contrarian, intellectual spirit. This spirit did not develop late in life, after Katz secured both recognition and honor for his work, but was present already in his first published essay—a withering review of a book proclaiming the historical inevitability of the

---

1. Jacob Katz, *With My Own Eyes: The Autobiography of an Historian*, translated by Ann Brenner and Zipora Brody (Hanover, N.H.: 1995), p. 2.

2. *With My Own Eyes*, p. 168.

decline of Judaism.[3] It remained a constant feature of Katz's work up to his final book, whose opening chapter excoriated historians afflicted with what he saw as the malady of postmodernism.[4] The intervening years between first and last publication revealed many incarnations of this fierce spirit, and perhaps for the better, since Katz faced more than a modicum of adversity in his long career. At the same time, the long passage from first to last publication exposed the shifting winds of historiographical discourse, as Katz moved from radical methodological innovator at the outset of his career to defender of scholarly orthodoxy by the end. The mission of this paper is to focus on the less well-known but formative stages of Katz's early career, highlighting a number of important and innovative themes in his work that have become pillars of Jewish historical scholarship at large.

I.

Born in 1904 in rural Hungary, Katz was compelled to learn to negotiate within and between competing cultural universes. The Jews of his town, although strictly observant, were not numerous enough to sustain either a synagogue or school. As a result, the young Katz studied in a local Protestant school in which he came to admire Martin Luther—to the point of deeming him "a most revered, almost celestial light," a sentiment bitterly crushed when Katz read Heinrich Graetz's portrayal of Luther in his *History of the Jews*.[5] It is interesting to note, though, that Katz was better able to gain a youthful appreciation for Luther than he was to win friends among his Protestant classmates. As he observed in his autobiography, the Jews of his village "had no social links to their environment; their contact with non-Jews was limited to business."[6] Clearly, sensitivity to the complicated nature of social and commercial relations between Jews and Christians came early to Katz, and would later inform his pioneering studies of medieval and early modern Jewish history (e.g., *Exclusiveness and Tolerance, Tradition and Crisis*, and *Out of the Ghetto*).

If Magyargencs exemplified a social dynamic that Katz labored to understand in his scholarly work, then Frankfurt am Main represented an important

---

3. Katz's review of Otto Heller's *Der Untergang des Judentums* was published as "Das untergehende Judentum" in *Nachalath Z'wi* 3 (1933): 219–26, 281–89.

4. Katz, "Historyah ve-historyonim, ḥadashim ke-yeshanim," *'Et laḥkor ve'et lehitbonen: Masa historit 'al darko shel bet Yisrael mi-az tse'eto me-artso ve-'ad shuvo eleha* (Jerusalem: 1998/9), pp. 11–45.

5. *With My Own Eyes*, p. 4.

6. *Ibid.*, p. 5.

variation of that theme. It was there that the tension between two core sensi-bilities in Katz reached their tautest point: the first, his ongoing commitment to a fully observant, halakhic existence, and the second, his voracious appetite for fields of study, scholarly methods, and languages that fell outside of the traditional Jewish canon.

Before arriving in Frankfurt, Katz became well acquainted with the yeshi-vah world of Hungary and Slovakia, in whose precincts he traveled from the age of twelve. Over the course of his studies, Katz encountered new trends in Hungarian Orthodoxy calling for increased stringency in ritual obser-vance. Katz's own father was swept up in this current, though the teenage Katz assumed "a firm stand against the new trend, particularly because of its negative attitude toward secular studies."[7] In fact, it was the pervasiveness of that negative attitude in yeshivah circles that led Katz to make his way to Frankfurt in 1928. Katz had every intention of continuing Talmud study, but he would do so in a setting quite unlike that of Hungary. The Frankfurt yeshi-vah to which he moved was inspired by the *Torah im derekh erez* philosophy of the nineteenth-century Neo-Orthodox rabbi, Samson Raphael Hirsch. Although calling for steadfast adherence to the precepts of rabbinic Judaism, the Hirschian philosophy maintained a proud openness to secular literature and culture. At the same time, Rabbi Hirsch insisted on a community of followers separate and distinct from the mainstream Jewish community of Frankfurt. After his death, leadership of the separatist community fell to the hands of his son-in-law, R. Solomon Breuer, who established a yeshivah based on the ideal of *Torah im derekh erez*.

Jacob Katz had encountered nothing like the Hirsch-Breuer community in his previous travels. The community was noteworthy not only for its bourgeois affluence, but also for its dual, and somewhat bewildering, com-mitments to a fierce intellectualism born of secular learning, on the one hand, and complete segregation from the mainstream Jewish community, on the other. Moreover, in the figure of Dr. Isaac Breuer, son of R. Solomon Breuer, Katz encountered a learned iconoclast who not only ably managed those dual commitments, but served as a model of integrity for Katz.[8]

Consistent with the precepts of the Breuer community, Katz was encour-aged to pursue an expansive curriculum of secular studies, including at the university. The major obstacle preventing him from meaningful progress in

---

7. *Ibid.*, p. 31.

8. It must be noted that Katz, already a budding Zionist, disagreed vigorously with Isaac Breuer's unrelenting opposition to Zionism. Consequently, Katz was explicitly requested not to discuss political matters with R. Breuer's sons. *With My Own Eyes*, p. 67.

this regard was his inadequate mastery of the German language. In order to
pass the external matriculation exam required for university admission, Katz
had to improve his command of written German. He began to work with
another foreign student in the Frankfurt yeshivah, the Moravian-born
Baruch Kurzweil, with whom Katz would go on to have a vexing relationship in Israel, culminating in a bitter polemic over the possibility of historical
objectivity in 1965.[9] But back in Frankfurt, Kurzweil was of great assistance
to Katz, helping him to achieve a level of German necessary for the matriculation exam.

Shortly thereafter, in 1930, Katz entered the University of Frankfurt. Up
to that point, he had covered a great physical and intellectual distance,
moving from small-town Hungary to cosmopolitan Frankfurt. In thinking
of this journey, one cannot help being struck by the fact that, at almost every
turn, Katz demonstrated a stubborn independence of mind that eschewed
commonplace assumptions about political or intellectual matters. This trait
made him an unusually discerning university student, particularly so for a
first-year foreigner with imperfect German. For example, Katz relates his
considerable pleasure at studying philosophy with Paul Tillich and Theodor
Adorno, but his strong dislike for Max Horkheimer, who, in Katz's eyes,
"seemed to lack any inspiration."[10] Katz's attitude was not merely a matter
of personal chemistry. Horkheimer presided over Frankfurt's Institut für
Sozialforschung, where adepts of the newly emerging Critical Theory attempted to rethink conventional philosophical, political, and cultural categories from a neo-Marxist perspective. Katz's own intellectual curiosity was
never drawn to the Frankfurt School, which makes understandable his great
reverence for a social theorist of a different stripe, Karl Mannheim. Katz's
affinity for Mannheim emanated from their shared Hungarian origins,
though Mannheim's background reflected the other, highly assimilated, end
of the Hungarian-Jewish spectrum.[11] As a young man in Budapest, Mannheim had fallen under the influence of the Marxist theorist Georg Lukacs,
but later foreswore his youthful leanings. In Katz's recollection, this act was
an essential step in Mannheim's "becom(ing) a sociologist who espoused a
method of empirical criticism."[12]

9. See D. N. Myers, "The Scholem-Kurzweil Debate and Modern Jewish Historiography," *Modern Judaism* 6 (1986): 261–86.
10. *With My Own Eyes*, p. 77.
11. *With My Own Eyes*, p. 78.
12. *With My Own Eyes*, p. 78.

Indeed, Mannheim's commitment to a scientifically grounded empirical criticism attracted the young Katz. By contrast, it was this commitment that drew the critical ire of Max Horkheimer.[13] Horkheimer attacked Mannheim's objectivist illusions in an essay from 1930, the same year in which both Katz and Mannheim joined the University of Frankfurt. Horkheimer's criticism of Mannheim may well have solidified Jacob Katz's dislike of the former and affinity for the latter, both on the grounds of intellectual disposition and, perhaps, out of a sense of tribal loyalty for his fellow Hungarian. In any event, Katz fell under Mannheim's sway soon after joining his Frankfurt seminar on the historical origins of liberalism. Mannheim had earlier published an important study on the function and varieties of conservative thought (1925); his seminar on liberalism was, according to another student, "an empirically oriented, interdisciplinary" extension of that earlier work.[14] Katz's own task in this seminar was to begin work on a collective project on Jewish assimilation and liberalism. This resulting research was to leave a deep imprint on his intellectual development. Indeed, the critical attitude he developed to modern liberalism became one of the conceptual pillars of his Frankfurt dissertation, "The Origin and Ideology of Jewish Assimilation in Germany."[15]

Apart from his encounter with Mannheim, Katz found further inspiration in the work of Hans Weil, another Frankfurt sociologist of Jewish origin. Before beginning to teach in the Department of Education at Frankfurt, Weil had written a doctoral dissertation at Göttingen on the origins of the German ideal of *Bildung* in 1927.[16] The dissertation sought to trace the emergence of

---

13. See Max Horkheimer, "Ein neuer Ideologiebegriff?" *Grünbergs Archiv* 15:1 (1930) and the helpful discussion in Martin Jay, "The Frankfurt School's Critique of Karl Mannheim and the Sociology of Knowledge," in his *Permanent Exiles: Essays on the Intellectual Migration from Germany to America* (New York: 1986), p. 70.

14. See the unattributed reference in the intellectual biography by David Kettler and Volker Meja, *Karl Mannheim and the Crisis of Liberalism: The Secret of These New Times* (New Brunswick, N.J.: 1995), p. 132. Mannheim jointly offered the seminar with the economist Adolf Löwe, and drew a diverse array of students and colleagues.

15. Written in 1933, this text was published in Frankfurt in 1935, a point to which we shall return later.

16. Weil's dissertation was published in 1930 as *Die Entstehung des deutschen Bildungsprinzips*; I have relied on the second edition with a new preface published in New York in 1967. Weil left Germany for Italy in 1937, and then settled in the United States in 1940. Unfortunately, little is known of Weil's subsequent life in the United States.

the ideal of *Bildung* out of German pietism in the latter half of the eighteenth
century. Rooted in the dual values of worldliness (*Weltlichkeit*) and inward-
ness (*Innigkeit*), this ideal found its chief expression in an elite cohort of
German intellectuals, a *Geistelite*, that served as a vital instrument of transition
between the traditional nobility and the new meritocratic bourgeoisie
(*Bildungsbürgertum*).[17] In tracing the path of this *Geistelite*, Weil melded intellectual history *à la* Dilthey with Weberian sociological tools. Thus, his intent
was not to delve into the earliest chronological roots of the *Bildung* principle,
but rather to attempt a synchronic study "of the interplay of individual intellectual concepts on one hand and socio-cultural constellations and recep-
tivity on the other."[18] As we shall see, Jacob Katz was much taken by the
subject and method of Weil's book in his own dissertation. In fact, he later
remembered Weil as "my guide to the structure of German society within
which the first stages of Jewish assimilation had occurred."[19]

   In general, the intellectual culture of Frankfurt, in which Jacob Katz found
himself from 1928, was a cauldron of ferment, particularly in the areas of
sociology and social theory. With the Critical Theorists, on one hand, and
Mannheim, on the other, sociology was subjected to new and innovative
approaches, building upon the earlier efforts of Max Weber to place that field
at the pinnacle of the *Geisteswissenschaften* (human sciences). Katz threw
himself into the swirling theoretical channels of Frankfurt, tending to the
more conservative political and methodological inclinations of Mannheim.
This tendency is on display in his first published article, in which Katz used
his recently acquired sociological prowess to attack Otto Heller's *Der Untergang des Judentums*—a book described by its author as "a historical-materialist
presentation of the overarching problem of the Jewish question."[20] Katz
rejected Heller's assertion that the Jews were an economic caste best suited
for a primitive economic order—and hence destined to assimilate into
modern society given their vanishing economic utility. Such claims of the
inexorability of Jewish assimilation were deeply misguided. Contra Heller,
Katz declared that even in the most extreme modern case: "There is no fall
of Jewry in Germany. There are only (individual) fallen Jews."[21]

---

17. Weil, pp. 5, 210ff.

18. Weil, p. viii.

19. *With My Own Eyes*, p. 79.

20. Heller, *Der Untergang des Judentums* (Vienna and Berlin: 1931), p. 5.

21. "Das untergehende Judentum," 288.

Notwithstanding that judgment, Katz chose to devote his early research precisely to the *movement* of Jewish assimilation in the late eighteenth century. In retrospect, we notice the convergence of several important intellectual vectors marking Katz's interest: his own personal experience of Jewish-gentile relations in Hungary and Germany; the provocative and unsatisfactory theories of Jewish group identity advanced by Heller and others (e.g., the earlier sociologist Werner Sombart); and the inquiry by sociologists such as Mannheim and Weil into the origins of German society at the cusp of Enlightenment.

We must also mention another factor that explains the salience and extraordinary sensitivity of Katz's chosen topic. On the eve of and during the Nazi rise to power, Jewish assimilation had become more than a matter of mere academic or communal concern. Rather, it was a matter of official state deliberation in an era in which Jews were beginning to be segregated from "Aryans." Because of the delicate nature of his subject, Katz was unable to find a publishing house (including the renowned Schocken house) to print his dissertation, with the sole exception of the David Droller firm associated with the Breuer community.[22] For a similar reason, Katz's nominal advisor at Frankfurt, the historian Georg Künzel, made a curious request. When Katz presented a complete draft of his dissertation to him in the spring of 1934—after Jewish professors, including Karl Mannheim, had been summarily dismissed from the university—Künzel asked that Katz add a disclaimer that made it clear that, despite his research on the origins of Jewish assimilation into German society, he *did not* regard assimilation as "the solution to the Jewish question."[23]

The disclaimer that Katz included in the preface to his dissertation made note of the fact that "the historic turn of 1933 had transformed the scholarly question (of assimilation) into a matter of great significance." Among other momentous effects, this turn signaled to Katz the end of the very process of Jewish assimilation into German society. But rather than facilitate dispassionate study of this stunted process, the "turn of 1933" invariably pushed Katz toward "an extra-scientific point of view."[24] Who could blame Katz, the devoted Jew and astute observer of Jewish life, for his strong interest in the tortuous path of German-Jewish integration? Still, it is quite striking to see a young Hungarian-Jewish doctoral student proceed with work on such a

---

22. *With My Own Eyes*, p. 95.

23. *With My Own Eyes*, p. 93.

24. *Die Entstehung der Judenassimilation in Deutschland und deren Ideologie* (Frankfurt: 1935), "Vorwort."

topic in Germany through 1934 and in an institutional setting singularly hostile to Jews. Was it the folly of youth? Was it Katz's status as a foreigner navigating between, but not fully at home in, parallel worlds, that of the Frankfurt neo-Orthodox and the Frankfurt sociologists? Or was it his confidence, borne of a firm Zionist faith, that he would imminently depart Germany for Palestine, and hence avoid both assimilation and its foil, anti-Semitism? Without dismissing any of these possibilities, we should not neglect another factor: Katz's intellectual audacity, a quality masked beneath his quite demeanor, but present from his earliest days as a yeshivah student.

II.

Sixty-five years after its publication, Jacob Katz's dissertation on the origins of Jewish assimilation hardly seems radical. On the contrary, it is rather commonplace to identify the late–eighteenth-century *Maskilim* as the transitional figures between tradition and modernity, as the first cohort of Jews to participate in a "neutral" (or later "semi-neutral") society.[25] Yet, the very vocabulary of a "neutral society"—and, moreover, the close attention to the social processes that underlay it—that have figured so prominently in subsequent scholarship received an initial airing in Katz's dissertation. Likewise, the sociological method Katz employed blazed a novel path in scholarly accounts of the modern Jewish experience. This method, with which Katz became acquainted in Frankfurt, had been refined over years of struggle between sociology and history, the latter of which had exerted a dominant influence on German humanistic scholarship through the *fin-de-siècle*. It may be helpful to examine briefly this disciplinary contest, since Katz's own method developed as a reaction to existing historical scholarship.

When Katz arrived in Frankfurt, an air of malaise had been hanging over the enterprise of history for decades. Even before the historian Ernst Troeltsch declared a crisis of historicism in 1922, the discipline of history had come under attack from at least two competing camps: theologians and philosophers, who decried the lack of holism and interpretive naïveté of historians; and empiricists of various sorts who bemoaned the lack of scientific rigor in historical method. Concurrent with this latter critique was the emergence of new modes of social scientific analysis—the *Sozialwissenschaften* (as distinct from the *Geisteswissenschaften*)—in German intellectual circles.

By the turn of the century, historians began to confront these new analytical modes. In one celebrated case, the German historian Karl Lamprecht attempted to transform history from its idiographic orientation, based on the

---

25. See the various references in *Die Entstehung der Judenassimilation*, pp. 25, 28, 32ff.

description of a single event, into a scientific enterprise whose goal was an historical typology drawn from a series of individual data.[26] Lamprecht was disturbed by the "micrology" of historical scholarship—its tendency to focus on the minutiae rather than the large structures of history.[27] His impulse to overcome the hyper-specialization of historical research, though challenged by many fellow historians, was shared by historically minded sociologists like Max Weber and Werner Sombart, who came to prominence in the first decades of the twentieth century. Weber set a new standard for theoretical sophistication and historical breadth in the emerging sociological discipline. In particular, his use of the "ideal type," rather than the individual datum, as a basic unit of scholarly investigation sought to lift sociology above the atomized state of history. At the same time, Weber's work introduced another sea change into the study of the past. Through books such as *The Protestant Ethic and the Spirit of Capitalism*, *Ancient Judaism*, and *Economy and Society*, Weber redirected the focus of research away from political and diplomatic developments toward economic, social, and cultural factors.[28]

The impulse to focus on larger social structures rather than particular historical details became a defining feature of sociological research. And yet, in seeking to differentiate their discipline from history, Weber and succeeding generations of sociologists were not anxious to dismiss the contextualizing work of the historian. For instance, Jacob Katz's own teacher, Karl Mannheim, recognized the importance of historical contextualization in his analysis of major ideological types (liberalism, conservatism, and socialism) that inform modern Western society. Moreover, sensing that the attack on

---

26. See, for example, Lamprecht, "Die geschichtswissenschaftlichen Probleme der Gegenwart," *Die Zukunft* 17 (1896): 300–11, as well as Horst Walter Blanke's discussion in *Historiographiegeschichte als Historik* (Stuttgart-Bad Cannstatt: 1991), pp. 397–98.

27. Blanke, p. 405.

28. See Guenther Roth's chapter, "Duration and Rationalization: Fernand Braudel and Max Weber," in Roth and Wolfgang Schluchter, *Max Weber's Vision of History* (Berkeley: 1979), p. 172. It should be noted that Weber's direction was not unique to Germany. In neighboring France, a debate was raging in the first decade of the twentieth century between defenders of the historical old guard and upstart sociologists. The latter, taking aim against what they saw as "German fact-grubbing," sought a more systematic scholarly analysis of past and present society. One of the chief representatives of this position, Emile Durkheim, called for sociology to supplant history as the chief method of investigation of the "human sciences," with the latter consigned to mere fact-gathering. See Carole Fink, *Marc Bloch: A Life in History* (New York: 1989), pp. 29–33.

historicism had gone too far in his day, Mannheim wrote a long theoretical
essay in 1924 underscoring both the ubiquity and virtue of historicism.[29] At
this point, the gap between sociological and historical method, which had
been widening since the turn of the century, began to close.

One of the hallmarks of Jacob Katz's mature career was his ability to bridge
the methods of history and sociology. And yet, as a young scholar in Frankfurt, Katz was intent on challenging the hegemony of history, particularly the
underlying assumptions of what he called "liberal (Jewish) historiography."[30]
In his dissertation, Katz set out to rebuff previous historians', particularly
Heinrich Graetz's, anxious embrace of Moses Mendelssohn as the harbinger
of progress after centuries of decline. Seven years after Salo Baron's famous
"Ghetto and Emancipation" (though without any hint of knowledge of it),
Katz echoed Baron's rejection of a post-Enlightenment Manicheanism
whereby the pre-modern world of darkness was set against the modern era
of light.[31] Thus, Katz noted early in his eighty-page dissertation that "(o)ne
cannot sustain the claim of intellectual stagnation in pre-assimilatory times."
To do so was to reveal a strong bias against rabbinic culture.[32] Katz's own
intimate acquaintance with the textual sources of pre-modern Judaism, as
well as his ongoing commitment to religious Orthodoxy, led him to regard
with suspicion the triumphalist view of modernity characteristic of German-
Jewish liberalism.

As noted earlier, Katz's critical reserve toward the modern liberal project
owed a good deal to his encounter with Karl Mannheim. Katz began to study
with Mannheim in a seminar on liberalism just after Mannheim had published *Ideology and Utopia* (1929). In that work, Mannheim does not appear

29. See Mannheim's analysis in "Historismus," *Wissenssoziologie* (Berlin: 1924), pp.
    246–307, or the English version, "Historicism," reprinted in Mannheim, *Essays
    in the Sociology of Knowledge* (London: 1952). See also Henk Woldring's discus-
    sion of Mannheim's essay (acknowledging its debt to Hegel) in his *Karl Mann-
    heim: The Development of His Thought* (Assen/Maastricht: 1986), pp. 103–19.

30. *Die Entstehung*, p. 9. For Katz, the emblem of this historiographic tradition was
    Heinrich Graetz, for whom Moses Mendelssohn marked the advent of Jewish
    assimilation into German society. Although Katz deliberately veered from the
    path of previous historians, he also assumed a course quite distinct from Jewish
    scholars operating under the banner of sociology at the beginning of the cen-
    tury. One thinks immediately of Arthur Ruppin with his statistically oriented
    analysis of contemporary Jewry.

31. Salo Baron, "Ghetto and Emancipation," *The Menorah Journal* (June 1928):
    515–26.

32. *Die Entstehung der Judenassimilation*, p. 10.

as a one-dimensional anti-liberal, but rather as a critic of the lifeless abstraction of idealism, which he cast as liberalism's chief philosophical expression.[33] Following his teacher, Katz was not an indiscriminate critic of liberalism. For instance, he did not believe that Jewish assimilation, nurtured by liberal ideas, prompted total "severance from the historical religion" of Judaism. But it did produce a gradual loosening of attachment to traditional ritual practices, as well as the characteristic state of social ambiguity of the modern Western Jew.[34]

Katz's unsentimental view of modern Jewish liberalism, and particularly of liberal Jewish historiography, was an important feature of his evolving intellectual personality. And yet, what makes Katz interesting is the presence of another, radically innovative, side to him. Though not yet armed with an articulate rationale, Katz attempted in his dissertation to move definitively away from an historical method rooted in what the French sociologist François Simiand once labelled *l'histoire événementielle* (event-based history). Katz *would* provide an articulate rationale for this method thirty years later in a well-known essay, "The Concept of Social History and Its Possible Use in Jewish Historical Research." There, he asserted that for both the sociologist and social historian, "ignoring details" was an essential requirement.[35] Rather than focus on the individual detail, both had "to observe the structure and functional efficiency of a certain society" by focusing on the general, representative, or typical features of that society.[36]

It was this methodological principle that guided Katz already in his dissertation. As against previous practitioners of *Wissenschaft des Judentums*, Katz eschewed the individual for the general, the intellectual for the social, the stark rupture for the subtle shift. Thus, in seeking to identify the origins of Jewish assimilation in Germany, Katz consciously ignored the efforts of single individuals in penetrating the surrounding intellectual culture. By contrast,

---

33. The first substantial piece of what would become *Ideologie und Utopie*, including an extended discussion of liberalism, was published in 1929. See Mannheim, *Ideology and Utopia: An Introduction to the Sociology of Knowledge*, translated by Louis Wirth and Edward Shils (San Diego: 1985), pp. 220–22. See also the discussion in Kettler and Meja in *Karl Mannheim and the Crisis of Liberalism*, pp. 15–25.

34. *Die Entstehung der Judenassimilation*, p. 49.

35. Katz, "The Concept of Social History and Its Possible Use in Jewish Historical Research," originally published in *Scripta Hierosolymitana* 3 (1956), and republished in Katz, *Emancipation and Assimilation: Studies in Modern Jewish History* (Westmead, England: 1972), p. 178.

36. "The Concept of Social History," pp. 180, 182.

he focused on the conditions in which a social cohort resituated itself outside of an exclusively Jewish world. In this approach, Katz consciously drew upon Hans Weil's work on the origins of *Bildung*, adapting the key notion of a *Geistelite* to the late–eighteenth-century Jewish context.[37] Similar to Weil's argument in the case of German *Aufklärer*, Katz was intent on identifying the social conditions in which a Jewish *Geistelite* emerged.[38]

The challenge for Katz was to identify the point of "synthesis of Jewishness and the *Zeitgeist*." It was at that point that a "neutral society" or "third sphere" (as he later called it) took rise.[39] Unlike the historian Selma Stern, whose work he admired and quoted amply, Katz did not believe that this point was reached in the person of the early–eighteenth-century Court Jew, Jud Süß. Rather, it came in the midst of a broad structural change in German society. Katz's sociological perspective led him to focus on a number of developments marking this structural change: first, a previously closed host group demonstrated a new openness to share its way of life and thought; and second, a recipient group was prepared to embrace this new way of life and thought, including language, dress, and food.[40] These developments were accompanied by a more or less coherent ideology of change that reached fruition in the *Haskalah* movement. In Katz's scheme, this mix of structural and ideological change was reached in the late eighteenth century, when a Jewish social cohort was at last able to find its way into a non-Jewish cultural universe. Emblematic of this moment were figures such as Gottsched Gumpertz, Markus Herz, Moses Mendelssohn, Naphtali Herz Wessely, and David Friedlander. In a telling illustration of the new social world that this cohort now inhabited, Katz quoted Mendelssohn's salutation in a letter to Herder: "Moses the Man writes to Herder the Man, not the Jew to his Superintendent."[41]

---

37. *Die Entstehung der Judenassimilation*, p. 32.

38. Katz held that, among historians of his day, Selma Stern shared his appreciation of Jewish assimilation as a "slow process," especially in her *Der preußische Staat und die Juden* (Berlin: 1925). See *Die Entstehung der Judenassimilation*, pp. 12–13, 25.

39. *Die Entstehung der Judenassimilation*, p. 27. For a discussion of the "third sphere" that mediated between established Jewish and Christian spheres, see Katz, *Tradition and Crisis: Jewish Society at the End of the Middle Ages*, translated by B. D. Cooperman (New York: 1993), p. 222.

40. *Die Entstehung der Judenassimilation*, p. 8.

41. *Die Entstehung der Judenassimilation*, p. 50.

Despite this citation, Katz had little enthusiasm for Mendelssohn. At one point, he suggested that Mendelssohn's view of Judaism paved "the theoretical ground for the renunciation of the religious law."[42] It may well be that Katz's antipathy for Mendelssohn was exacerbated in the period in which he wrote his dissertation—at the advent of the Nazi reign, in which the Mendelssohnian vision of cultural ecumenism seemed so defeated. Or it may simply be that Katz objected to the overemphasis of previous historians in depicting Mendelssohn as a great prophet of change rather than as a representative figure at the crossroad of structural and ideological change in Jewish history. This latter idea is advanced in the closing chapters of *Tradition and Crisis*, first published in 1957, where Katz again links his vision of historical change to the convergence of social and ideological forces. In that seminal work, Katz affirms that the crystallization of a Jewish intellectual/spiritual elite around Enlightenment principles signaled the culmination of an important social transformation. No longer did Jew and Gentile interact with one another purely on a utilitarian basis. The new values of "enlightenment came to serve as a basis for social grouping" such that Jew could meet Gentile as an equal in intellectual conversation.[43] Katz would later elaborate on, and somewhat modify, this thesis in *Out of the Ghetto: The Social Background of the Jewish Emancipation* (1973), which offers a book-length treatment of the Jewish *Geistelite*.[44]

The focus on the mix of social and ideological factors also shaped Katz's intriguing study of Jewish-Christian relations in medieval Europe: *Exclusiveness and Tolerance* (1961). There, he repeatedly highlighted the tension and inevitable reconciliation between long-standing halakhic norms and dynamic social conditions. Although others have noted Katz's innovative use of rabbinic sources in these studies, it is important to emphasize a different point here: namely, Katz's persistent quest to identify the nexus between social change and ideological warrant—or in the particular case at hand, between "law and practice."[45] In a more general sense, we may say that this commit-

---

42. *Die Entstehung der Judenassimilation*, p. 68.

43. Katz, *Tradition and Crisis*, p. 221.

44. Katz, *Out of the Ghetto: The Social Background of Jewish Emancipation* (Cambridge: 1973). It is in this work that Katz modifies his notion of a "neutral society" to that of a "semi-neutral" society. *Ibid.*, pp. 50–54, 231.

45. Katz, *Exclusiveness and Tolerance: Studies in Jewish-Gentile Relations in Medieval and Modern Times* (New York: 1961), pp. 28–30. See *Out of the Ghetto*, as well as two studies that explore the historical dynamism of halakhah: *The "Shabbes Goy": A Study in Halakhic Flexibility* (Philadelphia: 1989), and the recent collec-

ment to embed ideas or ideology in a rich social context stands as a hallmark of Jacob Katz's scholarly approach—as well as an important shift away from many of his historiographical forebears, for whom ideas or laws stood sovereign over social activity.

III.

Jacob Katz did not possess the classical etiological impulse of the historian, who seeks to excavate the earliest-known traces of a later phenomenon. That is not to say that Katz was uninterested in origins. However, his excavations, in good sociological fashion, were lateral. Like Hans Weil, he sought to trace the point at which discrete social elites, armed with distinctive norms, overlapped; at that point, innovation and transformation occurred. Such an approach was largely unknown to previous students of Jewish history, even Simon Dubnow, who issued a call in 1925 for a "sociological corrective" of earlier *Wissenschaft des Judentums*.[46] As Katz would later observe, Dubnow fundamentally misunderstood sociological method as its foremost practitioner, Max Weber, had intended it. Dubnow's "organological" approach to the Jewish past, which assumed the indivisibility of the "national body," was "an almost perfect barrier against the sociological approach."[47]

One of the main tasks of the sociologist or social historian, in Katz's view, was to mark the spot at which an individual is no longer a mere individual, but part of an incipient movement. It was this criterion that led him to minimize the import of Jud Süß and emphasize figures such as Markus Herz, Moses Mendelssohn, Naphtali Herz Wessely, and David Friedlander. These *Maskilim* represented an "open group" prepared to enter the social mainstream by surrendering a number of particularist features of traditional Jewish life, such as the use of the Yiddish language and the predominant focus on talmudic study.[48] In so doing, they symbolized a drift away from traditional communal life that was accentuated in the next generation, when German Jews moved further, though not totally, from the distinctive *Lebensformen* (social norms) of Judaism.[49]

---

tion of studies, *Divine Law in Human Hands: Case Studies in Halakhic Flexibility* (Jerusalem: 1998).

46. Katz challenged Dubnow's use of the term "sociological" in "The Concept of Social History," p. 189, n. 27.

47. "The Concept of Social History," pp. 189–190, n. 27.

48. *Die Entstehung der Judenassimilation*, p. 8.

49. *Die Entstehung der Judenassimilation*, p. 7.

A later example of Katz's sociological, rather than etiological, search for origins can be seen in his well-known article from 1950 on the "forerunners of Zionism" (*mevasre ha-Ziyonut*). In contrast to previous scholars of Zionism, including the Jerusalem historian, Ben-Zion Dinur, Katz was not interested in exhuming vague and scattered allusions to Zion from centuries past.[50] Consistent with his method, he saw the emergence of Jewish nationalist sentiments as part of an incremental social process that commenced with the late–eighteenth-century Enlightenment. Whereas Mendelssohn and his contemporaries appear at the beginning of the quest for emancipation, the "forerunners of Zionism" appeared at the culmination.[51] What distinguished these figures—Rabbi Yehudah Alkalai, Rabbi Z. H. Kalischer, and Moses Hess—from any other Jew who had ever conjured up the idea of a return to Zion was not their ideational similarity or occasional communication with one another, but a number of other properties: first, the "common marginal position" they held within their respective national and Jewish societies;[52] and second, the impetus provided by this position not only to call for the return to Zion, but to search for an appropriate social vehicle to carry that idea forward.

Katz's attempts at clarifying the term "forerunners of Zion" were not altogether successful. It was not simple to make a convincing case for a cohesive social group of "forerunners" from the 1850s or 1860s, given their geographic dispersion and cultural diversity.[53] Nevertheless, Katz's interest in revisiting the idea of "forerunners" reflects his desire to move beyond a one-dimensional analysis of ideas to a more textured sociological reading of the origins of Jewish nationalism. This kind of reading, in turn, led him to grasp the tension-filled, dialectical nature of the social processes he was exploring. For instance, in the case of Jewish nationalism, Katz labored to show how the "forerunners" both accepted and rejected elements of the traditional,

---

50. See Katz's critique of previous scholars of Zionism's *Vorgeschichte* in "The Forerunners of Zion," translated and republished in *idem, Jewish Emancipation and Self-Emancipation* (Philadelphia: 1986), pp. 104–6.

51. See Katz's "The Forerunners of Zionism," pp. 110–11, as well as "The Jewish National Movement: A Sociological Analysis," also reprinted in *Jewish Emancipation and Self-Emancipation*, p. 99.

52. Katz, "The Forerunners of Zion," p. 115.

53. Yosef Salmon has noted that Katz modified his view of Kalischer's and Alkalai's role as "forerunners" in subsequent writings. See Salmon's essay on Katz's notion of Zionist precursors, "The Historical Imagination of Jacob Katz: On the Origins of Jewish Nationalism," *Jewish Social Studies* 5:3 (1999): 164.

divinely inspired view of a return to Zion.[54] And in the case of Jewish assimilation, he sought to demonstrate that the impulse toward social integration
neither spelled the complete disappearance of Jewish ritual observance nor
was absent in those who defined themselves as Orthodox or "Torah-true"
Jews. It is a measure of Katz's intellectual range and openness that he wrote
with great insight about the opposing ends of the spectrum of modern Jewish
identity, the assimilationist and Orthodox, and yet confounded conventional
assumptions regarding both.

His ability and urge to do so may well extend back to his encounter in
Frankfurt with two distinct universes—the sociological circles dominated by
assimilated Jews and the neo-Orthodox community inspired by Samson
Raphael Hirsch. An illuminating reminder of Katz's mediation between
these two worlds comes in an early review he wrote of a book entitled
Heimkehr ins Judentum. Written by the Frankfurt-born Simon Schwab, later
to become an important rabbinic presence in the Breuer community of
Washington Heights, this book represents a youthful turn away from the
Hirschian ideal of *Torah im derekh erez*. Rather than seek to accommodate
secular learning to Torah-true Judaism, Schwab argued that the Hirschian
principle was no longer valid. In its time, that principle was "a necessary evil,
halakhically speaking, a הוראת שעה (a temporary decree)."[55] Now, however,
the force of acculturation was so powerful as to require its renunciation, and
concomitantly, a return back (*Heimkehr*) to an insular Jewish world dominated by "Lernen." Personifying this "return" himself, Schwab had left the
confines of the Frankfurt community to study in the Eastern European yeshivot of Telz and Mir.

Having travelled in an opposite geographic and cultural direction, Jacob
Katz found Schwab's proposal to be little more than "dilettantism" (*Dilettantismus*).[56] Writing in the journal of the Breuer community, *Nachalath Z'wi*,
Katz offered a spirited defense of the principle of *Torah im derekh erez*. But in
doing so, he expounded a notion that resonated beyond the confines of that
limited circle. Not only was it naïve to assume that modern Judaism, Orthodoxy included, could remain insulated from the cultural currents swirling
around it. But the entire history of Judaism was full of—indeed, animated by
—encounters with the surrounding Gentile culture.[57] To cease contact with
this culture, as Simon Schwab seemed to advocate, was a form of atavism.

---

54. "The Forerunners of Zion," p. 111.
55. "Umkehr oder Rückkehr," *Nachalath Z'wi* 5 (1935): 92.
56. "Umkehr oder Rückkehr," p. 96.
57. This is an adumbration of Gerson Cohen's more unabashed position in *The*

Katz's harsh view of Schwab was rooted in his strong personal conviction that confrontation with a modern secular world and adherence to Jewish ritual commandments were not mutually exclusive. At the same time, Katz's vision of Orthodoxy as a product of modernity—no less than assimilation— developed into a firm commitment to integrate the study of "traditionalist" currents into modern Jewish history.[58] Although Katz readily acceded that secularization "affected the role played by religion generally," it did not "succeed in ousting religion nor in effacing the particular characteristics" of Judaism. On the contrary, it altered the visage of traditional Judaism to the point of creating new denominational camps, including Orthodoxy.[59] Hirschian Judaism, with its unapologetic allegiance to secular study, was one result of that reconfiguration. But so too were other forms of Orthodoxy, which, though far less open to secular study, still defined themselves in response to modern cultural and intellectual norms—as Katz showed in his highly empathic study of the Hatam Sofer.[60]

Through such insights, Jacob Katz came to understand that tradition and modernity need not be seen as polar opposites. Rather, they inhabited an historical continuum full of dialectical inversions.[61] Katz's own appreciation

---

Blessing of Assimilation in Jewish History (Commencement Address/Hebrew Teachers College), (Brookline, Mass.: 1966).

58. For a prominent example of this trend, see *Ha-halakhah be-metsar: mikhsholim 'al derekh ha-ortodoksyah be-hithavutah* (Jerusalem: 1992).

59. See Katz's 1968 essay, "Judaism and Christianity against the Background of Modern Secularism," reprinted in *Emancipation and Assimilation*, p. 125. Katz's student, Mordechai Breuer, offered an extended elaboration of this vision of Orthodoxy in *Modernity within Tradition: The Social History of Orthodox Jewry in Imperial Germany*, translated by Elizabeth Petuchowski (New York: 1992).

60. In this study, Katz argued that the "Hatam Sofer did not negate the value of engagement in 'external wisdom' (secular studies)," but drew the line at the point of philosophical inquiry. See "Towards a Biography of the Hatam Sofer," in *Divine Law in Human Hands*, p. 432. This point is further illustrated by Katz's student, Michael Silber, in his discussion of the descendents of the Hatam Sofer among Hungarian Ultra-Orthodox. Ultra-Orthodoxy, as Silber understands it, is "not an unchanged and unchanging remnant of pre-modern, traditional Jewish society, but as much a child of modernity and change as any of its 'modern' rivals." See Michael K. Silber, "The Emergence of Ultra-Orthodoxy: The Invention of a Tradition," in Jack Wertheimer, ed., *The Uses of Tradition: Jewish Continuity in the Modern Era* (New York: 1992), p. 24.

61. For a sense of this continuum, see Katz's distinction between traditional and modern societies in his 1960 article, "Ḥevrah mesortit ve-ḥevrah modernit," reprinted in Katz's *Le'umiyut yehudit* (Jerusalem: 1983), pp. 155–66.

of this dialectical quality is evident in the titles of some of his most important monographs: *Exclusiveness and Tolerance, Tradition and Crisis,* and *Jewish Emancipation and Self-Emancipation.*

What emerges from these books is the sense that historical change occurred less in time than space. That is, change did not result from the sequential supplanting of one event by another, but from a series of subtle social encounters within a given milieu. Even when Katz illumined these encounters through use of ideal typical models, they did not become mere swatches of stasis. His penchant for the dialectical would not permit this.

The novelty of Katz's sociological sensibility makes understandable his exclusion from the Hebrew University for a decade and a half (until 1949). For his outlook stood in sharp contrast to—even represented a critique of— the archive-based historiography of the University's Jewish historians, Yitzhak Baer and Ben-Zion Dinur.[62] Given the forcefulness and consistency with which Katz presented his views, it is no surprise that two of the major disciples of Baer and Dinur in Jerusalem, Shmuel Ettinger and Haim Hillel Ben-Sasson, felt compelled to defend the legacy of their masters by attacking the bold methodological tack taken by Katz in *Tradition and Crisis.*

And yet, over time, Katz's persistence, as well as the shifting winds of historical study, led to a new situation. He eventually gained acceptance in the Hebrew University, assuming important administrative posts and cultivating disciples within and without. In his wake, Katz's students have made important contributions to the study of "traditionalism" and Orthodoxy, as well as assimilation, in modern Jewish history.[63] Moreover, Katz's views of Jewish-Christian encounters in medieval times paved the way for studies of intercommunal relations that did not rest on theological animus.[64] Likewise, his pioneering use of halakhic sources considerably expanded the canvas of Jewish history, adding important and neglected dimensions to the perspective of his predecessors.[65]

---

62. See Myers, *Re-inventing the Jewish Past,* pp. 109–50.

63. Among the prominent students of Katz who have contributed to clarification of these terms are Jacob Toury, Mordechai Breuer, Immanuel Etkes, Israel Bartal, Michael Silber, David Ellenson, and Haym Soloveitchik.

64. I am thinking here primarily of Yisrael Yuval, whose controversial article on Jewish attitudes of vengeance and their absorption by medieval Christians, acknowledged Katz's *Exclusiveness and Tolerance* as "the most comprehensive and important study of Jewish attitudes towards Christianity." See Yuval, "Hanakam veha-kelalah, ha-dat veha-'alilah," *Zion* 58 (1993): 33, n. 1.

65. For an early appreciation of Katz's use of Halakhic sources, see Isadore Twersky's review in *Jewish Social Studies* (old series) 21 (1959), especially pp.

Few if any of Katz's disciples have replicated the sweep of his historical reconstruction. For that matter, few possessed the intimate familiarity with two discrete bodies of knowledge that enabled such a sweep. Effortlessly moving between the sea of the Talmud and the currents of modern European history, Katz ultimately completed a task that seemed at odds with his formative scholarly calling. That is, his early training prompted him to reject the narrative reductionism of previous Jewish historians. But he ended up producing a thickly textured *narrative* of Jewish social history that extended from the medieval period (*Exclusiveness and Tolerance*) through the early modern (*Tradition and Crisis*) to the modern (*Out of the Ghetto* and *From Prejudice to Destruction*).

This narrative reconstruction constitutes a unique—and ironic—achievement in twentieth-century Jewish historiography. In light of the marginal methodological and institutional position he occupied at the outset of his career, it is no small wonder that Katz became, by the end of his life, the most venerated Jewish historian of his age. Curiously, at both points in time, the historical discipline was facing a crisis of faith—in interwar Europe, as well as in late–twentieth-century Israel. In the first instance, Katz joined other young intellectuals in challenging the hegemony of historicism; in the latter, Katz sought to beat back the advances of "post-Zionist" scholars who questioned the conceptual foundations of Israeli historiography. In both cases, Katz proved to be an energetic, self-reflective, and often contrarian scholar. In fact, we might profitably conclude by calling Jacob Katz a conservative revolutionary—not in the same sense as the Weimar intellectuals who sought a third way between the paths of socialism and fascism.[66] Rather, it was Katz's constant mediation between the poles of tradition and modernity, as well as of assimilation and Orthodoxy, that calls this term to mind. Likewise, it was his early rejection of the tenets of "liberal Jewish historiography," paired with his implementation of a bold new methodological regime for the study of the Jewish past, that merits this designation. And it is this dual legacy that ensures Katz a prized place in the annals of twentieth-century Jewish scholarship.

249–51. Katz's student, Haym Soloveitchik, elaborated on Katz's use of these sources in "Can Halakhic Texts Talk History?" *AJS Review* 3 (1978): 52–196 and *Shu"T ke-makor histori* (Jerusalem: 1990).

66. On the conservative revolutionaries, see Roger Woods, *The Conservative Revolution in the Weimar Republic* (New York: 1996).

JACOB KATZ ON HALAKHAH AND KABBALAH

Israel Ta-Shma

The Hebrew University, Jerusalem

Jacob Katz lived to a ripe old age and there was no decline whatever in the quality of his work till his death at ninety-four. Katz blazed new trails in the study of Jewish history, in a variety of areas. One of the most interesting was his series of pioneering studies—there are six of them—on the historical relationship between halakhah and kabbalah. Five of them appeared almost simultaneously, between 1979 and 1982, and the last was published in 1984, when Katz was eighty years old. We will be concerned mainly with the first two articles of the series, "Halakhah and Kabbalah—First Contacts," published in the *Memorial Volume for Prof. I. Baer*, and "Halakhic Rulings in the Zohar," published in *Tarbiz* 50 (Jubilee Volume). Three other articles were devoted to "The Relationship between Halakhah and Kabbalah in the Generations after the 'Discovery of the Zohar'," one article with that title, published in *Da'at* 4, and two others concerned with specific examples: "*Tefillin* on the Intermediate Days of Festivals," in *Proceedings of the Seventh World Congress of Jewish Studies* and "Levirate Marriage and *Halitzah* in the Post-Talmudic Period," in *Tarbiz* 51. The subject of the sixth article, "Halakhah and Kabbalah as Rival Subjects of Study," is somewhat different; so I shall not deal with it here.

Despite the wide publicity achieved at the time, this series of articles aroused no reaction, positive or negative, and it had no echoes in subsequent historical research. In his 1988 ground-breaking work *Kabbalah—New Perspectives*, Moshe Idel devoted four lines to these articles at the very end of chapter 2, entitled "Remarks on Kabbalah Scholarship":

> Finally, the relationship between Kabbalah and such classical Jewish literary genres as Midrash and Halakha, has been largely neglected by modern scholarship, an outstanding exception being Jacob Katz's recent pioneering treatment of the relationship between Kabbalah and Halakha" (p. 16).

29

But no further information is provided and the results of Katz's pioneering efforts have remained unnoticed. As we all know, Katz's historical, religious, and social writings inspired detailed descriptions and summaries, as well as substantial discussions while he was still alive, and they continue to do so today. Some of those discussions were critical, others more friendly to Katz's ideas. Various historians took part in these discussions, some devoting important articles to his views on such subjects as the history of Hungarian Jewry, the history of Orthodoxy, harbingers of Zionism, Jewish-Christian relations during the last few centuries, and so on. However, his articles on the general development of halakhah in the Middle Ages and its interrelationship with society and environment, including his research on the relationship between halakhah and kabbalah in particular, stimulated no reaction and were not even summarized in succinct form. Katz was deeply interested in the history of halakhah; it was one of his research subjects all through his life, and he published extensively in the field, apart from his series on halakhah and kabbalah—but it elicited no response from historians, except for the excellent work of his student, Chayim Soloveitchik, whose work more than touches on Katz's theories. Most scholars' interest in, and understanding of, the subject are quite limited. However, it is surprising that scholars of kabbalah, too, have ignored Katz's series of articles. After all, these more than one hundred pages offer novel and interesting observations, carefully and precisely phrased, on subjects intimately bound up with kabbalistic literature. I am not a historian by profession, and certainly not a scholar of kabbalah, but I am deeply interested in the history and development of halakhah in the Middle Ages. For that reason, I would like to try and fill the gap myself, namely, to summarize Katz's views on the question of halakhah and kabbalah, and to offer a brief response.

The central, new issue raised in these articles may be summarized in a single sentence: How was halakhah integrated into kabbalistic literature of various periods, and how did the resulting mix, in turn, influence halakhic praxis? Katz's first two articles address the first part of the question, the other three deal with the "feedback," i.e., the influence of kabbalistic halakhah on halakhic praxis. As stated, I shall adhere to the first part only, that is, the ways in which halakhah was integrated into kabbalistic literature. Katz essentially splits this terse question into a string of more detailed inquiries: What parts of halakhah appear in kabbalistic literature? Can one discern any historical development in the integration process? What is the halakhic level of that integration—and of the person or group of persons responsible for it? Can one differentiate between levels of achievement in the course of time? What was the contribution of the integration to halakhic theory, if at all, and what was its purpose? How much creativity was involved? Were there any unique features in the kabbalists' perception of halakhah, beyond their special symbolic interpretation?

Katz's first article, "First Contacts," opens with *Sefer ha-Bahir*, the first book of kabbalah, and advances step by step, through R. Isaac the Blind and R. Ezra of Gerona, up to, but not including, the Zohar. The role of halakhah in the Zohar, which is the zenith of the study and its major desideratum, is the subject of the entire second article. The last three articles also deal, directly and indirectly, with the study of the Zohar, but are concerned with "feedback." Thus, Katz's research in the field covers the relationship between kabbalah and halakhah from first to last, from *Sefer ha-Bahir* almost to the present. His account of the overarching historical development of this relationship is as follows.

In *Sefer ha-Bahir* we find references to more than a dozen *mizvot* mentioned explicitly in the Torah. The book refers to them by name, cites one or more verses from the relevant biblical passage, and reinterprets them in a manner entirely at variance with the plain meaning and intention of the text—through "destructive" exegesis in the spirit of kabbalistic symbolism and its usual concerns. We do not know why these particular *mizvot* were selected; but it is quite clear that those chosen were *mizvot* to which the Sages themselves had already attributed some semi-mystical intent, such as the precepts of *tefillin* and *zizit*, which the rabbis claimed were worn by God Himself. This ancient interpretative substrate made it easier to introduce interpretations in the spirit of the new kabbalistic symbolism.

Two generations later, R. Isaac the Blind went farther and modified the closing-formula of the last benediction in the Grace after Meals,[1] basing his action not on halakhic grounds but entirely on kabbalistic considerations—quite an exceptional procedure in the traditional world of halakhah. The kabbalist R. Ezra of Gerona, who wrote a long chapter on the 613 *mizvot* and their rationale, adhered closely to those *mizvot* already "presumed" by the kabbalists since *Sefer ha-Bahir* to be open to kabbalistic interpretation. Indeed,

---

1. I do not intend here to go into details of the *halakhot* and laws that Katz discusses, but content myself with a few brief remarks. In this context, S. Abramson took a different approach in his book, *Inyanot be-Sifrut ha-Ge'onim* (Jerusalem: 1974), pp. 150–55, where he discusses the subject at great length and states categorically that the prayer in question is the Eighteen Benedictions and not the Grace after Meals; what the *Magen Avraham* had to say on the subject, Abramson believes, was exceptional. In this connection, however, Katz was right. At the time, Abramson was unaware of what R. Isaac of Acre wrote in *Me'irat Eynayim*, which clearly indicates the existence of an early tradition explicitly referring to the Grace after Meals, as Katz wrote.

those *miẓvot* did receive special attention from R. Ezra, but he also expanded and supplied kabbalistic explanations for other *miẓvot*, not previously held to be such. It is significant that R. Ezra concerned himself with the small, petty details of the law, even the most minor minutiae, to which he assigned regular meaning and function in the conceptual world of the kabbalah. As time went on, this tendency became more pronounced and the Zohar did not hesitate to take an active part in actually deciding the halakhah between two, or more, competing views. The Zohar contains previously unknown halakhic innovations, though Katz points out that not everything generally thought to be an innovation of the Zohar is indeed new, and that a considerable part of such "innovations" originated in earlier halakhic traditions.

When Katz initiated the discussion of how halakhah was woven into kabbalah, he took good advantage of his profound scholarship and thorough acquaintance with the world of halakhah, with its special concepts and unique patterns of thought. Presumably, it was the lack of these skills, or of most of them, that prevented previous scholars from entering this field of research; they tacitly assumed that halakhah and kabbalah reflect parallel and detached realms of thought and knowledge, radiating, as it were, parallel lines that never intersect. Here are, it was formerly conceived, two different views, or ideologies, of the content of the world of religious praxis, each view assigning a different conceptual significance to the same system of positive and negative *miẓvot*. Kabbalah, indeed, considers itself subordinate in all practical respects to the strictest commandments of halakhah, but, at the same time, believes the entire halakhic system derives most of its inner meaning from the kabbalistic world of symbols and entities. The differences between the two views lie in the field of ideas, thought, and symbol, and have nothing to do with the practical observance of halakhah, which is ruled, as all agree, by the absolute dictates of halakhah.

Katz disputed this supposed dichotomy. He showed that kabbalah incorporates many disputed halakhic questions and offers its own rulings, relating not only to disputes that had already—ostensibly—been resolved in the past, but also to disagreements concerning current issues. Moreover, at times its rulings contradicted the generally accepted ones, being reached in a new, specifically kabbalistic way, sometimes constituting an innovative, creative approach to halakhah. Katz showed that kabbalah enlisted in its service not only general principles of widespread halakhah, but delved into its most minute details. In addition, as far as the sefirotic symbolism attached to them was concerned, surprisingly it accorded equal treatment and sefirotic importance to all parts of halakhah—biblical law (*de'orayta*), rabbinic law (*de-rabbanan*), and custom (*minhag*), regardless of the quite different halakhic force and status of these three components. According to Katz, the kabbalah considers

halakhah, any part of halakhah, to be meaningful only in its all-inclusive total-
ity, as a rounded and "finished product," in its accepted practice, ignoring the
many legal differences and nuances in the background. Katz rightly stresses
that it is here, in relation to the small details of the *miẓvot*, that the attitudes
of philosophers to the world of halakhah differ essentially from those of the
kabbalists. Although medieval philosophers also considered themselves subordinate to halakhah and its dictates, endeavoring to explain the underlying
reasons for various *miẓvot* and assign them a rational meaning, they could not
consistently explain the myriad minutiae of the *miẓvot*—those fine details that
make up the main content and significance of each *miẓvah* but, for the philos-
opher, must remain obscure and unexplainable, as Maimonides explicitly
admits in his *Guide of the Perplexed*. The kabbalists, on the other hand, joyfully
embraced all those details, considering them all of equal and precise sefirotic
importance, without arranging them in any hierarchy of intrinsic significance. By thus penetrating to the most basic substrate, as it were, of the
halakhic system, by assigning value and meaning to each and every detail of
religious observance, major or minor, the kabbalists showed no hesitation—
and, in fact, succeeded in an almost natural way—in innovating hitherto
unknown details and gestures, playing a creative, original role in renewing the
theoretical and practical aspect of halakhah.

At this point, Katz observes: "From now on, we are justified in asking
whether, in such innovations, halakhic considerations played any part whatever, or whether they fell by the wayside as a consequence of the proclivity
to kabbalistic interpretation" (p. 43). After discussing several issues and
examples, Katz reaches the conclusion that the motive for this creativity came
exclusively from the force of kabbalistic exegesis; halakhic considerations
were never brought into play by the author of the Zohar, who, Katz believes,
was a rather mediocre halakhist who never achieved the level of a halakhic
authority. That is why one finds various well-known examples in the Zohar
of religious laws diametrically opposed to accepted talmudic tradition—
serious deviations regarding which, in Katz's words, "no great halakhic
authority would ever have erred…, even when half asleep" (p. 50).

Katz's views of the matter may thus be summarized as follows. In a gradual
process, which lasted about one hundred years, from the first advent of
kabbalah on the historical stage in *Sefer ha-Bahir*, at the end of the twelfth
century, till the completion of the Zohar at the end of the thirteenth century,
the new movement of kabbalah became increasingly involved, qualitatively
as well as quantitatively, in halakhic matters. At the first stage, kabbalists
assigned mystical significance to an increasing number of *miẓvot* in the framework of kabbalistic symbolism; next, they totally brought to their domain the
entire body of halakhah as practiced in real life, with no consideration for the

inner hierarchy of biblical, rabbinic, and customary law; eventually they had no scruples even about changing the wording of benedictions on the basis of kabbalistic considerations and ruling on various disputes and practices. At the end of the process they acted quite independently, feeling free to create new halakhic details and new ceremonies—driven not by halakhic pretensions, but by motives and interests stemming from kabbalistic interpretation. Kabbalah, as it were, appropriated halakhah from the outside, without any inner authority or ability based on halakhic proficiency.

Notwithstanding the superficial purport of the thesis, the main importance and significance of those views pertain, I believe, primarily to the history of halakhah in the period of the Zohar and later on, and not so much to the history of kabbalah. This was indeed Katz's intention, for he was concerned all his life with the various social and religious aspects of the study of halakhah, whereas kabbalah interested him only as far as it affected those aspects of halakhah. Nevertheless, a more careful look at the conclusions of his research may reveal further directions of inquiry that may well lead to important historical conclusions in the area of kabbalah research.

A central issue in Katz's general approach to the relationship between halakhah and kabbalah is the extent of creative innovation to be found in the Zohar. In the course of his research, Katz proposed two mutually contradictory findings; he, himself, realized the inner tension between them, but nevertheless insisted that they coexist, complementing, rather than contradicting, each other. On the one hand, he maintained that halakhic creativity—that is, the creation of new ritual and halakhic details, unprecedented in the past—was the peak of the kabbalah's active intervention in the world of halakhah. However, on the other, there was the argument, or rather discovery, that many innovations normally credited to kabbalah are actually ancient traditions, although it is not always easy to trace them today in pre-zoharic literature and one must sometimes simply rely on impressions.

On the face of it, the second thesis cancels out the first, for, if it is true, there is no longer any measure of innovation present. Katz was aware of the apparent contradiction and, therefore, phrased his double thesis as follows:

> Even if a careful examination should prove that many rulings attributed
> to the Zohar have their sources elsewhere, and the Zohar only put its
> stamp on them and promoted their dissemination, it is still true that it
> considerably expanded the scope of ritual and ruled concerning *hala-
> khot* that were questionable or disputed prior to its time.

This rather tepid formulation is not necessarily correct. Indeed, if the origin of those laws, customs, and ritual details is elsewhere, their being mentioned in the Zohar does not necessarily imply any zoharic ruling, "stamp," or the like. All it implies is that those laws, etc., were practiced in the social circle of the author of the Zohar, and that what is reflected in the Zohar is the accepted practice of his cultural and halakhic environment, not his personal halakhic rulings. It should be noted that halakhic matters figure in the Zohar only as required by the kabbalistic content invested in them, and most of them are referred to only in passing. In such cases it seems clear that no deliberate halakhic ruling on any level is involved, but only existing circumstances. After all, it was Katz, himself, who always stressed the secondary role of the great luminaries of Jewish scholarship in the development of halakhah, in contrast to the decisive role of traditional Jewish society, which, guided by an inner religious sensitivity, carefully sifted out the permitted from the forbidden, discarding some practices and admitting others, thus itself determining halakhic norms. Only after such customs had taken root and become common practice among the many, were they brought to the professional, authoritative attention of halakhic luminaries, who generally tended to sanction accepted customs—though at times improving upon them or, more rarely, abolishing them. So why should we interpret halakhic matters in the Zohar as straightforward halakhic rulings, rather than reflections of generally accepted norms?

The following simple illustration should suffice. Katz devoted an entire article to the history of wearing *tefillin* on the intermediate days of a festival—one of the series of six articles under discussion here. He points out that R. Isaac Caro, uncle of R. Joseph Caro, who lived in the last generation before the expulsion from Spain, wrote that the universal practice in Spain was to follow the rulings of R. Asher b. Jehiel (the Rosh), who wore *tefillin* on the Intermediate Days; however, ever since Spanish scholars found an injunction in the Zohar forbidding the practice, they rejected the Rosh's ruling. This is, indeed, a good example of the considerable authority attributed by some scholars to the Zohar in Spain during the second half of the fifteenth century. However, Katz's assertion that "the ruling of the Zohar in the matter of *tefillin* on the Intermediate Days of festivals received attention at an early stage" is untenable. Katz, himself, shows in the same article that, although the Rosh's ruling agrees with the halakhic tradition of Franco-Germany, all the great Spanish scholars, up to and including the Rosh's lifetime, unanimously agreed that one should not wear *tefillin* on the Intermediate Days; it was the Rosh who changed the ancient Spanish practice from his time on, by virtue of his great personal and public authority. The Zohar, however, which was written around the time of Nahmanides, followed the accepted usage of all Spanish scholars up to and including its own time, thus forbidding *tefillin* on the Intermediate Days in conformity with what was customary in that part of the Jewish world. It seems self-evident that the Zohar was by no means

ruling or settling some previous controversy, but simply expressing what was
accepted at that time. The author of the Zohar could not, of course, have
known that the Rosh would come to Spain some thirty or forty years later,
reject the accepted Spanish custom, and reverse the ruling. Only scholars of
later generations, such as R. Isaac Caro, on the eve of the expulsion, who
were familiar with the Rosh's practice as that of their own country, might
have regarded the zoharic injunction as a halakhic ruling that could reverse
an existing situation.

To return to our main inquiry, how much innovation is discernible in the
halakhic component of the Zohar, that halakhic—or semi-halakhic—component for which we know of no literary or other precedent, and that may
be considered the Zohar's own creation and what is the real extent of that
component? Now, despite the importance of this question, I believe a much
more important question needs to be asked. It concerns the halakhic component of the Zohar that is clearly derived from some source outside the Zohar,
whether by way of halakhic ruling as seen by Katz, or as an accepted practice
of the environment, as might be argued were it not for Katz's work. Can one
point to some common source for those practices or, at least, to some underlying basis common to all or most of them? Or were these elements culled
from different sources and simply admitted if they agreed with the needs of
the appropriate kabbalistic interpretation? Katz did not deal with this important question, which will occupy us in what follows.

Truth to tell, the fifteen examples that Katz adduced to demonstrate the
existence of an earlier source for *halakhot* previously believed to have been
innovated by the Zohar all originate in Ashkenazi custom and in halakhic
literature written in the sphere of Franco-German Jewish culture. Katz did
not notice this point (or ignored it as accidental and insignificant), being
troubled, rather, by a question of principle: How could the Zohar, written
by Moses de Leon in Spain, have drawn on an Ashkenazi source? As he wrote,
after claiming that a single example could be shown to have possibly been
derived from an Ashkenazi source: "The Zohar's adoption of what was
probably an Ashkenazi custom [namely, that the levites wash the priests'
hands before the priestly blessing – I.T.S.] should not surprise us, for many
Ashkenazi customs were known before that time in Spain, as will be demonstrated in the following case"—namely, the recitation of the words *el melekh
ne'eman* before the *Shema*, a subject that I had already dealt with in much detail
and associated with the Zohar, and Katz, indeed, cited my work to prove his
point. However, as already noted, not only these two but all Katz's examples
of early origins come from Franco-Germany. I decided to examine that phenomenon in depth.

I quickly realized that a proper examination could not be carried out without a thorough check of the whole book of the Zohar, to locate all its submerged halakhic matters, including questions of liturgy, which actually demand separate treatment. Since such an extensive project was out of the question, I confined myself to the explicit occurrences of such themes in the Zohar, the result being my short book *Ha-Nigleh sheba-Nistar*. That inquiry clarified the extent to which Ashkenazi rite figures in the Zohar. The basic halakhah of the Zohar is unmistakably Spanish, almost always following Maimonides. This is the case, for example, for the aforementioned injunction against wearing *tefillin* on the intermediate days of festivals; the same holds true for the basic liturgy of the Zohar. Nevertheless, there are many details of laws and rules occurring in the Zohar that originate in Ashkenazi practice and in Franco-German rabbinic literature.[2]

The phenomenon in question clearly indicates the degree of Ashkenazi influence on the circle of the Zohar—not ideological, philosophical, or mystical influence in any way, but the immediate, practical influence of everyday religious ritual, whose myriad of details forms what is usually known as "Ashkenazi custom." Although I am by no means arguing that all Ashkenazi custom, with all its details and minutiae, was absorbed into the Zohar —and there is certainly no proof of such extensive absorption—we, nevertheless, have a large body of Franco-German life experience inside Spain. This is, to my mind, the most important message to emerge from the analysis of Katz's series of articles, although it appears there not explicitly but implicitly.[3]

I have referred to Katz's central observation that the kabbalists concerned themselves with halakhah in its final form, as actually practiced, paying little attention to underlying theoretical elements; they considered it a single, unified corpus, homogeneous in structure, with equal strength and importance attributed to general principles and details alike. They assigned precise kabbalistic-sefirotic meanings to all components of the relevant *halakhah* in equal degree, completely ignoring the tripartite hierarchic structure and inner subdivision of halakhah according to levels of strictness—biblical law, rabbinic law, and custom. This approach rightly surprised Katz, for any person

---

2. After *Ha-Nigleh sheba-Nistar* had been published, I found further very interesting examples of the phenomenon. I published them in two articles that appeared in the English-language journal *Kabbalah*.

3. In *Ha-Nigleh sheba-Nistar* I wrote at length on the broader significance of this discovery for our understanding of the background and immediate message of the Zohar. I also note further points of contact between the Zohar and various Ashkenazi elements reflected in it. In this essay, however, I am concerned solely with the content of Katz's research and my reaction.

doing so reveals himself to be not much of a scholar, someone unprepared or incapable of considering every law against the background of the underlying, complex scholarly debate. Rather, such an individual is "taking a shortcut" to mystical-symbolic interpretation by treating all components equally. If I am not mistaken, this approach was the main basis for Katz's conclusion that the author of the Zohar was not an accomplished scholar. However, the difficulty inherent in Katz's conclusion is the tremendous familiarity with the Talmud and the midrash obvious on every page of the Zohar. True, this familiarity mostly relates to aggadic material, in which case we could view the author of the Zohar to be someone well-versed in aggadah, yet not a professional scholar, as seen by his avoiding complicated and superfluous analyses of halakhic issues. This is, more or less, Katz's conclusion.

I believe that the solution to this rather perplexing situation is quite different. Basically, the zoharic approach to halakhah is typical of the Ashkenazi halakhist, which is quite different from the widespread classical, geonic-Spanish, approach. The world of Ashkenazi halakhah assigned a very important place to custom, far beyond that implied by the usual talmudic norm, which treats custom as the lowest rung on the ladder of halakhic importance. In the Ashkenazi world of values, however, custom heads the hierarchy, in the simple sense that it has the power to supplant accepted law, in the spirit of the rule "Custom circumvents the law."[4] The common talmudic hierarchy—biblical, rabbinic, custom—expresses the level of severity from the standpoint of punitive measures, that is, the attitude toward a person who transgresses the law; it does not reflect the degree of importance of the individual details of the *miẓvah* for a person who observes it faithfully. With regard to this positive aspect, custom had pride of place; in essence, it was observance of the traditions of ancestral custom, passed down from one generation to the next in all their minute details, that constituted religious observance—not observance of the specific law *per se*. In different places, where the observance of a given *miẓvah* was governed by different customs, local Jews were obligated to observe it in exactly the same way as their ancestors had observed it there, unchanged. This approach was a radical mental about-face for anyone schooled in the classical talmudic way of thinking, as well as its later manifestations in geonic literature and the works of the Spanish authorities, from Maimonides to the *Shulḥan Arukh*. On the other hand, it represents an elementary religious-cultural reality for anyone familiar with

---

4. I discussed this principle at great length in my book *Minhag Ashkenaz ha-Kadmon* ("Early Franco-German Ritual and Custom"), where I pointed out that the basis for this approach came from Eretz Israel and where I elaborated upon its historical and literary background.

medieval Franco-German rabbinic literature—its implications are still with us to this day in the Ashkenazi Haredi society.

Within the confines of this essay I cannot possibly relate the entire extent of the Ashkenazi approach. However, a few words should suffice to resolve much of the surprise expressed by Katz. In the classical Ashkenazi perception, custom does not reflect folkloristic episodes and popular culture—these are viewed by halakhah with some disdain and treated, at best, patiently. On the contrary, custom as prevalent among the people is the main content of each *mizvah*; the slightest deviation from custom is forbidden, even if it seems to contradict halakhah. In fact, the basic form of every *mizvah* is the form in which it is observed in that particular place. Essentially, Katz's observation of the unscholarly nature of zoharic halakhah is the best illustration of the Ashkenazi character of the zoharic world of halakhah.

Jacob Katz on Jews and Christians in the Middle Ages

David Berger
Brooklyn College and the Graduate Center, CUNY

Few scholars indeed have produced seminal works of abiding value in areas outside their primary field of expertise. Jacob Katz's *Exclusiveness and Tolerance*, which is precisely such a work, is remarkable testimony to the power of wide learning, penetrating insight, and exceptional instincts to overcome significant lacunae in the author's command of relevant material.[1] Katz was not a medievalist; he was not deeply conversant with Christian sources; and he did not study the full range of Jewish texts relevant to the relationship between medieval Christians and Jews. Thus, Christian works play virtually no role in any facet of his analysis. His discussion of the motivation of Christian converts to Judaism, for example, makes no reference to the one memoir by such a convert that addresses this question explicitly, and his assertion that the doctrine of Jewish toleration was not fully worked out until Aquinas provides a somewhat misleading impression that probably results from lack of familiarity with earlier texts by churchmen of lesser renown. Apart from the famous Paris disputation, to which he devotes an important chapter, he makes virtually no use of Jewish polemical literature, so that we find precisely one reference to *Sefer Yosef ha-Meqanne*, the central polemical text in thirteenth-century France, and no reference at all to the *Niẓẓaḥon Vetus*, a major compilation of anti-Christian arguments in medieval Ashkenaz, which is the

---

1. The English version was published by Oxford University Press in 1961. The Hebrew, *Bein Yehudim le-Goyim* (Jerusalem: 1960), appeared earlier but, according to the preface, was written later and hence, says Katz, takes precedence. In a number of quite important instances, the Hebrew is superior not because of revisions but because at that point Katz's command of written English was not fully adequate to the task and whoever assisted him did not always capture the necessary nuances.

41

sphere of culture standing at the center of his work.[2] Yet this little volume, described by Katz himself as a collection of essays rather than a sustained study, has deservedly become the starting point for all serious discussion of Jewish approaches to Christianity in medieval Europe.

When a scholar writes a book about a subject that he is not fully trained to address, the question of motivation arises in more acute fashion than usual. I strongly suspect that Katz was drawn to this theme as a result of a religious concern that he acknowledges and an ethical one that he downplays. His autobiography describes the inner struggles of Orthodox Jewish university students in interwar Germany. "The dilemma for most of my fellow students seemed to be rooted in a sense of contradiction between the Jewish tradition by which they lived and the scientific concepts and universal values encountered during their academic studies. The apologetic efforts of Orthodox Judaism…were aimed at creating an ideology to bridge this abyss."[3] He maintains, however, that he himself was not bothered by the discrepancy between traditional Judaism and an "external system of concepts and values"; his concern was with evidence for historical development within a purportedly closed, unitary tradition whose authority seemed to rest on its imperviousness to change.

Although I do not doubt that Katz was disturbed by the latter tension, I doubt very much that he was unconcerned about the former. It cannot be unalloyed coincidence that the theme of *Exclusiveness and Tolerance* unites both issues by examining the development of Jewish law with respect to the standing of Gentiles, perhaps the quintessential area in which Judaism was accused of violating the requirements of universal values. Rabbi David Zvi Hoffmann, the leading German rabbi in the late-nineteenth and early twentieth centuries, was impelled to write an apologetic work on Jewish attitudes toward believers in other faiths.[4] We now know that Rabbi Jehiel Jacob Weinberg, the distinguished leader of the Berlin Rabbinical Seminary at the

---

2. Although *Sefer Yosef ha-Meqanne* had not yet been published in its entirety, much of the work was available in print. See Judah Rosenthal's summary of the publication history in his edition (Jerusalem: 1970), Introduction, p. 32. The *Niẓẓaḥon Vetus* had been published by Johann Christoph Wagenseil, *Tela Ignea Satanae*, vol. 2 (Altdorf: 1681), pp. 1–260.

3. Jacob Katz, *With My Own Eyes: The Autobiography of a Historian* (Hanover and London: 1995), p. 82.

4. *Der Shulchan-Aruch und die Rabbinen ueber das Verhaeltnis der Juden zu Andersglauebigen* (1894).

very time that Katz studied in Frankfurt, was profoundly troubled by this problem.[5]

Moreover, Katz himself provides us with several indications of his own sensitivities and sympathies. He argues that a historian has the right to use the term "shortcoming" as an expression of moral judgment with respect to earlier societies without violating the principle that later values alien to those societies should not be imposed in the process of historical assessment. His justification for this position rests on the argument that even the medievals had some sense of a universal humanitarian standard, although they would regularly suspend it in the face of what they perceived to be the demands of their religion; it is precisely their awareness of such a standard that allows a historian to render judgment as to the degree of their fealty to it. One cannot help but wonder if Katz would really have avoided all moral judgment if he were studying a society that he considered bereft of any universal humanitarian concern. He appears to be straining to find an academically plausible argument allowing for the infiltration of an explicitly ethical prism into his historical analysis, thereby satisfying both his moral and his historical conscience.

In the last few lines of the preface to the Hebrew version, he allows us a fleeting glimpse into his hope and conviction that the book is not irrelevant to the issues of the day.

> The roots of contemporary problems extend to the far reaches of the past, and Jewish-Gentile relations even today cannot be understood without knowing their earlier history. A historian is permitted to believe that when he distances the reader from the present, he does not sever him from it; rather, he provides him with a vantage point from which he can more readily encompass even the place where we now stand.[6]

In *Exclusiveness and Tolerance* as well as his other essays on our theme, Katz saw himself as a rebel against dubious apologetics. He does not hesitate to state flatly that a key contention of Hoffmann's work arguing that medieval Jews had declared their Christian contemporaries free of idolatry is misleading.[7] In

---

5. See Marc B. Shapiro, *Between the Yeshiva World and Modern Orthodoxy: The Life and Works of Rabbi Jehiel Jacob Weinberg 1884–1966* (London and Portland, Oregon: 1999), pp. 182–83.

6. *Bein Yehudim le-Goyim*, p. 8.

7. "Sheloshah Mishpatim Apologetiyyim be-Gilguleihem," reprinted in Jacob Katz, *Halakhah ve-Qabbalah* (Jerusalem: 1984), p. 285. "Misleading" is an accurate but not quite adequate translation of the stronger original (*eino ella maṭ‘eh*).

the wake of Katz's analysis, it is difficult for us to recapture an environment in which excellent scholars affirmed that Ashkenazic Jews of the Middle Ages had utterly excluded Christianity from the category of *avodah zarah*, the technical term imprecisely translated as idolatry. Katz reminds us that such assertions were made not only in explicitly apologetic works; Hanokh Albeck, for example, in a major study of the Mishnah, asserted that the views of medieval Jewish authorities are encompassed in the position of R. Menahem ha-Meiri, which is, in fact, striking in its atypical liberalism.[8] At the same time, I do not doubt that Katz was impelled to study ha-Meiri's posture, which he describes as "undoubtedly a great achievement,"[9] precisely because it afforded him the opportunity to highlight Jewish tolerance without sacrificing scholarly integrity.

Whatever Katz's motivations, it is time to turn to the substance of his work. I would like to examine the scope of his interest in medieval Jewish–Christian relations, his methodology, his contribution to the state of the question when he wrote, the validity of his arguments in and of themselves, and the degree to which they stand up in light of later scholarship and the sources he failed to examine.

One of the hallmarks of Katz's approach, which has little if any precedent in earlier historiography, is the great significance that he assigns to instinct. Visceral reactions, he argues, can weigh more heavily than texts. Thus, Jewish revulsion at Christian rituals and symbols is no less important than formal halakhah in determining that Christianity is *avodah zarah* and inspiring the decision of martyrs.[10] Katz ascribes this emotional reaction to Ashkenazic Jews—correctly, in my view—despite his awareness that pawnbroking put them into contact with Christian *sancta* and produced serious temptations to relax taboos against benefiting from such presumably idolatrous objects.

Sensitivity to a different sort of popular instinct plays a major role in a later work in which Katz examined the evolution of legal approaches to the use of Gentiles for work on the Sabbath. Here again, he argues that texts can occasionally be subordinated to "ritual instinct," so that ordinary Jews will ask for permission to violate serious prohibitions that do not repel them while

---

8. On this point, Katz notes that even Hoffmann recognized the uniqueness of ha-Meiri's approach. See Katz, "Sovlanut Datit be-Shitato shel R. Menaḥem ha-Meiri ba-Halakhah u-be-Pilosofia," in *Halakhah ve-Kabbalah*, p. 191, n. 1.

9. *Bein Yehudim le-Goyim*, p. 128 (my translation); *Exclusiveness and Tolerance*, p. 128.

10. *Bein Yehudim le-Goyim*, p. 34; *Exclusiveness and Tolerance*, p. 23.

refraining from seeking dispensation to engage in behavior that is less objectionable to the legal mind but unthinkable in light of deeply entrenched emotions.

Standards for evaluating assertions about instinct can be elusive. Thus, I will sometimes be discussing my instinct about Katz's instinct about the instinct of medieval Jews. Evidence, of course, is not irrelevant to this enterprise, nor was it irrelevant in medieval discourse. One of Katz's great strengths is that he recognizes this. For all his emphasis on the primacy of emotions, instinct, and a sense of social identity, he is not carried away by his insight. It is only on the rarest of occasions that he loses sight of the interplay of these factors with more disciplined intellectual pursuits, whether theological or halakhic. Except in those rare moments, his work is a model of balance, as a supple and subtle mind reconstructs the delicately poised interweaving of unexamined, primal reactions, economic and social needs, and the reasoned examination of authoritative texts.

Even Katz's marginal, poorly informed discussion of polemic reveals this strength. Thus, he appreciates the significance of the intellectual dimension of what many observers have seen as static and uninteresting ritual combat and he points to the internalizing of anti-Christian exegesis as evidence of the deep Jewish sensitivity to Christian arguments. Thus, he says, both R. Joseph Bekhor Shor and R. Isaac Or Zarua assert that Deuteronomy 6:4 affirms not merely that the Lord is God but that He is *our* God, thereby proclaiming that no other nation can claim Him as its own.[11] Still, Katz does not regard intellectual arguments as the Jews' primary line of defense. They were decidedly secondary to the emotions of group identification and the attraction of Judaism's entrenched symbols.[12]

Katz underscores this approach in his more detailed discussion of martyrdom. Ordinary Jews, he says, martyred themselves not because of familiarity with the niceties of their halakhic obligations but because they had been reared on *stories* of heroic self-sacrifice.[13] Despite these observations, historians debating the roots of Ashkenazic martyrdom—and other instances of extreme behavior—are not as sensitive to this point as they should be. To take an example outside the purview of medieval Ashkenaz, a Christian writer tells the story of Moses of Crete, a fifth-century Messianic pretender, who persuaded all the Jews to jump into the Mediterranean with the assurance that

11. *Bein Yehudim le-Goyim*, p. 30. The English version (*Exclusiveness and Tolerance*, p. 19) is so truncated that the point is almost completely lost.

12. *Bein Yehudim le-Goyim*, p. 32; *Exclusiveness and Tolerance*, p. 21.

13. *Bein Yehudim le-Goyim*, p. 91; *Exclusiveness and Tolerance*, pp. 84–85.

the sea would split to facilitate their journey to the Promised Land. Historians have retold the story with a sense of amazement at such mass credulity or skepticism as to the historicity of the account.[14] Although I am by no means prepared to assert confidently that these events occurred, the plausibility of the narrative increases dramatically once we appreciate the impact of stories about heroic faith absorbed from childhood.

A well-known rabbinic legend relates that the Red Sea split only after Naḥshon ben Aminadav of the tribe of Judah demonstrated his unquestioning faith by leaping into the roiling sea.[15] Today, every school child receiving a traditional Jewish education is familiar with this story. We cannot know if this was the case in fifth-century Crete, but if it was, the probability that Jews could have been capable of such behavior is enhanced exponentially. In the safety of a classroom, there is no price to pay for expressions of smug disdain for the lack of faith displayed by pusillanimous skeptics standing at the edge of the sea. But as the Jews of Crete looked out at the Mediterranean facing a potentially deadly choice, the natural resistance to irrational action would be sorely challenged by a lesson ingrained from the inception of their religious consciousness.[16]

---

14. Salo Baron expressed both reactions, the first in a general discussion of messianic figures and the second in a more detailed account of Moses. The reasons for skepticism, he says, are the Christian author's emphasis on Jewish credulity and his assertion that those saved by Christian fishermen accepted baptism. See *A Social and Religious History of the Jews* (New York, London, and Philadelphia: 1960), vol 3, p. 16, and vol. 5, pp. 366–67. Gerson Cohen, who excluded messianic movements attested only in Christian sources from his analysis of the messianic stances of medieval Jewish communities, remarked during a Columbia University colloquium in the mid–1960s that his own skepticism about the historicity of this account is rooted in the fact that the Jews' credulousness regarding false messiahs combined with their rejection of the true one is a standard, polemically useful Christian topos. Cohen's policy of excluding messianic accounts by non-Jews has recently come under attack. See his "Messianic Postures of Ashkenazim and Sephardim," in *Studies of the Leo Baeck Institute*, ed. by Max Kreutzberger (New York: 1967), p. 123, n.11, and Elisheva Carlebach, *Between History and Hope: Jewish Messianism in Ashkenaz and Sepharad. Third Annual Lecture of the Victor J. Selmanowitz Chair of Jewish History* (New York: Touro College, 1998), pp. 12–13.

15. See the references in Louis Ginzberg, *The Legends of the Jews* (Philadelphia: 1928), vol. 6, pp. 75–79 (n. 388).

16. Lest I be accused of equating Moses son of Amram with Moses of Crete and ignoring the earlier miraculous events that presumably justified Naḥshon's

Let us now return to the martyrs of Ashkenaz. A vexed question central to recent historical debate asks if the justification for suicide and the killing of others emerged out of almost routine analysis of texts or if it was molded by emotional considerations and the need to justify the actions of sainted ancestors. This is not the occasion to survey the state of this question in its fullness. Nonetheless, there remains much to be said both for Katz's general approach and for his specific observations. He noted, for example, a highly unusual formulation in *Tosafot* that persuasively underscores the impact of martyrdom's extraordinary emotional resonance on halakhic discourse. The tosafists remark that the ordinary processes of halakhic reasoning appear to yield the conclusion that it is permissible to commit idolatry under threat of death provided that the act does not take place in the presence of ten Jews. *Tosafot* does not merely reject this position. Rather, we are witness, at least initially, to what Katz properly describes as an extraordinary phenomenon— a *cri de coeur* instead of an argument. "God forbid that we should rule in a case of idolatry that one should transgress rather than die."[17]

In the current debate, Avraham Grossman and Yisrael Ta-Shma have taken issue with Haym Soloveitchik's position that the willingness of Ashkenazic authorities to justify suicide and even the killing of children in the face of enforced idolatry cannot have emerged from a straightforward application of legal reasoning but rather from the need to justify the behavior of the martyrs. Soloveitchik's argument rests in part on the resort of these authorities to aggadic sources; his critics, however, assert that Ashkenazic Jews drew no material distinction between halakhah and aggadah, so that

---

decision, let me put these obvious distinctions on the record. They do not, in my view, undermine the essential psychological observation.

17. *Tosafot Avodah Zarah* 54a, s.v. *ha be-ẓin'a*. See *Bein Yehudim le-Goyim*, pp. 90– 91; *Exclusiveness and Tolerance*, pp. 83–84. I have a personal stake in this argument. Without any conscious memory of the passage in Katz's book, I was struck by precisely the same formula while studying that *tosafot* for reasons unrelated to history, and I presented his point as my own when writing the introduction to *The Jewish-Christian Debate in the High Middle Ages* (Philadelphia: 1979) in the mid–1970s. While the book was in press, I re-read Katz and discovered to my combined pleasure and disappointment that my "discovery" had already been made. The printed version (pp. 25–26), therefore, contains a footnote attributing the point to *Bein Yehudim le-Goyim* with the observation that the English version is so bland that "the emotional force of the argument is virtually lost." (It renders *ḥas ve-shalom*, which I have translated "God forbid," as "Far be it from us.") When I related the story to Katz years later, he told me how pleased he had been with this insight when it had originally struck him.

their arguments from texts that Soloveitchik would place out of bounds are entirely consistent with their own worldview.[18]

I think it is fair to say that even in medieval Ashkenaz, the first resort of rabbinic decisors would be to texts that we would describe as halakhic. At the same time, I do not believe that they would dismiss evidence from an aggadah by saying, "I do not recognize this genre as authoritative in a legal discussion." Thus, when mainstream authorities issue a problematic ruling based entirely on aggadic material, we are justified in asking pointed questions about motivation, as long as we do not insist that the resort to aggadah demonstrates in and of itself that highly unusual processes must be at work. In short, our antennas should be raised, though we may ultimately decide that nothing extraordinary is happening.

With respect to our issue, I am not even certain that it is appropriate to characterize all the sources adduced in the medieval discussion as aggadic;[19] nonetheless, I am strongly inclined to think that a deeply emotional need to validate the heroism of the martyrs did play an important role in Ashkenazic decision-making. Katz's *tosafot* is highly relevant here, but an even more significant text has not, in my view, been given its due by either side in this controversy, even though all the parties know it very well.

Rabbi Meir of Rothenburg, the great thirteenth-century decisor, was asked whether atonement is necessary for a man who had killed his wife and children (with their consent) to prevent their capture by a mob demanding conversion to Christianity. He responded that suicide can be defended in such a case, but it is much more difficult to find a justification for the killing of others. Nonetheless, he rose to the challenge by proposing an original extension of a rabbinic midrash on a biblical text. Defenders of martyrdom by suicide had long cited the assertion in *Bereshit Rabbah* 34:19 that the word "but" (*akh*) in Genesis 9:5 limits the scope of the prohibition against suicide that immediately follows.[20] R. Meir suggested that this word, and hence this

---

18. See Haym Soloveitchik, "Religious Law and Change: The Medieval Ashkenazic Example," *AJS Review* 12 (1987): 205–21; Avraham Grossman, "Shorashav shel Qiddush ha-Shem be-Ashkenaz ha-Qedumah," in *Qedushat ha-Ḥayyim ve-Ḥeruf ha-Nefesh: Kovetz Ma'amarim le-Zikhro shel Amir Yekutiel*, ed. by Isaiah Gafni and Aviezer Ravitzky (Jerusalem: 1993), pp. 99–130; Israel Ta Shma, "Hitabbedut ve-Reẓaḥ ha-Zulat al Qiddush ha-Shem: Li-She'elat Meqomah shel ha-Aggadah be-Massoret ha-Pesiqah ha-Ashkenazit," in *Yehudim mul ha-Ẓelav: Gezerot Tatn"u ba-Historiah u-ba-Historiographiah*, ed. by Yom Tov Assis et al. (Jerusalem: 2000), pp. 150–56.

19. See the following note.

20. Even though *Bereshit Rabbah* is an aggadic text, this passage has the sound and

limitation, also governs the remainder of the verse, which prohibits murder. It follows that killing others may be permitted under the same circumstances that justify suicide. He prefaced this suggestion with the observation that "the position that this is permissible has spread widely, for we have seen and found many great men who slaughtered their sons and daughters," and he followed it with the powerful assertion that "anyone who requires atonement for this is besmirching the name of the pious men of old."

Though large questions of this sort cannot be settled definitively by a single source, this responsum, it seems to me, is as close to a smoking gun as we could ever expect. An Ashkenazic rabbi of the first rank tells us that (1) it is a challenge to find grounds for permitting the killing of others; (2) the reason for seeking such grounds is the fact that the practice has been widespread among great rabbis; (3) one can permit this by an [unattested, innovative] expansion of a rabbinic midrash on a biblical verse [a very rare procedure in thirteenth-century halakhic discourse];[21] and (4) anyone who disagrees with this original proposal to accomplish an admittedly problematic task is besmirching the name of the pious men of old.

Soloveitchik himself cites this responsum only to underscore its tragic character and to note that R. Meir "was hard put to find a reply" to the question. He goes on to assert that "for the murder of children few could find a defense, and almost all passed that over in audible silence." The lengthy footnote to this sentence makes no reference to R. Meir, and readers are given no indication of the main point of his responsum.[22] Even though he never wrote the words, "This is permitted," it is beyond question that this is the thrust of R. Meir's ruling. The greatest decisor in thirteenth-century Germany composed an emotion-laden responsum that provides powerful evidence for Soloveitchik's—and Katz's—position.

Despite R. Meir's initial reluctance to extend the permission to commit suicide to include the killing of others, the unhesitating readiness of some Ashkenazic Jews to do so is not, I think, an impenetrable mystery. Once

feel of halakhah, so that Soloveitchik's argument that suicides were justified by aggadah pure and simple probably requires qualification. It would be going very far indeed to expect Ashkenazic Jews to shrink from relying upon an explicitly legal formulation solely because it appears in a non-halakhic midrash.

21. In my "Ḥeqer Rabbanut Ashkenaz ha-Qedumah," *Tarbiẓ* 33 (1984): 484, n. 6, I made the point that R. Meir's determining a halakhah on the basis of a partially original midrash on a biblical verse is highly unusual among medieval authorities. In private conversations, two learned scholars insisted that they do not consider such a practice strikingly atypical, but I am not persuaded.

22. "Religious Law and Change," pp. 209–10.

again, I am inclined to assign pride of place to instinctive and emotional considerations. But let me begin by proposing a formal argument that may well have been taken for granted though it is unattested in the medieval sources and has not been noted in the current debates. A much-cited passage in *Da'at Zeqenim mi-Ba'alei ha-Tosafot* to Genesis 9:5 indicates that unnamed Ashkenazic Jews had clearly and apparently unself-consciously applied the passage in *Bereshit Rabbah* not only to suicide but to the killing of children as well. If we turn to that midrashic passage, we find that it points to the death of Saul as one of the paradigmatic exceptions to the prohibition against suicide. But Saul initially asked a servant to kill him; it was only after the servant refused that the king killed himself. (I leave aside the more complicated issue of the subsequent story in II Samuel 1 where an Amalekite tells David that Saul's suicide attempt was not wholly successful and that he acceded to a royal request to complete the task.) The reader of the midrash has every right to assume that the exception made for Saul includes his initial request as well as his final action.[23]

At the same time, I do not believe that such arguments went through the minds of Jews preparing to commit suicide in the blood-stained arenas of Mainz and Worms. Let us imagine the scene. A large group of Jews is facing the certainty of death or conversion. To save themselves from slaughter at the hands of the crusading hordes—or from the prospect of descending into the maelstrom of idolatry in the face of torture—they decide to take their lives. They know that they will be instantaneously transported to a world of eternal light at the side of Abraham, Isaac, Jacob, and Rabbi Akiva. Do they take their children with them to eternal bliss or do they leave them to wander among the bloody corpses of their parents until they are found and raised to live a life of idolatry? I am tempted to say that the choice is clear. In fact, it is not. The choice to slaughter your children is never clear, and the agonies of that choice are evident in the chilling chronicles of those terrible events. None-

---

23. Cf. Radak's commentary to I Samuel 31:4, which states—citing our midrash—that Saul did not sin, without proffering the slightest hint that the initial request, reported in the very same verse, was improper.

Shortly after I submitted this article to the editor, Prof. Ephraim Kanarfogel called my attention to his discussion in a forthcoming article of Rabbenu Tam's position on the fear of succumbing to torture as a halakhic justification for suicide. See Kanarfogel's "*Halakhah* and *Meẓiut* (Realia) in Medieval Ashkenaz: Surveying the Parameters and Defining the Limits," scheduled to appear in *Jewish Law Annual* 14 (2001), where he analyzes the relevance of the talmudic assertion (*Ketubbot* 33b) that Hananiah, Mishael, and Azariah would have bowed to the statue made by Nebuchadnezzar had they been beaten. I thank Prof. Kanarfogel for affording me the opportunity to read the typescript.

theless, the choice was made, and I think it far more likely that it was made on the basis of an instinctive reaction than on the basis of textual analysis. Once it was made, subsequent Jews, at least for the most part, had little emotional choice but to react like R. Meir of Rothenburg, though he agonized over the question far more than most, and his transparent struggle has much to teach us about the interaction between heart and mind.

One element in Katz's own formulation of the martyrological psychology of Ashkenazic Jews may even be too weak. He poses the medievals' question as to the permissibility of suicide or the killing of children "to avoid religious compulsion and the temptation to apostasy." He goes on to say that "the answer of Ashkenazic rabbis was inclined toward stringency from the outset ..., and it is clear that they were not concerned that this stringency fell into the category of a decree that the masses are unprepared to withstand."[24] In other words, not only the rabbis but even the masses were inclined toward such a response. If so, we may well ask ourselves about the propriety of the term "stringency" here. The question posed was whether suicides and killings were permissible, and the answer was in the affirmative. In any other context, an affirmative answer to a question beginning, "Is it permissible?" would be characterized as lenient, not stringent. For all his deep understanding of the psyche of medieval Ashkenazic Jews, Katz could not avoid the unconscious imposition of his (and our) instincts upon theirs by transforming a *qulla* into a *ḥumra*, a leniency into a stringency. Difficult as it is for us to fathom, these medieval Jews *wanted* the answer to be, "It is permissible."

Many years ago, my interest in the centrality of martyrdom for the Ashkenazic psyche was piqued by a passage in the *Niẓẓaḥon Vetus*, which impelled me to draw attention to both Katz's *tosafot* and R. Meir of Rothenburg's responsum. That passage, which would surely have caught Katz's sharp eye had he read the text, transmutes the story made famous by Judah Halevi's *Kuzari* into a celebration of the willingness to be martyred as the hallmark of the true faith. As in the *Kuzari*, the soon-to-be-converted ruler is impressed by the fact that Judaism is the second choice of both Muslim and Christian, but he is even more impressed when the Jew is prepared to sacrifice his life where the others are not.[25]

Finally, Katz makes the telling observation that the talmudic concept of *parhesia* describing a public act underwent an illuminating transformation in the Middle Ages. For the talmudic sages, an act fell into the category of *parhesia* if it was done in the presence of ten Jews. In the formal, legal sense, this

24. *Bein Yehudim le-Goyim*, p. 91. The English version (*Exclusiveness and Tolerance*, p. 84) does not quite convey the point.

25. *The Jewish-Christian Debate in the High Middle Ages*, pp. 26–27, 216–18.

did not change, but when medieval Jews described the death of martyrs in a public setting, they usually referred to the intent to sanctify God's name by projecting devotion to the non-Jewish world. It was this confrontation that gave the act of martyrdom its critical context and its transcendent purpose.

In citing concrete evidence for this important and penetrating insight, Katz can, nonetheless, overreach. The Hebrew version contains a footnote asserting that the intent of the martyrs to have Christians recognize the truth of Judaism is made explicit (*nitparesh*) in a comment by R. Solomon b. Shimshon.[26] The comment cited certainly expresses the Jews' fervent expectation that Christians will recognize that truth, but the instrument of this recognition is not Jewish martyrdom but the Lord's eschatological vengeance against Christendom. Because of this divine punishment, Christians will perceive the outrageous injustice that they had perpetrated by spilling the blood of Jewish babies in the name of a false belief.

Both the Ashkenazic variant of the *Kuzari* story and the hope for eschatological Christian enlightenment bring us to Katz's discussion of converts. Once again, his instincts guide him very well even in the absence of an extensive evidentiary base. He understands, of course, the full spectrum of motivations for Jewish conversion to Christianity, from pragmatic interests to genuine conviction. His tendency, however, predictably inclines toward social explanation: in a profoundly religious age, Jews attracted by the values of Christian society would express this attraction by embracing the religious form in which those values expressed themselves.[27] Though I would assign somewhat more force than did Katz to the attraction of Christian arguments, I am, nonetheless, inclined to think that his emphasis is correct. He intuits this psychological process despite the fact that his entire discussion of the motivations of Jewish apostates takes place with virtually no reference to Christian sources, which appear in one footnote containing a reference to a few pages in two secondary works.[28] I have already alluded to the fact that our one detailed personal memoir of the conversion experience by a Jewish convert to Christianity, Herman of Cologne's *Opuscula de Conversione Sua*, is entirely absent from the analysis—an inconceivable omission for anyone with real familiarity with Latin materials. And yet, Herman's account strikingly reinforces Katz's point, subordinating, though not ignoring, intellectual arguments, and emphasizing an attraction to the values of simple piety.[29]

---

26. *Bein Yehudim le-Goyim*, p. 97, n. 41.

27. *Bein Yehudim le-Goyim*, p. 83; *Exclusiveness and Tolerance*, p. 76.

28. *Bein Yehudim le-Goyim*, p. 83, n. 46; *Exclusiveness and Tolerance*, p. 75, n. 6.

29. Gerlinde Niemeyer, ed., *Hermannus quondam Judaeus opusculum de conversione*

Similarly, Katz argues with no concrete evidence that the reason why medieval Ashkenazic Jews persisted in converting Christians despite the obvious difficulties is that they saw every instance of conversion to Judaism as a proof and declaration of the truth of the Jewish religion to the outside world.[30] The *Niẓẓaḥon Vetus* strikingly confirms this intuition—not only in the story of the Emperor that we have already encountered but also in a passage dealing frontally with the implications of conversion writ large.

> With regard to their questioning us as to whether there are proselytes among us, they ask this question to their shame and to the shame of their faith. After all, one should not be surprised at the bad deeds of an evil Jew who becomes an apostate, because his motives are to enable himself to eat all that his heart desires, to give pleasure to his flesh with wine and fornication, to remove from himself the yoke of the kingdom of heaven so that he should fear nothing, to free himself from all the commandments, cleave to sin, and concern himself with worldly pleasures. But the situation is different with regard to proselytes who converted to Judaism and thus went of their own free will from freedom to slavery, from light to darkness. If the proselyte is a man, then he knows that he must wound himself by removing his foreskin through circumcision, that he must exile himself from place to place, that he must deprive himself of worldly good and fear for his life from the external threat of being killed by the uncircumcised, and that he will

---

sua, *Monumenta Germaniae Historica: Quellen zur Geistgeschichte des Mittelalters*, vol. 4 (Weimar: 1963), esp. p. 108. (The text had been published twice before Niemeyer's edition.) See Jeremy Cohen, "The Mentality of the Medieval Jewish Apostate: Peter Alfonsi, Hermann of Cologne, and Pablo Christiani," in *Jewish Apostasy in the Modern World*, ed. by Todd Endelman and Jeffrey Gurock (New York: 1987), pp. 20–47; and Karl F. Morrison, *Conversion and Text: The Cases of Augustine of Hippo, Herman-Judah, and Constantine-Tsatsos* (Charlottesville and London: 1992), which also contains an English translation. Well after Katz wrote his book, Avrom Saltman argued that the *Opusculum* is, in fact, a fictitious work by a born Christian; see his "Hermann's *Opusculum de Conversione Sua*: Truth or Fiction?," *Revue des Etudes Juives* 47 (1988): 31–56. The most recent discussion of this question is Jean-Claude Schmitt, *Die autobiographische Fiktion: Hermann des Juden Bekehrung* (Kleine Schriften des Arye-Maimon Instituts 3; Trier, 2000). Since no one had doubted the authenticity of this work when Katz wrote, I have referred to it as Hermann's in my discussion. As Schmitt argues, many relevant insights can be gleaned from it even if it is essentially fiction.

30. *Bein Yehudim le-Goyim*, p. 85. The English version (*Exclusiveness and Tolerance*, p. 77) is considerably less forceful.

lack many things that his heart desires; similarly, a woman proselyte also separates herself from all pleasures. And despite all this, they come to take refuge under the wing of the divine presence. It is evident that they would not do this unless they knew for certain that their faith is without foundation and that it is all a lie, vanity, and emptiness. Consequently, you should be ashamed when you mention the matter of proselytes.[31]

Katz's related argument that the generally positive attitude toward converts in the Middle Ages reflects an active quest for Jewish triumph[32] is less than compelling in and of itself, but is in my view confirmed by the pervasive tone of Jewish polemic and considerable evidence from Christian sources, none of which played any role in forming Katz's conclusion. Although I do not believe that we should go so far as to speak of a medieval Jewish mission, there is strong reason to believe that Jews confronted Christians on the streets of Europe to pose religious arguments and took great satisfaction in producing a sense of discomfiture or defeat in the mind of their interlocutor.[33]

That Jews reviled apostates is self-evident, and yet they insisted that such converts retain the legal status of Jews. Katz devoted an article to the application of the talmudic formula "even though he sinned he is an Israelite" to the abiding Jewishness of the apostate.[34] He proved the validity of an earlier suggestion that Rashi was responsible for the use of this expression to establish the standing of apostates as Jews; then he proceeded to examine the larger social context of the new understanding and wide popularity of this formula. The explanation, he says, is neither halakhic logic in itself nor Rashi's personal predilections but the real struggle carried on by the Jewish community against conversion and forced apostasy.[35]

On the one hand, there are legal and psychological advantages in seeing the apostate as non-Jewish. He does not generate a levirate relationship, so that his widowed, childless sister-in-law can marry without asking him for a release; you can lend him money at interest; you can indulge your utter rejection of him. In this connection, Katz makes another acute observation

---

31. *The Jewish-Christian Debate in the High Middle Ages*, #211, English section, pp. 206–7.

32. *Bein Yehudim le-Goyim*, p. 88; *Exclusiveness and Tolerance*, p. 81.

33. See my "Mission to the Jews and Jewish-Christian Contacts in the Polemical Literature of the High Middle Ages," *American Historical Review* 91 (1986): 576–91.

34. "Af al Pi she-Ḥata Yisrael Hu," in *Halakhah ve-Qabbalah*, pp. 255–69.

35. "Af al Pi she-Ḥata," p. 262.

about the transformation of a talmudic term. For the Sages, one who habitually violated a particular injunction was a *mumar* with respect to that injunction (*mumar le-x*); for medieval Jews, *mumar le-* became simply *mumar*—an apostate whose very essence is the transgression of the Torah.

But there were countervailing concerns of considerable, ultimately decisive emotional and pragmatic impact. Jews wanted to demonstrate that baptism has no force, that it could not effect a transformation of identity, and they also wanted to encourage converts to return to Judaism.[36] To these considerations I would add a third: Jews wanted to see all the sins of apostates as sins. To be sure, the conversion itself, barring future repentance, sealed their fate. Nonetheless, as long as they remain Jews, every desecration of the Sabbath, every taste of forbidden food increases the temperature of the hellfire prepared for them.

Katz's instincts about Jewish attitudes toward Christianity can sometimes not be tested at all. He asserts, for example, that Ashkenazic Jews were sincere both when they prayed for the peace of the government and when they prayed for its ultimate destruction.[37] I am inclined to believe that he is right, but I cannot think of an easy way to prove it. The complex interaction of attraction and revulsion toward the Christian world is particularly difficult to pin down. Citing the work of Yitzhak Baer, Katz affirmed that we now know that religious phenomena in both communities emerged out of a common trend, but the medievals themselves, he argued, did not know this. For them, these very religious impulses strengthened the instinct to recoil from the other

---

36. "Af al Pi she-Ḥata," pp. 262–65.

37. *Bein Yehudim le-Goyim*, p. 60; *Exclusiveness and Tolerance*, p. 51. The difference between the Hebrew and English versions of this passage is so striking that for all Katz's insistence that he spurned apologetics, it is difficult to avoid the impression that he or his English stylist softened the formulation for a non-Jewish audience. The Hebrew reads, "The vision of the end of days signifies the overturning of the current order, when the dispersed and humiliated people will see its revenge from its tormentors. The hope for a day of revenge and the prayer for the arrival of that day may be considered as conflicting with a profession of loyalty to the government...." Here is the English: "A reversal of the existing order was envisaged in the messianic age, when the dispersed and humiliated Jewish people was to come into its own. The entertaining of such hopes, and the prayer for their fulfillment, might well be considered as conflicting with a profession of loyalty...."

On the much debated question of whether Ashkenazic Jews looked forward to Christian conversion or annihilation at the end of days, see my "Al Tadmitam ve-Goralam shel ha-Goyim be-Sifrut ha-Pulmus ha-Ashkenazit," in *Yehudim mul ha-Ẓelav* (above, n. 18), pp. 74–91.

religion.[38] With all the substantial progress that has been made since *Exclusiveness and Tolerance* to enhance our understanding of both the openness and the hostility of Ashkenazic Jewry to its Christian environment,[39] Katz's assessment has, in the main, withstood the test of time.

Katz places great emphasis on the Jewish instinct that Christianity is *avodah zarah*, asserting that any economically motivated change in this perception would appear to stand in absolute contradiction to the classic perception that the world is unconditionally divided between Israel and the nations.[40] A bit later he argues that retaining this perception was necessary to safeguard the community against absorption and conversion.[41] There is certainly much truth in this, but to test it one would have to introduce at least some comparative dimension. How did Jews under Islam handle this problem? They surely regarded Muslims as part of "the nations," and with sufficient effort it was possible to classify them as idolaters;[42] nonetheless, neither Maimonides nor the great majority of rabbinic authorities took this step. Though Katz makes no reference to Islam in this context, he does allude to the small size of Ashkenazic communities and the intense missionary efforts exerted by Christians as factors that increased the Jewish need for self-defense. I do not believe that this is enough to explain the different reactions under Christendom and Islam, particularly since the intensity of missionary efforts in Northern

---

38. *Bein Yehudim le-Goyim*, pp. 98–99; *Exclusiveness and Tolerance*, pp. 93–94.

39. See my discussion and references in Gerald J. Blidstein, David Berger, Shnayer Z. Leiman, and Aharon Lichtenstein, *Judaism's Encounter with Other Cultures: Rejection or Integration?*, ed. by Jacob J. Schacter, pp. 117–25, as well as in "Al Tadmitam ve-Goralam shel ha-Goyim" (above, n. 37). See also Ivan Marcus, *Rituals of Childhood: Jewish Acculturation in Medieval Europe* (New Haven and London: 1996); Israel J. Yuval, *Shenei Goyim be-Bitnekh* (Tel Aviv, 2000); and much relevant discussion in Avraham Grossman's *Ḥakhmei Ashkenaz ha-Rishonim* (Jerusalem: 1981) and *Ḥakhmei Zarfat ha-Rishonim* (Jerusalem: 1995) and in Ephraim Kanarfogel, *Jewish Education and Society in the High Middle Ages* (Detroit: 1992).

40. *Bein Yehudim le-Goyim*, p. 36; *Exclusiveness and Tolerance*, p. 25. The formulation in the English version is not as sharp.

41. *Bein Yehudim le-Goyim*, p. 46; *Exclusiveness and Tolerance*, p. 37.

42. So the anonymous rabbi attacked by Maimonides in his *Epistle on Martyrdom*; see Abraham Halkin and David Hartman, *Epistles of Maimonides: Crisis and Leadership* (Philadelphia: 1993), pp. 16, 21. Cf. also *Ḥiddushei ha-Ran* to *Sanhedrin* 61b. (The author is not Rabbi Nissim Gerondi but a somewhat earlier Spanish talmudist.)

Europe through the twelfth century is very much in question.[43] Katz acknowledged that the theological chasm separating Judaism from Christianity played some role here, and in this instance I think that the actual content of Jewish and Christian beliefs deserves pride of place. We shall soon encounter the emphasis by R. Menahem ha-Meiri on the deep and genuine divide between Christianity and paganism, but in the final analysis it is a daunting task to argue that worship of Jesus of Nazareth as God is not *avodah zarah* by the standards of Jewish law.

In his final work, Katz did utilize medieval Jewish-Muslim relations as a tool for evaluating the causes of the tense relationship between Jews and Christians in the same period.[44] Here he endorsed the position that tensions were much greater in the latter case because the truth of one religion depended on the falsehood of the other only in the Jewish-Christian relationship. This stray remark requires elaboration. As I wrote on another occasion with respect to polemical literature,[45] the Jewish-Christian encounter was more stressful because of both its greater intimacy and its greater difference. Since the Hebrew Bible played a considerably less important role in Islam than it did in Christianity, arguments over its meaning, including, of course, the identity of True Israel, were incomparably more significant in the Jewish-Christian interaction. With regard to theology, it was the greater gap between Jews and Christians that was decisive in exacerbating tensions. "Islamic monotheism left no room for the creative rancor that produced the philosophical dimension of Jewish-Christian discussions, which addressed such issues as trinity and incarnation."[46] In our context, sharper terminology may be in order. Christianity was *avodah zarah*; Islam was not.

A comparative dimension might also have been useful in testing one aspect of Katz's controversial hypothesis about the difference between medieval Ashkenazim and their sixteenth- and seventeenth-century counterparts. Katz asserts that by the seventeenth century, Ashkenazic Jews had spiritualized the ideal of martyrdom and were far less aggressive in confronting Christianity. These changes, he says, resulted from greater insularity. Christianity had become less of a psychological reality, and the sense of spiritual threat or temptation had diminished.[47]

---

43. See my "Mission to the Jews" (above, n. 33).

44. *Et Laḥqor ve-Et le-Hitbonen* (Jerusalem: 1999), p. 54.

45. "Jewish-Christian Polemics," *The Encyclopedia of Religion* 11: 389.

46. "Jewish-Christian Polemics," 389.

47. "Bein Tatn'u le-Ta'ḥ Ta't," in *Halakhah ve-Qabbalah*, pp. 311–30.

This is not the forum to address the controversy over this thesis in detail. I think that Katz was wrong about spiritualization and right about aggressiveness, but his reason for the decline in aggressiveness is highly speculative. We would do well to ask why medieval Provencal, Italian, and Spanish Jews were less aggressive than those of Northern Europe in their anti-Christian works. Were those Jews less tempted by Christianity? Was it less of a psychological reality for them? In these societies, it is likely that differences in cultural attitudes and norms of expression were at work. But then, as the Middle Ages wore on, there was fear. This is certainly evident in late medieval Spain, where the Tortosa disputation took place in a profoundly different atmosphere from the one that had prevailed in Barcelona a century and a half earlier, but there were similar transformations in Ashkenaz as well. Rabbi Yehiel of Paris did not dare to address Nicholas Donin in the manner that his contemporary Ashkenazic coreligionists wrote or even, I am inclined to think, still spoke to Christians on the street. Later—but still well before the period identified by Katz—Yom Tov Lipmann Muehlhausen was much less caustic than Joseph Official, and he found it necessary to deny the obvious meaning of pejorative Jewish terms applied to Christian *sancta*.[48] The public aggressiveness of Ashkenazic Jewry changed because it had to change.

Katz's social explanations for the stance of medieval Jews on legal issues in the Jewish-Christian relationship always make intuitive sense, but on rare occasions his formulation is problematic or the evidence is pushed too hard. Thus, he points to an assertion in *Sefer Ḥasidim* that penance is needed for a Jew who desecrated the Sabbath to save a gentile and contrasts it to the injunctions in the same work to fight a Jew who is attempting to kill an innocent gentile and to take up arms in support of Christian allies who fulfill their obligations to their Jewish partners. The contrast in these positions certainly requires explanation, and Katz suggests two distinctions that somehow appear to merge. There is a difference, he says, between reflective and spontaneous reactions and between the response to an individual Christian and the approach to Christians as a stereotyped group. The reflective reaction requires penance; the spontaneous one requires you to help. The individual is entitled to your assistance; the representative of the group is not.[49]

In this instance, however, these are problematic distinctions. It is hard to see why saving someone on the Sabbath involves less of a direct, spontaneous emotion than saving him from a Jewish murderer, or why the former is a stereotypical Christian while the latter is an individual. I think that Katz is

---

48. *Sefer Niẓẓaḥon* (Altdorf: 1644), p. 194.

49. *Bein Yehudim le-Goyim*, p. 105; *Exclusiveness and Tolerance*, pp. 100–1.

correct in his further assertion that the imperative to help the gentile may well emerge from a direct human reaction that transcends self-interest, but I cannot prove this. Even if this is so, the distinction between the cases can result from the conviction, or even instinct, that indifference to the life of a gentile may—and should—be overridden far more readily than the prohibition against violating the Sabbath.

In another instance, I believe that Katz's intuition is correct, but he presses the evidence to the point of misrepresentation. Medieval Jews had a powerful incentive to permit the deriving of benefit from gentile wine; at the same time, they did not drink it and in most cases did not want to drink it. As Katz presents it, Rabbenu Tam permitted benefit on the basis of an argument that should logically have permitted drinking as well. When Ri objected by pointing to this implication, Rabbenu Tam withdrew his argument and produced a different one that would not lead to the unwanted conclusion. Katz points out that the Talmud itself makes no distinction between benefit and drinking, so that only the extra-halakhic concern prevented Ri and Rabbenu Tam from endorsing a consistent position.[50]

In a footnote found only in the Hebrew version, Katz concedes that R. Tam's statement "can be interpreted to mean that his ruling was reported inaccurately, but even if this is so one can still wonder why Ri would have been upset by the conclusion that Rabbenu Tam reached in the form it was reported to him."[51] First of all, R. Tam's statement cannot just be *interpreted* to mean that his position was misreported; that is the only thing it can mean. Second, although the Talmud does not generally distinguish between deriving benefit from Gentile wine and drinking it, in a critically relevant line in this discussion it does. Ri objected to a permissive ruling that was both unprecedented and contrary to accepted practice. What is really striking is R. Tam's reaction, "God forbid," to Ri's assertion in his name, a reaction that powerfully supports Katz's fundamental thesis about the depth of the instinct at work here. We have already seen an instance in which Katz was acutely sensitive to the significance of this formula. In this case he did not pick it up, apparently because he was committed to the position that R. Tam had changed his mind. The deep aversion of Ashkenazic authorities to permitting the drinking of gentile wine really does emerge here, but Katz has constructed a misleading scenario regarding both the unfolding of R. Tam's position and its presumed inconsistency.[52]

---

50. *Bein Yehudim le-Goyim*, pp. 55–56; *Exclusiveness and Tolerance*, pp. 46–47.

51. *Bein Yehudim le-Goyim*, p. 56, n. 36.

52. After writing this, I had the benefit of reading the typescript of Haym Solo-

In his analysis of the perception of Christianity as *avodah zarah*, Katz frequently reiterates what he presents as a fundamental characteristic of halakhic literature: the limited, local application of a principle mobilized to deal with a particular problem. The point is that formulations implying that medieval Christians are not idolaters were not generalized beyond the narrow context that produced them. I do not doubt that this characteristic of halakhic literature, which Haym Soloveitchik has called "halakhic federalism,"[53] is real, and Katz uses it convincingly to refute scholars who equated the tosafists with the Meiri by attributing to them a principled denial that medieval Christians worship *avodah zarah*. But on a matter so fundamental to the self-perception of Ashkenazic Jewry and its relationship with its environment, we are entitled to ask whether the overwhelming instinct that Christianity is *avodah zarah* should inform our understanding of the local contexts themselves. Did medieval Ashkenazic halakhists ever mean to say—even in narrow applications—that Christianity is not *avodah zarah*?

The answer to this question may very well be no. In some of those cases, Katz appears willing to interpret the relevant statements so narrowly that they do not make any assertion about the Christian religion itself. Thus, the declaration that the gentiles among us (or "in this time") are not worshippers of *avodah zarah* means only that they are not particularly devout.[54] The most important example of this issue, *Tosafot*'s assertion that "association" (*shittuf*) is not forbidden to non-Jews, elicits a more ambiguous treatment. Katz's own

---

veitchik's study, "Saḥar bi-Stam Yenam be-Ashkenaz—Pereq be-Toledot ha-Halakhah ve-ha-Kalkalah ha-Yehudit bi-Yemei ha-Beinayim," which will have appeared in *Tarbiẓ* before the publication of this article. I am grateful to Prof. Soloveitchik for providing me with this typescript, which contains an important analysis of the exchange between Ri and Rabbenu Tam and argues persuasively for the existence of a deeply ingrained instinctive revulsion among Ashkenazic Jews at the prospect of drinking gentile wine.

Katz's report of a tosafist position in another case also requires correction, but the misleading formulation is only slightly off the mark. He tells us that Ri permitted taking interest from gentiles beyond the requirements of bare sustenance, because Jews were now a minority among the gentiles (*Bein Yehudim le-Goyim*, p. 40; *Exclusiveness and Tolerance*, p. 30). This is a category Katz uses to explain a larger pattern of halakhic adjustment. So he mobilizes it here, when in fact Ri grounded his permissive ruling not on the numerical status of the Jews but on the related fact that they are subject to economic persecution.

53. *Halakhah, Kalkalah, ve-Dimmuy Aẓmi* (Jerusalem: 1985), pp. 79–81.

54. "Sheloshah Mishpatim Apologetiyyim be-Gilguleihem," in *Halakhah ve-Qabbalah*, p. 284.

presentation in an earlier article, as well as in his book, indicates that he understands the term to refer to worship of God along with something else. Thus, Christianity would not be *avodah zarah* for gentiles. This principle, however, was applied only in the narrow context in which it arose, to wit, accepting an oath from a Christian in a business dispute.[55] In the article, however, he proceeds to discuss "meticulous jurists" (*baalei halakhah dayqanim*) who understood the tosafists to mean only that gentiles may take an oath in God's name while also thinking of another entity; they never meant to suggest that gentiles may associate God with something else in worship. Nonetheless, Katz does not retract his earlier interpretation, and in the Hebrew version of the book he reiterates it without going on to discuss the meticulous jurists. If, as is very likely, *tosafot* never meant to say that Christian worship is not *avodah zarah* for gentiles, there is no example of narrow application here. There was never any principle that could have been generalized.[56]

One of the weaknesses of halakhic federalism is that it cannot easily survive scrutiny. When exposed to the light, it withers. And so we come to ha-Meiri, where one of Katz's points is precisely that federalism withers, to be replaced by an all-embracing principle excluding Christians from the category of idolaters. Many of Katz's best characteristics emerge in this analysis: sensitivity to language, to pitch, to tone—not just ha-Meiri's new formula describing Christians and Muslims as nations bound by the ways of religions, but the celebratory language and the elimination of other arguments as unnecessary. We find once again a remarkable instinct that cuts to the core of a phenomenon even where hard evidence is thin: in this case, the instinct that philosophy is somehow at work here even though the evidence Katz adduces for this is not utterly compelling and the position to be explained is the opposite of that of Maimonides. In other instances we have seen Katz's intuitions

---

55. "Sheloshah Mishpatim" p. 279. Cf. *Bein Yehudim le-Goyim*, p. 163. The English version, *Exclusiveness and Tolerance*, p. 163, omits the reference to worship. As we shall see, this may well be a better understanding of *Tosafot*, but in light of the two Hebrew discussions, I doubt that it represents Katz's true intent at this point in his analysis.

56. There is an additional interpretive option that was proposed to understand this *tosafot* that Katz does not address in the article or in the Hebrew version of the book, but it makes an appearance in the English. *Shittuf* may mean nothing more than the inclusion of references to God and something else—in this case the saints—in the same oath. Christian worship remains *avodah zarah* even for gentiles. I have discussed the various interpretations of this *tosafot* in Appendix III of *The Rebbe, the Messiah, and the Scandal of Orthodox Indifference* (London and Portland, Oregon: 2001).

confirmed by polemical works; in this case, Moshe Halbertal has demonstrated the essential correctness of Katz's instincts by reference to philosophical and other texts.[57]

Finally, the question of Christianity as *avodah zarah* is intimately connected to the question of the damnation or salvation of Christians. On two occasions, Katz noted a passage in the Hebrew account of the 1240 Paris disputation where R. Yehiel indicated that Christians can be saved if they observe the seven Noahide laws.[58] Katz does not directly address the transparent problem that *avodah zarah* is one of those commandments. Nonetheless, his discussion of this passage and of the disputation as a whole is extremely perceptive, and his insight that the need to respond to Christian attacks on the Talmud could lead to the growth of genuine tolerance has significance beyond the geographical and chronological arena that concerns him in this chapter.[59]

Let us conclude, then, by returning to Katz's introductory comment about the contemporary relevance of his work. Within the medieval universe of discourse, we can unhesitatingly speak of both tolerance and intolerance when discussing the dominant religions. When you have the power to kill or expel—and these options are realistic within your universe of discourse—you exhibit tolerance if you refrain from exercising that power. When you kill or expel one group but not another, you have shown tolerance toward the group that remains. The more tolerant the society, the higher the standard an individual or subcommunity must meet to be considered tolerant.

57. Moshe Halbertal, *Bein Torah le-Ḥokhmah: Rabbi Menaḥem ha-Meiri u-Baʿalei ha-Halakhah ha-Maimunim bi-Provence* (Jerusalem: 2000), pp. 80–108. Katz laid special emphasis on ha-Meiri's remarkable assertion that a Jewish convert to Christianity is entitled to the rights accorded to civilized believers, whereas an unconverted heretic is not (*Bein Yehudim le-Goyim*, pp. 124–25; *Exclusiveness and Tolerance*, pp. 123–24). On a similar assertion by Moses ha-Kohen of Tordesillas, see my "Christians, Gentiles, and the Talmud: A Fourteenth-Century Jewish Response to the Attack on Rabbinic Judaism," in *Religionsgespraeche im Mittelalter*, ed. by Bernard Lewis and Friedrich Niewoehner (Wiesbaden: 1992), p. 126. Note, too, Yom Tov Lippman Muehlhausen, *Sefer Niẓẓaḥon*, p. 193.

58. "Sheloshah Mishpatim," p. 273; *Bein Yehudim le-Goyim*, p. 115; *Exclusiveness and Tolerance*, p. 113. See my discussion of this passage in "Al Tadmitam ve-Goralam shel ha-Goyim," pp. 80–81.

59. See my observations in "Christians, Gentiles, and the Talmud," p. 130.

For a relatively powerless minority, the situation is quite different. We can speak of theoretical tolerance and intolerance, but because the group in question has no authority to enforce its norms, we sometimes slip into a usage in which intolerance becomes synonymous with hostility. This equation, however, blurs important distinctions. Bernard of Clairvaux, for example, was hostile to Jews, even very hostile, but he was simultaneously tolerant, even—by medieval Christian standards—very tolerant.[60] No medieval Jew can be judged by this standard, because no Jew was confronted with the temptations or restraints of power.

Powerlessness confers freedom to express hostility without the need for a real confrontation with the consequences. One can curse one's enemies, condemn them to hellfire, list the innumerable offenses for which they should be executed and the many obligations that they must be compelled to discharge —and then go to bed. Power brings responsibility and subjects its bearers to the discipline of governing.[61] Powerlessness provides the luxury of both untested tolerance and untested zealotry. Neither the tolerance nor the zealotry may survive the transition to power.

Whether we frame the issue as hostility versus cordiality or tolerance versus intolerance, Katz's studies reveal how medieval Jews confronting a Christian society dealt with the normative texts that they had inherited. Though their strategies often carried significant practical consequences, the effects were limited by the reality of exile. Katz, on the other hand, wrote in an age of restored Jewish sovereignty. He certainly welcomed this, but he also saw the dangers and no doubt hoped that his work, free of the unhistorical apologetics of an earlier generation, would provide guidance as well as understanding. This dimension of his achievement is difficult to assess. But within the four ells of scholarly endeavor, the impact of his oeuvre is beyond cavil. Every scholar of the Jewish experience is indebted to Jacob Katz for setting a standard of erudition, insight, and clarity that we can only strive to approach.

---

60. See my "The Attitude of St. Bernard of Clairvaux toward the Jews," *Proceedings of the American Academy for Jewish Research* 40 (1972): 89–108.

61. Note the discussion of some of these sometimes surprising complexities in Kenneth R. Stow, "Papal and Royal Attitudes toward Jewish Lending in the Thirteenth Century," *AJS Review* 6 (1981): 161–84.

EARLY MODERN ASHKENAZ IN THE WRITINGS OF JACOB KATZ

Elisheva Carlebach
Queens College, CUNY

Jacob Katz's pioneering trilogy, *Tradition and Crisis, Exclusiveness and Toler-ance*, and *Out of the Ghetto*, paved new paths for the exploration of Jewish society in an age of transition.[1] Katz introduced and legitimated the methods and goals of social history into a field that had been dominated by religious and intellectual history. Close to a half century after the publi-cation of Katz's first works, the field has grown and expanded upon Katz's foundational insights. Possibilities for mining new resource collections con-tinue to grow, and disciplines such as comparative religion, sociology, and anthropology continue to enrich the perspectives from which the Jewish past can be understood. The great strides taken by scholars in both methodology and accessibility of sources allow for a reexamination of Katz's original assumptions, directions, and choices from the perspective afforded by time, hindsight, and genuine progress in the field Katz shaped. Like every great originator, Katz challenged many of the dominant methodological assump-tions of Jewish historiography in his work, even while his own conceptions, like those of every scholar, were informed by implicit values, opinions, and notions.

---

1. *Tradition and Crisis* (Glencoe, N.Y.: 1961; trans. Bernard Dov Cooperman, 1993; repr. Syracuse: 2000); *Exclusiveness and Tolerance: Studies in Jewish-Gentile Relations in Medieval and Modern Times* (London: 1961; New York: 1973); *Out of the Ghetto: The Social Background of Jewish Emancipation, 1770–1870* (Cam-bridge, Mass.: 1973; New York: 1978). Bernard Cooperman's essay, "After-word: *Tradition and Crisis*, The Study of Early Modern Jewish History," remains an invaluable analysis of the place of *Tradition and Crisis* in Jewish historiography. I thank Professors Israel Bartal and Haym Soloveitchik for their discussions of my remarks, although only my own views are reflected herein.

In his introduction to *Exclusiveness and Tolerance*[2] Katz defined his subject in three ways: first, by its chronological focus, the early-modern period; second, by its geographical/cultural locus, Ashkenaz; and third, by its subject, Jewish-Gentile relations. Let us examine each of these in turn.

As for periodization, Katz was virtually the first historian of the Jews to view the Early Modern period as a discrete age of transition. As the model for a broad-based analysis of an age of transition, no synthesis parallels Katz's collective oeuvre.[3] His predecessors tended either to see a radical break between medieval traditional Jewish life and modern conditions[4] or, alternatively, to elevate insignificant developments to the status of "precursors" of later historical currents, although they were not necessarily related.[5] At the

---

2. Original Hebrew title, *Beyn yehudim le-goyim: Yahas ha-yehudim li-shekhenehem bi-yeme ha-beinayim u-vi-tehilat ha-zeman he-hadash* (Jerusalem: 1960).

3. European historiography of the spirit and culture of a transitional age has a notable pedigree. Johann Huizinga's Dutch masterpiece, *The Autumn of the Middle Ages*, trans. Rodney J. Payton and Ulrich Mammitzsch (Chicago: 1996) and Jakob Burckhardt's *Civilization of the Renaissance in Italy*, trans. S.G.C. Middlemore (London and New York: 1990) exemplify the tradition. In linking the Early Modern period and the notion of a society whose values were in crisis, Katz's venerable predecessors include Paul Hazard, *La crise de la conscience européenne (1680–1715)* (Paris: 1935); Geoffrey Parker and Leslie Smith, eds., *The General Crisis of the Seventeenth Century* (London: 1997); cf. Chimen Abramsky, "The Crisis of Authority within European Jewry in the Eighteenth Century," in Siegfried Stein and Raphael Loewe, eds., *Studies in Jewish Religious and Intellectual History Presented to Alexander Altmann* (University, Ala.: 1979), pp. 13–29.

4. Many of the larger narrative histories of the Jewish people depict a sudden shift from the darkness of the medieval period into the light of the age of Moses Mendelssohn, with little intervening age of transition. For example, see Heinrich Graetz, *Divrei Yemei Yisrael* (trans. S.P. Rabinowitz), v. 8, pp. 526–27:

   עוד רבה המהומה במחנה ישראל בין שני הרבנים...
   והנה רבו אותות זמן חדש הממשמש ובא באירופה:
   החכם שבישראל ר' משה בן מנחם והחכם שבאומות העולם אפרים לעסינג
   כרתו ביניהם ברית אהבה וידידות

   The superb collective effort *German-Jewish History in Modern Times*, Michael Meyer, ed. (New York:1996), perhaps due more to organizational than ideological imperatives, breaks sharply between the Early Modern and subsequent periods (v. 1, pp. 260–62).

5. Azriel Shoḥat, *Im ḥilufei tekuphot: Reshit ha-haskalah be-yahadut germanyah* (Jerusalem: 1960), provides some examples of the latter tendency; cf. the sophis-

same time that Katz sharpened the chronological framework, he attempted
to dissolve and transcend political and geographical lines. Katz defined his
geographical/cultural scope, as "the province of Ashkenazi Jewry in the
wider sense, i.e. from the Jewries of Northern France and Germany in the
middle ages and from the life of their descendants in Germany and eastern
Europe (Poland and Lithuania) between the sixteenth and the eighteenth
centuries." With this broad definition, Katz posed questions concerning the
modernization of medieval Jewry that remain of the greatest significance for
students of Jewish history. What defines the common parameters that allow
us to draw parallels and even to erase the boundary lines between Jews of one
national, political and historical experience and those of a different milieu?
What commonalities allow us to speak of a Jewish transition to modernity,
rather than a French-Jewish, German-Jewish, English-Jewish, etc.? Where
must we acknowledge that firm lines exist?[6]

By advocating the value of a general rather than particularistic picture,
Katz' work highlighted the need for a form of comparative historical analysis
that has only recently begun to blossom in Jewish historiography.[7] But by
privileging the concept of "Ashkenaz" as his primary unit of analysis, Katz
eliminated one set of constraints only to adopt another that already occupied
a formidable position in the Jewish historiographical imagination. Many
meanings have been projected onto the elastic term "Ashkenaz." As Ismar
Schorsch has described in his insightful essay, German maskilim rejected
medieval Ashkenaz as symbolic of Jewish cultural insularity and turned to

---

ticated analysis of maskilic precursors by Shmuel Feiner, "Ha-haskalah ha-
muqdemet be-yahadut ha-meah ha-shemonah esreh," *Tarbiz* 67 (1998): 189–
240. Jonathan Israel's *European Jewry in the Age of Mercantilism, 1550–1750* (Oxford:
1985) analyzed the transitional age of European Jews from a perspective completely different from Katz's, essentially arguing that changing economic imperatives of the European states opened new doors for both Ashkenazic and
Sephardic Jews in Western Europe.

6. See Katz's formulation, *Tradition and Crisis*, 5–9, 255, n. 2.

7. On this methodology, see Todd Endelman's introduction to *Comparing Jewish
    Societies* (Ann Arbor: 1997), pp. 1–21. Endelman cites Katz's work as exemplary
    of an extreme tendency to survey "broad expanses of Jewish history, collapsing
    differences among communities and subcommunities in order to force their
    varied experiences into a uniform model or framework," For examples of a
    comparative approach, see Yosef Hayim Yerushalmi, "Assimilation and Racial
    Anti-Semitism: The Iberian and the German Models," Leo Baeck Memorial
    Lecture no. 26 (New York: 1982) and the recent volume, Michael Brenner,
    Rainer Liedtke, and David Richter, eds., *Two Nations: British and German Jews
    in Comparative Perspective* (Tübingen: 1999).

medieval Sepharad as the model of cultural openness.[8] They criticized the
educational system that they hoped to reform, as "insular, ungraded, and
adult orientated"; they advocated the inclusion of secular subjects, the
curbing of talmudic exclusivity, the study of Hebrew grammar, and the training for independent thinking, for which the ideal paradigm remained the
Sephardic school system. For *Wissenschaft* historians, classical medieval
"Ashkenaz" signified the continuity of rabbinic scholarship into the medieval period, a sign of the vitality of Judaism in its exilic period and, therefore,
to be evaluated as a basically positive and desirable development. Only in the
later period had Ashkenazic Jewry, overcome by persecution and suffering,
lost its original vitality, veering onto a course of spiritual degeneration and
intellectual decline. Graetz saw the emergence of kabbalah as the result of a
twisted exilic mentality. "Despite its foreign origins and its roots in the imagi-
native faculty, they called it 'Hokhmat ha-emet.'...It emerged in the course
of controversy and always fomented dispute and disunity."[9] He characterized
the fruits of the work of Mahari"l and Isaac Tyrnau as "a mere unspiritual
cataloging of custom,"[10] whereas Moritz Güdemann blamed the hyper-
trophy of *minhag* on the Black Plague.[11] These historians defined Ashkenaz
in an essentialist manner; developments that did not quite fit into their ideal,
they disdained as accretions that did not emerge from the essence of
Ashkenaz.

Possibly intending to correct the derisive judgment of his predecessors,
Yitzhak Baer posited an Ashkenaz that preserved its inner Jewish core, that
created from the authentic wellsprings of the Jewish past, and that avoided
the intellectual arrogance that doomed the Sephardic Jews to collective apostasy in the face of crisis. Baer characterized the distinctiveness of medieval
Ashkenaz in its religious piety, and contrasted it favorably to rationalist
Sephardic Jewry that had become distanced from its Jewish roots.[12] Some-

8. Ismar Schorsch, "The Myth of Sephardic Supremacy," *Leo Baeck Institute Yearbook* 34 (1989): 47–66. See also John Efron, "Scientific Racism and the Mystique of Sephardic Racial Superiority," *Leo Baeck Institute Yearbook* 38 (1993): 75–96.

9. Graetz, *Divrei Yemei Yisrael* (trans. S. P. Rabinowitz), 5:69.

10. Cited in Y. Dinari, "Ha-minhag ve-ha-halakhah be-teshuvot ḥakhmei Ashenaz ba-me'ah ha–15," in E.Z. Melamed, ed., *Benjamin de Vries Memorial Volume* (Jerusalem: 1968), p. 197.

11. Moritz Güdemann, *Geschichte des Erziehungswesens und der Cultur der abendländischen Juden während des Mittelalters* (trans. into Hebrew, Friedberg, *Sefer ha-torah veha-ḥayim be-artzot ha-ma'arav be-yemei ha-beinayim*; Warsaw: 1899).

12. David N. Myers, *Re-inventing the Jewish Past: European Jewish Intellectuals and the*

what paradoxically, Baer believed that medieval Ashkenazic society had absorbed many of its most admirable features from the surrounding Christian society, including its representative and democratic mode of self-government, its martyrological ideology, its exegetical-polemical tradition, and its internalization of the Christian penitential pietism that shaped *Hasidut Ashkenaz*.[13]

Modern scholarship has applied its own associations to the cultural characteristics clustered with Ashkenaz, often to construct a polemical ideal type. To Gerson Cohen, Ashkenaz signified rabbinic elitism, intellectual fundamentalism, rampant anthropomorphism, political quietism, willingness to martyrdom, and messianic passivity.[14] For the curators of a museum exhibit on the cultural legacy of Ashkenaz, "Ashkenazi heritage [w]as a unique cultural phenomenon that developed in German lands during the Dark Ages and persisted…in German lands….[It consisted of a] nearly unbroken and astonishingly uniform flow of thought and action." Ashkenazi hallmarks were: "discipline, meticulousness and persistence," the modern notion of the "yekke" superimposed on the medieval past.[15] *The Encyclopedia Judaica* [following the entry in *Encyclopedia Ivrit*] defined the Jews of Ashkenaz as "fundamentalist and rigorist, consonant mainly with internal Jewish sources, ideas, and customs…circumscribed by study of the Bible and Talmud."[16] Dan Miron ascribed to modern Hebrew [Ashkenazic] literature a conception of medieval Ashkenaz that served as the foil for Jewish modernity. "To the modern Jewish imagination, at least to that which found its expression in modern Hebrew literature, medieval Ashkenaz was the non plus ultra of the

---

Zionist Return to History (New York and Oxford: 1995), pp. 120–23.

13. Yitzhaq Baer, "Ha-megamah ha-datit—ḥevratit shel 'Sefer Ḥasidim'" *Zion* 3 (1938): 1–50, esp. 3–5; cf. the quite different interpretation of Haym Soloveitchik, "Three Themes in Sefer Ḥasidim," *AJS Review* 1 (1976): 311–58, esp. 317.

14. Gerson Cohen, "Messianic Postures of Ashkenazim and Sephardim," Leo Baeck Memorial Lecture no. 9 (New York: 1967); repr. in Marc Saperstein, ed., *Essential Papers on Messianic Movements and Personalities in Jewish History*, (New York: 1992), pp. 202–233, esp. pp. 212, 219 (references are to the latter edition.) Cf. my "Between History and Hope: Jewish Messianism Between Ashkenaz and Sepharad" Annual Lecture of the Selmanowitz Chair of Jewish History, Touro College, (New York: 1998) pp. 1–30.

15. Sylvia Hershkowitz, introduction to Gertrude Hirschler, ed., *Ashkenaz: The German Jewish Heritage* (New York: Yeshiva University Museum, 1988), p. xiii.

16. *EJ* 3: 720, *s.v.* "Ashkenaz." Ephraim E. Urbach, *Encyclopedia Ivrit s.v.* "Ashkenaz."

Jewish exilic experience [their embrace of martyrdom...]. It conjured up
Jewish civilization most deeply rooted in Galut." This symbolic Ashkenaz
"huddled physically in narrow ghettoes...voluntarily in their cultural spiritual ghetto."[17] Jacob Katz, too, constructed a medieval Ashkenaz to serve as
a contrast to the Early Modern Jewish society he analyzed, particularly in its
relationship to the Christian world.

Before we approach Katz's Ashkenaz, let us acknowledge the complex
history of the term's usage, and some of the earlier meanings invested in it.
Medieval users of "Ashkenaz" intended highly specific geographical or
cultural referents.[18] Recall one of the few surviving secular poems from
medieval Ashkenazic lands, in which the French author skewers the Jews of
Ashkenaz:

When I left France and	יום מצרפת יצאתי
journeyed down to Germany,	אל ארץ אשכנז ירדתי
I found a people there as cruel	ועם אכזר מצאתי
as ostriches in the desert.	כיענים במדבר
Oh, Israel is not forsaken...	כי לא אלמן ישראל...
I searched up and down Alsace	חפשתי אלזוש ארכה
but could find nothing of note,	ולא ידע אנוש ערכה
except that, —Oh, perversity!	לולא שלא כדרכה
—there the women ride over the men.	האשה על האיש תגבר
Oh, Israel is not forsaken...	כי לא אלמן ישראל...
I am heartily sick of these Ashkenazim.	קצתי מאוד באשכנזים
They are grim faced and	כי הם כולם פנים עזים
have beards like goats.	אף זקנם כמו עזים
Don't believe a word they breathe.	אל תאמן להם דבר!
Oh, Israel is not forsaken...	כי לא אלמן ישראל...

(The editor notes that the Hebrew word *alman* (אלמן) echoes the French
"allemand," so that the phrase can be read satirically: "A German [Jew] is not
an Israelite.")[19] Already for this fourteenth-century author, the term Ashke-

---

17. Dan Miron, "Ashkenaz: Modern Hebrew Literature and the Pre-modern
      German Jewish Experience," Leo Baeck Memorial Lecture no.33 (New York:
      1989), pp. 14–16.

18. On the history of the term Ashkenaz, see *inter alia*, Shlomo Eidelberg,
      "Ashkenaz," in Gertrude Hirschler, ed., *Ashkenaz: The German Jewish Heritage*
      (New York: Yeshiva University Museum, 1988); *EJ* 3: 720, *s.v.* "Ashkenaz."

19. Poem, translation, and note from T. Carmi, *The Penguin Book of Hebrew Verse*
      (New York: 1981), p. 453.

naz referred to a set of cultural characteristics as well as to a specific geographic
entity. The term has enjoyed a long and flexible career in this dual capacity.
Yet so long as a relatively cohesive and stable Jewish settlement endured in
one cultural and geographical realm, we can accept that the self-definition of
its members included some sense of belonging to a collective tradition, reaching back over time. Katz is certainly justified in stating that some form of
Ashkenazic collective identity can be posited for the medieval centuries.

The methodological difficulties begin when Katz stretches the medieval
conception of a cultural unit forward into the Early Modern period and
equates cultural identity with historical reality. His idealized depiction of
Jewish-Christian relations in the medieval world contrasts handily with an
equally homogenized Early Modern Ashkenazic Jewry. Katz characterized
Jewish-Christian relations in the Middle Ages as having a high degree of
economically vital interaction, leading to an intense awareness of Christians
and Christianity within medieval Jewry. The modified definition of Christians in the thought of the Meiri stands as the highwater mark of this development. According to Katz, such a strong level of interaction with Christians
no longer existed in the Early Modern period, when Jews simply stopped
relating to the Christian world altogether. Katz viewed this as a negative
development, characterizing this insularity as "lethargy" of mental attitude.[20]
Only the breakdown of traditional Jewish patterns of thought with the advent
of Haskalah and Hasidism eventually led Jews of Ashkenaz to renewed ties
with the Christian world and a reinvigorated mental life. If Katz had written
his assessment of the Early Modern period slightly later, he might have chosen
the title "The Closing of the Ashkenazi Mind."

Katz arrived at this picture by insisting that the conceptual unity of
Ashkenaz operated as an historical entity, in his oft repeated definitions: "The
Jews of France and Germany, and their descendants in central and eastern
European countries....These Jews underwent great changes between the
fifteenth and the seventeenth centuries."[21] Katz went out of his way to justify
his inclusion of Polish Jewry. He wrote of the eastward migration of German
Jews and of Polish Jews who regarded themselves as a branch of Ashkenaz as
defined by the linguistic commonality of Yiddish. Katz continued, on this
basis alone, to argue: "No justification, therefore, is necessary for the inclusion of Polish Jewry in a study that aims at tracing the development of Jewish-
Gentile relations within Ashkenazi Jewry. We shall in fact, fail to find any
marked difference between German and Polish Jewry in this period, and we
must regard both as historical descendants of Ashkenazi Jewry of the Middle

20. *Exclusiveness and Tolerance*, pp. 136–37.

21. *Exclusiveness and Tolerance*, p. 131.

Ages."[22] Katz concluded this point by saying that "divergences" that occurred, nevertheless, could be attributed to "historical factors." This is precisely where he has blurred the boundaries: the essentialist entity called
Ashkenazic Jewry may have different "historical conditioning" wherever it
may be, but because it shares the consciousness of belonging to Ashkenazic
Jewry, it can be treated as an historical unit.

Here, we must pause to assess this sweeping inclusiveness. In terms of commercial and family ties we may indeed speak of a meta-Ashkenazic inter-
connecting web of relationships in the Early Modern period. Often conducted in Yiddish, private correspondence, wills and testaments, business
documents and chronicles do, indeed, provide ample evidence of intricate
networks of family and business connections (although Katz barely relates to
the worlds of Yiddish writing). In other realms, "Ashkenaz" is far from a historically valid construct.[23] Historical consciousness of belonging to a cultural
cluster does not mean that historical experience, even in the broadest sense,
is parallel. David Ruderman has already commented on the "difficulty of
treating Poland, Lithuania, Bohemia and German lands as one continuous
landscape."[24] In his attempt to draw the definitive picture of Ashkenazic
society at the end of the Middle Ages, Katz glossed over some very critical
distinctions existing within the world of Ashkenaz.[25]

Rabbinic sources served as Katz's most important guides in the construction of his norm; yet even sources from the realm of *halakhah* and *minhag*
cannot sustain Katz's picture for the Early Modern period. It is certainly true
that the elite of sixteenth-century Polish halakhists, such as Maharsha"l,

---

22. *Exclusiveness and Tolerance*, p. 132.

23. I thank Hillel Kieval for introducing this notion in his comments at the
      conference. Bernard Weinryb, *The Jews of Poland: A Social and Economic History
      of the Jewish Community in Poland from 1100 to 1800* (Philadelphia: 1973), p. ix,
      argues that although there were myriad economic contacts and partnerships
      between the Jews of Poland and European Ashkenazic Jewry, their economic
      structure, their economic interrelations with the Christian society around
      them, and many of their economic activities differed fundamentally.

24. David Ruderman, *Jewish Thought and Scientific Discovery in Early Modern Europe*
      (New Haven: 1995), p. 67.

25. It is perhaps superfluous to mention that by not specifying in his titles that he
      is dealing with "Jewish-Christian" relations whenever he writes "Jewish-
      Gentile" relations, Katz seems to be positing that the central experience of Jews
      in the diaspora was that of Jews within the Christian world. For an example of
      a fruitful comparative approach, see Mark R. Cohen, *Under Crescent and Cross:
      The Jews in the Middle Ages* (Princeton: 1994).

Rem"a, and Levush, regarded themselves as heirs and defenders of Ashkenazic halakhic tradition against the powerful incursion of Sephardic influences,
particularly of the *Shulḥan Arukh* and Lurianic kabbalah; in this sense it is
certainly fair to accept their "Ashkenazic" self-assessment.[26] However, although Polish halakhists of the sixteenth century may have regarded themselves as Ashkenazic to the core vis-à-vis Sepharad, they regarded themselves
as having superseded the geographical Ashkenazim [the German scholars] in
their level of scholarship.[27] Contemporary German halakhists often bemoaned the lack of sensitivity by Polish halakhists to authentic traditions of
Ashkenaz. R. Chaim of Ulm (b. 1575) defended the ancient customs of
Ashkenaz against the "new arrivals recently come to Ashkenaz, rabbis from
Poland."[28] R. Hayim of Friedberg, brother of Mahara"l, chastised the editor
of Rem"a's *Torat Ḥatat*: "The preface of the proofreader mentions explicitly
[that the work is appropriate for] Poland, Russia [Ukraine], Bohemia and
Moravia…and perhaps any place where the language of Ashkenaz [Yiddish]
is spoken. The printer then added, of his own accord, an explicit mention of
'Ashkenaz' as well as on the title page…in order to increase sales."[29] R.
Hayim protested the inclusion of German Jews in the publisher's blurb. Any
tendency to fold the halakhic precedents and customs of German Jews into
those of the larger entity now called Ashkenaz was anathema to him, and he
is merely one representative figure. Early modern halakhists operated with no
clear-cut definition of who belonged within "Ashkenaz." In a recent illuminating study, Joseph Davis has analyzed just how difficult it was to establish
a consensus of who was "Ashkenaz" vis-à-vis the acceptance of the authority
of the *Shulḥan Arukh*. Some halakhists advanced a definition based on territory, some on family descent, and still others advocated an individualistic and
largely voluntary corporate conception.[30] Moreover, in the specific realm

26. On this, see *i.a.* Elchanan Reiner, "The Ashkenazi Élite at the Beginning of
    the Modern Era: Manuscript vs. Printed Book," *Polin* 10 (1997): 85–98.

27. Jacob Elbaum, *Petichut ve-histagrut: ha yetzirah ha-ruchanit- ha-sifrutit be-Polin u-
    ve-artzot Ashkenaz be-shilhei yemei ha-me'ah ha-shesh esreh* (Jerusalem: 1990), p.
    15, n. 12, cites from several *tshuvot* of Maharsha"l (#72, #85) that bespeak
    disdain for the scholarly level of "hakhamim benei Ashkenaz."

28. Eric Zimmer, *Gahaltan shel Hakhamim* (Beer Sheva: 1999), pp. 232, 234. See
    pp. 210–16 on R. Hayim b. Bezalel of Friedberg's vociferous opposition to
    halakhists who glossed over the Ashkenazic—German-Jewish—precedent,
    and pp. 220–37, which originally appeared in *Sinai* 102 (1988): 226–40.

29. Zimmer, *Gahaltan*, p. 213.

30. I thank Professor Joseph Davis of Gratz College for allowing me to read, prior

that Katz emphasized Jewish-Christian relations, the very circles he cited to construct the seamless ideal unity were aware of the profound difference between German and Polish circumstances.[31]

In one of his most innovative emphases, Katz noted that he would not merely analyze Christian attitudes toward Jews, the conventional focus of most studies of medieval and Early Modern Jewish-Christian relations, but that he intended to study the "changes of attitude on the part of Jews toward their non-Jewish environment." He further defined,

> Attitude…implies, first of all, some ideological appreciation of the nature and essence of the society with which the group in question is confronted.…[It] also has a practical bearing. The existence of the Jews was dependent upon economic relations with Gentiles: but were not these relations impeded by the mutually exclusive religious affiliations of the parties? The same question is even more relevant with regard to social intercourse.

Here, we enter into another methodological difficulty, for it is one thing to discuss an ideological posture and another to equate it with historical experience. In the realm of Jewish-Christian relations, Katz employed the rubric "social history" to undermine the processes of history itself: "At any time, Jewish-Gentile relations may appear to have differed according to the country concerned, but the differences were in reality no more than mutations of the same pattern."[32] Yet, to take only the most obvious example from

---

to its publication, his essay, "The Reception of the Shulkhan 'Arukh and the Formation of Ashkenazic Jewish Identity," forthcoming in *AJS Review*.

31. See Elbaum, *Petichut ve-histagrut*, 12, citation from Isserles: במדינות אלו... אין שנאתם גוברה [כך] עלינו כמו במדינת אשכנז and similarly, R. Hayim ben Bezalel Friedberg, who observed that Jews were not as downtrodden in Poland as they were in German lands. While in Poland no Gentile would dare to harm a Jew, in German lands Jews were freely persecuted even in their own spaces:
במדינת הרב [רמ"א] ידוע שת"ל עם ה' אינו בזוי ושסוי כ"כ כמו במדינות אלו [ארצות אשכנז] וכל גוי הבא ברחוב היהודים אימת הציבור עליו וירא לעשות נבלה בישראל; אבל...במדינות הללו...כל איש יהודי נגוש ועשוק ורצוץ כל היום ואין הגוי ירא או מתבייש מלרדות את הישראל אף בביתו...שם [בפולין] חדלו פרזון וכולם יושבים בקהילות, ...אבל בארצות אלו שרוב יושביה[ן] ישוב ורחוקים מן הקהילות...
Thus, in the very respect that Katz emphasized, the thinkers and leaders were aware of profound differences in circumstances.

32. *Exclusiveness and Tolerance*, p. xi.

this period, the historical patterns of German and Polish Jews could not have differed more. In the first decades of the sixteenth century, most German Jews were expelled from the Imperial cities, culminating with the Regensburg expulsion of 1519. Just as Polish Jewry reached a critical mass with new and secure Jewish settlement, German Jewry approached its nadir of insecure and very sparse population distribution. This shift changed the demographic profile of German Jewry. With the exception of Frankfurt and Worms, none of the urban centers associated with German Jewish settlement persisted. The dominant profile was a scattered, isolated one, often just several households. These tiny communities did not exist behind ghetto walls, and although Jews tended to live close together, this was not always the case.[33] The early-modern demographic shift also marked a decline in the intellectual profile of German Jews. With the sole exception of Frankfurt, large yeshivot ceased to exist or to attract students in German lands. German Jews sent their best students to Poland and often hired private tutors and rabbis from there, but could rarely count on local scholarship to produce Jewish intellectual leaders.[34] The *Landjudenschaften*, which organized the scattered German Jews into loose confederations, cannot compare in terms of power and influence to the *Va'ad Arbah Aratzot*, the council of Four lands, nor could local *kehillot* function on the same level except in the largest communities.[35]

Jews living in small groups among a Christian population with whom they interacted on an ongoing basis for every need differed in their relations to their Christian environment from those in larger clusters with hundreds of families who could more easily afford to isolate themselves from their sur-

---

33. Microhistories of Jewish communities in the Early Modern period in German lands that fit this pattern abound. For an example, see Claudia Ulbrich, *Shulamit und Margarete: Macht, Geschlecht und Religion in einer ländlichen Gesellschaft des 18. Jahrhunderts.* (Aschkenas. Zeitschrift für Geschichte und Kultur der Juden. Beiheft 4; Vienna-Cologne-Weimar: Böhlau Verlag, 1999).

34. Khone Shmeruk, "Bahurim me-Ashkenaz be-yeshivot Polin," in Shmuel Ettinger, Salo Baron, Ben Zion Dinur, Yisrael Halperin, eds., *Sefer yovel le-Yitzhaq Baer* (Jerusalem: 1961), pp. 304–17.

35. On the organization of German Jewry in this period, see Daniel J. Cohen, "Die Landjudenschaften in Hessen-Darmstadt bis zur Emanzipation als Organe der jüdische Selbstverwaltung," *Neunhundert Jahre Geschichte der Juden in Hessen* (Wiesbaden: 1983); Eric Zimmer, *Harmony and Discord: An Analysis of the Decline of Jewish Self Government in 15th Century Europe* (New York: 1970); idem, *Jewish Synods in Germany during the Late Middle Ages* (New York: 1978); Mordechai Breuer in *German-Jewish History in Modern Times*, Michael Meyer, ed. (New York: 1966), pp. 194–208, and source cited at p. 398.

roundings. The "ghetto mentality" (for there was no enforced Jewish space in Poland for Jews in this period), of "intensely Jewish life of the ghetto, a relationship dominated by Jewish exclusiveness" that Katz associated with Polish Jewry was not the reality for most Jews in German-speaking lands.[36] Ironically, in cities that imposed real ghettoes, whether Venice, Frankfurt, or Prague, Jewish minds were never closed to the Christian world, and Judaism there cannot be characterized as a "closed system of thought."

The astonishing growth, settlement patterns, and economic role of Jews in Poland in this period differed fundamentally from the conditions in German lands. Salo Baron saw in the rapid expansion of Polish Jewry an "epochal transformation." In terms of rapid re-adjustment to a less hostile environment and myriad economic opportunities, Baron viewed Polish Jews as closer to the Jews of medieval Islam or Christian Spain: "Population growth of the dimensions experienced by Polish-Lithuanian Jewry during the crucial century and a half before the Cossack uprising of 1648 also helped give rise to a revolutionary transformation in the general social and economic structure of Ashkenazic Jewry."[37] Jews and Christians in Poland worked together in a variety of economic activities, a far richer pattern of continuous interaction than Katz's depiction allows.[38] Those cities that adopted the policy *de non tolerandis judaeis* did so out of fear of Jewish economic competition, a testimony to Jewish success in penetrating vital aspects of the Polish urban economy.[39]

Katz defined insularity as "the disappearance of tension with the outside world," characterized by three important changes. First, that "polemics virtually cease." This hallmark characterized only Early Modern Poland. In German and central European lands, polemical encounters continued, although sporadically; indeed, all the exceptions to the rule that Katz cites refer to German-speaking lands. The presence or absence of polemical en-

---

36. *Exclusiveness and Tolerance*, pp. 132–33.

37. Salo Baron, *A Social and Religious History of the Jews* (New York: 1976), v. 16, pp. 214–15.

38. On the population of Polish Jews, see Shaul Stampfer, "Gidul ha-uchlusia ve-hagira be-yahadut Polin-Lita be-et ha-ḥadashah," in Israel Bartal and Israel Guttman, eds., *Kiyum ve-shever: Yehudei Folin le-doroteihem* (Jerusalem: 1997), v. 1, pp. 263–85. On their economic integration, see Moshe Rosman, "Yehudei Polin ad shenat 1648: Megamot politiyot, kalkaliyot, ve-hevratiyot," pp. 59–82, in the same volume; Edward Fram, *Ideals Face Reality: Jewish Law and Life in Poland, 1550–1655* (Cincinnati: 1997), ch. 1.

39. Jacob Goldberg, *Ha-hevrah ha-yehudit be-mamlekhet Polin-Lita*; trans. Sophia Lassman (Jerusalem: 1999), pp. 9–80.

counters between Jews and Christians in this period had much less to do with internal change of attitude on the part of Jews than with external factors. The Reformation in German lands led to periodic bouts of interest in Jewish conversion; the lack of any central political power in German lands (as Richard Kiekheffer has argued in another context) kept conversionary interest off political agendas through most of the Early Modern period. In Poland the virtually total lack of interest in Jewish conversion by the Polish Church in this period, rather than mental isolationism on the part of Jews, determined the absence of polemical "tension."[40]

The second hallmark of Early Modern insularity noted by Katz was a lack of interest in seeking proselytes and a contradictory attitude toward apostates. This is a somewhat unusual criterion, for surely the seeking of proselytes among Christians was not a common feature of medieval Jewish life, even if occasional exceptions occurred. In other respects, such as the facilitation of the return of penitent apostates, Katz is right on the mark for Polish Jewry, but not for German lands, where many *meshummadim* attested that vigorous communal efforts were made to prevent conversion out, and to facilitate the return of penitent apostates.[41]

The third basis for Katz's analysis was the reaction of Polish Jews to the pogroms of 1648–49. The willingness to martyrdom, he argued, along with the absence of polemical exchange, betrayed how distant the world of Polish Jews had grown from that of Christians, for the encounter was utterly devoid of Jewish polemical engagement. Here, recent scholarship has shown that only subsequent chroniclers saw *Qiddush Hashem* in these events; contemporary Jews were not generally given the choice of baptism or death. Later literary hands transformed murder into martyrdom.[42] Moreover, although it

---

40. Richard Kieckheffer, *Repression of Heresy in Medieval Germany* (Liverpool: 1979). On the lack of interest in converting Jews, see the recent work by Magdalena Teter, "Jews in the Legislation and Teachings of the Catholic Church in Poland (1648–1772)," Ph.D. dissertation, Columbia University, 2000, esp. ch. 3, "Beyond Adversos Judaeos."

41. Edward Fram, "Perception and Reception of Repentant Apostates in Medieval Ashkenaz and Premodern Poland," *AJS Review* 21 (1996): 299–339. Concerning the efforts made by German Jews to facilitate the return of apostates, see my forthcoming article "'Ich will dich nach Holland schicken': Amsterdam and the Reversion to Judaism of German-Jewish Converts," in Richard Popkin and Martin Mulsow, eds., *Secret Conversions in Amsterdam* (Archives of the History of Ideas Series, Kluwer Academic Publishers, forthcoming).

42. Edward Fram, "Creating a Tale of Martyrdom in Tulczyn, 1648," in Elisheva Carlebach, John Efron, and David Myers, eds., *Jewish History and Jewish Memory:*

is true that some Jews in German lands were still rejecting conversion as an alternative to death, many more were publicly embracing Christianity with no immediate coercion whatsoever.

But Katz did not set out to explore only internal Jewish attitudes. He also looked to the shift in the attitude of Christian society concerning the possibility of a place for Jews as individuals within society. Here the contrast between Polish and German Jewry could not be starker. The picture painted by Katz, especially in *Exclusiveness and Tolerance*, of a Jewry so completely insular that "Christianity never presented a temptation,"[43] may have been true for Polish Jewry, but it is the diametric opposite of the German experience. This is true both for the attitudes of Christian society to Jews as well as the reciprocal attitudes of Jews toward Christianity. In Germany, the Protestant Churches sporadically made serious attempts to reach out to Jews. Most notable among these, Jakob Spener's Pietist movement spawned several successful missionary offspring, the institutes of Edzard in Hamburg and Callenberg in Halle. More importantly, Christian Hebraists throughout German lands sustained a centuries-long effort to represent Judaism and Jewish life to a Christian audience. They employed Jews as tutors and informants. Their contact with Jews and knowledge of Judaism yielded a rich bounty in converts to Christianity and left virtually no corner of Jewish ritual life uninspected. Converts from Judaism as well as Christian Hebraists set out on a colossal project that spanned three centuries and produced translations into German of many Jewish texts, handbooks of Jewish customs as detailed as any *sefer minhagim*, and even dictionaries and guidebooks to instruct Germans in Yiddish. Any German Christian who wanted to prepare for an encounter with Jews could find ample material in his vernacular with which to inform and arm himself, and many did just that.[44]

No similar development took place in Poland. From the sixteenth century through the eighteenth century, the Catholic clergy of Poland fought on many fronts: "Not just German style Protestantism, but Greek Orthodoxy, and the Islam of the Tatars were some of the many religions and denominations contending for space." Even as the Catholic Church began to consolidate its power in Poland, conversion of the Jews remained the preoccupation

---

Essays in Honor of Yosef Hayim Yerushalmi (Hanover and London: 1998), pp. 89–112.

43. *Exclusiveness and Tolerance*, p. 155.

44. See my book, *Divided Souls: Converts from Judaism in Early Modern German Lands* (New Haven: Yale University Press, 2001) for aspects of mission and conversion in sixteenth- to eighteenth-century German lands.

of several individuals but never a concerted effort on the part of any establishment. The magnate economy still depended too heavily on the service of
Jews. Those members of the clergy who wished to approach Jews were
mocked for their utter lack of understanding of the basics of Judaism. They
tended to revert to the, by then, primitive method of citing biblical proof-
texts and, in some cases, the kidnapping of Jewish children for conversion.
No parallel movement to the Christian Hebraists of German lands took root
in Early Modern Poland. By and large, the Church in Poland through the
eighteenth century made no concerted overtures to the largest Jewish community within the Christian world.[45]

The crisis of traditional ideals represented by the German Haskalah was a
complex historical moment precipitated by many factors, internal and external, long-term and immediate. One strand of the move toward refashioning
Jews and their religion was the internalization of the Christian critique of
Judaism that had been articulated by the converts and Hebraists in the previous centuries. Many of the initial efforts at educational, economic, religious,
and even linguistic and sartorial reform of Judaism in late–eighteenth- and
early–nineteenth-century German lands focused on items that had been the
subjects of prior Christian critique. The "crisis" was not the result of purely
internal Jewish developments, but of the prolonged discussion of Jews and
Judaism in German to which the Jews were not impervious. Since no such
discussion took place in Poland in the sixteenth to eighteenth centuries, no
such absorption of Christian criticism could have taken place, regardless of
how frequent the social and economic exchanges.

The attempt to view all Ashkenaz with the same lens brought Katz to the
troublesome need to find an equivalent disintegration of Jewish attitudes in
Eastern Europe to the German Haskalah. He found it by drawing a purely
chronological line to the mid-eighteenth century, and viewed Hasidism as a
rupture from tradition, a move much criticized in subsequent historiography.
Of the two movements, only the German Haskalah represented an engagement with the opinions and arguments expressed in the Christian critique.

Other aspects of Katz's focus on Jewish attitudes toward Christianity in the
Early Modern period bear closer scrutiny as well. In order to construct the
Jewish norms, Katz chose sources produced primarily by two sets of Jewish
elite: the rabbinate, as represented both by halakhic sources as well as *drashot*
and *mussar* literature; and communal records that promoted a view of the
official community as run by its lay leadership. Katz saw communal institu-

---

45. Teter, *op. cit.*, ch. 3, and Jacob Goldberg, *Ha-mumarim be-mamlekhet Polin-Lita*
(Jerusalem: 1985).

tions as super-personal aggregates that also behaved according to norms, within which the individuals must function.[46] He maintained that these sources provided as good a picture of "tradition," the ideal past of Jewish society, as historians could ever get.

The use of Jewish thinkers such as Mahara"l and Rem"a to exemplify Jewish insularity is problematic even on its own terms. Their philosophy placed Christians and Christianity in particular spaces on an ontological plane, but each man's philosophical approach to non-Jewish life and thought did not even necessarily mirror his own pragmatic orientation, let alone the attitudes of his contemporaries from every social class. Mahara"l's thought is deeply significant for the intellectual history of the period, but for the social history? Katz' s statement "Mahara"l is an excellent example of a thinker whose ideas contradict the evidence of reality" suffices to make the point. Philosophical works cannot function as the basis for construction of a social-historical norm. Katz's assertion that there is only one unchanging and simple conception of Christianity in the Jewish world,

תפיסה אחת ומאחדת שליוותה את היהדות כמעט מאז עמדה על דעתה ההיסטורית

appears to simplify the more complex reality in conformity with the ideals of "social history," but it does not reflect historical realia.[47] Sources that reflect ideals held by the most articulate and leading segments of society cannot be read as constructions of the lived reality of the less articulate classes. Even *drashah* literature, arguably the most revealing among his sources of social norms and failures, was more of a literary genre than a record of social conditions, with scholars in this period often basing their sermons on precedents that tended to emphasize the scholarly and exegetical over practical concerns.[48] Sermons were carefully edited before publication and, like all homiletic literature, often exaggerated for the sake of emotional or rhetorical effect. In cities where intrusive Christian censors obsessed over subversive Jewish incitement against Christianity, Jews would have self-censored any statements in homiletic collections that could be construed as offensive to Christians and Christianity. In late–seventeenth-century Prague, for example, Jesuit influence brought the government to demand pre-censorship of Jewish sermons. Preachers would be required to present their sermons three

---

46. *Ibid.*, p. 300.

47. For a picture of a Jewish community whose profile deviates in so many ways from the idealized norm, see "The Prague Jewish Community in the Late 17th and Early 18th Centuries," *Judaica Bohemia* 36 (2000): 4–140. I thank Dr. Putík for sharing his work with me prior to its publication.

48. Elbaum, *Petichut ve-histagrut*, pp. 223–47.

days prior to delivery in Hebrew "with German translation."[49] How could any sermons published under such circumstances yield a true picture of Jewish attitudes toward Christians and Christianity?

By relying on the literature of the official classes, Katz did not include in his construction of the norm the vast vernacular world of Yiddish in Early Modern Ashkenaz, thus failing to reflect the lives and ideals of women and unlearned men, as Chava Weissler has argued for another context.[50] Her argument is particularly valid for the realm Katz wished to illuminate most, as Jewish women often served as the primary interfaces in the most quotidian realms of Jewish-Christian transactions. Jewish women engaged in a wide range of commercial and economic activities, traveling to fairs, lending money, and cottage-industry manufacturing. This ubiquitous access could easily lead to religious terrain. From the early sixteenth century in German lands, as the attention of Christian polemicists was drawn to the domestic and private sphere, Jewish women figured more prominently in their expositions of Jewish life and became direct targets of their appeals. Christian missionaries sought out Jewish wives and daughters when the family men proved intractable. Missionary-minded theologians formulated arguments specifically to persuade Jewish women and reached out to Jewish women directly as having the most to gain from conversion to Christianity. The missionary literature mocked the Jewish religion for assigning inferior roles to women in Jewish custom and liturgy, and criticized Jewish society for the gender differentiation in Jewish education. This became a common topos in the literature aimed at promoting conversion among German and Central European Jewish women.

The tensions, compromises, and exchanges that took place in the daily interactions between Jewish women and their Christian milieus are revealed in family chronicles, ethical wills and testaments, and private correspondence. To take some illustrative examples, when Christian Hebraist Johann Christoph Wagenseil hoped to lure a Jewish family to remain with him in Altdorf, he entered into a prolonged correspondence with Bella Perlhefter, the Prague native who adamantly refused his overtures.[51] A Yiddish will written by a

---

49. See the primary documents in Putík, "The Prague Jewish Community," appendix 1.

50. See the exchange between Katz and Chava Weissler, "Law, Spirituality, and Society," *Jewish Social Studies* 2 (1996): 87–98, 105–8.

51. Bernard Weinryb, "Historisches und Kulturhistorisches aus Wagenseils hebräischen Briefwechsel," *Monatsschrift für Geschichte und Wissenschaft des Judenthums*, N.S. 47 (1939): 325–41.

Jewish woman near Mannheim in 1713 contains a prolegomenon stating that if

> Heaven forbid, during my final illness, I will be induced by Others, …to thoughts or deeds against the One and Only God or his oral Torah, even against one tiny fraction thereof, I hereby pronounce before witnesses that they should be invalidated…and any thoughts against the Jewish religion should be as naught.[52]

Alternatively, when Parnas Abraham Jacob wrote his will, he included the Christian poor of his village.[53] Members of a society that lived completely insularly and without tension toward its surroundings would not have produced these cases. If, in fact, Polish Jewish women did not live with such frictions even though they were equally active in economic activities that brought them into contact with Christians, then the contrast deserves further study.

Although the methodological assumption that there was a Jewish popular or folk culture that ran counter to the elite, rabbinic culture is beset by serious difficulties, we can at least assume that rabbinic culture had long learned self-restraint regarding expressions that aroused the ire of official censors searching for anti-Christiana, whereas the less conspicuous stratum of culture that found its way into some Yiddish writing had never made similar adjustments. It constituted a private and hidden layer of Jewish culture and the posture toward Christianity embedded in it ought to be taken into account. It reflected a realm of daily transactions between Jews and Christians, the tensions that accompanied them, the strategies adopted by Christians to penetrate that world, and those adopted by Jews to repel conversion effectively that halakhic and official communal sources often did not reveal. Jewish resistance to Christian overtures was embedded deep within the culture of Ashkenaz and was expressed in many ways, some polemical and aggressive, others subtle, profound, and hidden. In their autobiographical and ethnographic texts, converts from Judaism to Christianity constantly alluded to a culture among common Jews that was different from the text-based image of the Jewish religion.

The omission of this type of source material is particularly regrettable because a pioneering work in Jewish social history should have given voice precisely to those classes that official history neglected. Katz's choice of sources precluded such a transformation within his own work. Yet Katz did

---

52. Joseph Bloch, "Le testament d'une femme juive au commencement du XVIIIe siècle," *Révue des études juives* 90 (1931): 156.

53. Ulbrich, *Shulamit und Margarete*, p. 315.

write one of the first attempts at a social history of Early Modern Jewry. His turn to social history was path-breaking and facilitated monumental changes in the research agenda of Jewish historians. Because Katz's turn to a new disciplinary mode came from a scholar who had clearly mastered the primary sources for intellectual history and wanted to expand the boundaries, his work had a profound impact on Jewish academe. Decades after his books were published, and despite the bodies of criticism from various angles, social history has become one of the fundamental ways to explore Jewish history and the Early Modern period has emerged as a separate unit in the design and construction of its periodization.

Jacob Katz as Social Historian

Paula E. Hyman
Yale University

Jacob Katz defined himself as a social historian and, indeed, he was a pioneer in the field of Jewish social history. In his memoirs, published in Hebrew in 1989 and in English in 1995, he attributed his attraction to social history to his graduate studies at the University of Frankfurt in the early 1930s. Karl Mannheim, the great sociologist of knowledge, became his mentor. As Katz writes, "At the very first class I knew beyond doubt that here was the person from whom I had the most to learn."[1] He describes his first articles as works of social history in their method and was not surprised that he was accepted into the Department of Sociology at the Hebrew University several years before he was invited to teach in the Department of Jewish History. There he subsequently felt isolated despite his personal friendship with several of his colleagues.[2]

Katz posited that social history necessitated both abstraction and generalization. In his 1956 article "The Concept of Social History," he asserted that "[i]n portraying a certain stratum of society the social historian is concerned solely with the typical and normative character of that stratum."[3] The successful social historian, then, would steep himself in the particular in order to

---

1. Jacob Katz, *With My Own Eyes: The Autobiography of an Historian*, trans. Anne Brenner and Zipora Brody (Hanover and London: Brandeis University Press, 1995), p. 78. Mannheim was not the official sponsor of Katz's dissertation because he had been expelled from the university by the time Katz submitted his thesis.

2. *Ibid.*, pp. 140–43.

3. Jacob Katz, "The Concept of Social History and Its Possible Use in Jewish Historical Research," in *Scripta Hierosolymitana*, Vol. III (1956), pp. 298–300. The citation is on p. 300.

create an ideal type of the phenomenon he was studying. What made the social historian different from the sociologist was not only his choice to examine the past but his regular inclusion of "time" (i.e., chronological development) in his consideration of his subject.[4] Still, the social historian used sociological method.

Katz considered social history ideally suited to the Jewish historian. Borrowing a line from the British historian G.M. Trevelyan, who stated in 1942 that social history might be considered (albeit wrongly) "history with the politics left out," he asserted that the Jews' lack of the conventional attributes of political power in the Diaspora meant that the common historical focus on political events could not be applied to the Jewish historical experience. A history that explored social processes and institutions "fit" the Jewish experience better than the time-honored political approach.

Katz's definition of social history appears idiosyncratic today largely because it is tightly linked to German sociological method, particularly as it found expression in the influential theoretical work of Max Weber. In Katz's student days what became known as the "annales" school was also taking shape in France. Adopting the sociological critique of conventional history, or "l'histoire évenementielle," the pioneer "annalistes" conceptualized history as a study of the processes of social or economic change over the "longue durée,"—decades, if not centuries.[5] Despite the fact that he would refer specifically to the Annales approach only in his last years, Katz's emphasis on generalization and abstraction was deeply rooted in the new historiographical currents of his time, which were imbued with sociological concepts. Although he became more concerned with detail as he became more self-consciously "historical," Katz never fully abandoned the approach he had developed in his student years in Frankfurt. He was also relatively untouched by the advances made in social history in both Europe and the United States in the last decades of his long and extraordinarily productive life.

There is no consensus as to what constitutes social history even today. The 1968 *International Encyclopedia of the Social Sciences* focused on the "unsatisfactory state" of the field, due to its "amorphous, invertebrate character, which derives very largely from the absence of a corpus of theory capable of providing concepts and hypotheses." In this view from the social sciences, social history, "ideally considered...is the study of the structure and process of human action and interaction as they have occurred in sociocultural contexts in the recorded past." But, in practice it was "not considered in such

---

4. *Ibid.*, p. 301.

5. The journal *Annales d'histoire économique et sociale* was established in 1929.

analytical [or] comprehensive [terms]."[6] Reflections on the field from social historians some three decades later emphasize not method but the subjects that social historians address, in particular, "groups of people...remote from the summits of power...the activities and beliefs of the working class, or peasants, or racial or ethnic minorities, or women, or youth." In addition, social historians wrote about "a range of social behaviors and ideas, not simply the formal political and intellectual strands that organize most conventional history."[7] As social history developed from the 1960s on, notes another historian, it focused on "history from below," on subordinated groups, but also increasingly on "'culture' rather than 'society.'"[8] In sum, historians defining social history agree that its practitioners are interested in social process rather than events, in the interaction of elements of social systems, and in analysis over time, but remain eclectic as to methodology.

Jacob Katz's definition of social history shares little with any of the scholarly assessments of the last thirty years except for his emphasis on "process," systemic interaction, and on "time." In fact, his insistence on abstraction, generalization, and the typical and normative as the central characteristics of social history dissented strikingly from the norms of most historians throughout the years of his career. His first book, *Tradition and Crisis*, implemented his methodological strategy, offering an ideal-type depiction of the traditional European Jewish community of the sixteenth through eighteenth centuries and, as he suggested in his theoretical essay, "ignoring details."[9] Not surprisingly, the book was strongly criticized by his colleagues at the Hebrew University, Hayyim Hillel Ben-Sasson and Shmuel Ettinger.[10] Despite the fact that the book was grounded in a careful reading of historical documents,

---

6. *International Encyclopedia of the Social Sciences* (ed. David L. Sills; n.p.: MacMillan Co. and The Free Press, 1968), Vol. 6, pp. 459, 455.

7. Peter Stearns, "Introduction," *Encyclopedia of Social History* (ed. Peter N. Stearns; New York: Garland Publishing, 1994), pp. vii–viii.

8. Pat Thane, "Social History," *The Social Science Encyclopedia* (2nd ed., eds. Adam Kuper and Jessica Kuper; London and New York: Routledge, 1996), p. 788.

9. *Masoret Umashber* was published in Hebrew in 1958 by Mossad Bialik and in an English translation, without footnotes and with some unanticipated elisions, by The Free Press in 1961. Bernard Cooperman's retranslation, published by New York University Press in 1993, restores the notes and provides a useful bibliography of Katz's sources. Katz, "The Concept of Social History," p. 297.

10. H.H. Ben-Sasson, "Concepts and Reality in Jewish History at the End of the Middle Ages," *Tarbiẓ* 29:3 (April, 1960): 297–312 and S. Ettinger, review of *Masoret Umashber, Kirjath Sepher* 35 (1959–60): 12–18.

especially responsa, its discussion of Ashkenazi Jewish society and its institutions in abstract terms rankled many historians, who enjoy grappling with
the particular and exploring difference and detail.

Like others of my colleagues, I find *Tradition and Crisis* a flawed book.
Katz posited that from the sixteenth to the eighteenth centuries Ashkenazi
Jewry from France in the West to Poland in the East constituted one socio-
cultural unit (an assertion with which one reviewer, Isadore Twersky, hap-
pily agreed). Such a position remains difficult to defend, given the sub-
stantially different contexts in which European Jews lived. The significance
of regional differences, not to mention national political variations, simply
disappeared in Katz's creation of a "typical" Ashkenazi community. As
Ettinger pointed out, Katz also violated his emphasis on "time" as the characteristic that differentiated the social historian from the sociologist. *Tradition
and Crisis* treated Ashkenazi Jewry as a virtually unchanging whole, for all the
years under consideration except for the very last.

Only at the end of the eighteenth century do forces for change appear—
Enlightenment in the West and Hasidism in the East. The development of
two such contrasting phenomena points to fundamental social, intellectual,
and political differences of long standing among the European countries in
which Ashkenazi Jews lived. But Katz has chosen to ignore these distinctions
in his presentation of Jewish society at the end of the Middle Ages, the subtitle
of his book. Because Enlightenment and Hasidism each stimulates change in
traditional Jewish society, Katz treats them as functional equivalents. Their
respective, quite different "messages" are subordinate to their purportedly
similar impact in challenging traditional Jewish authority. Each arouses
opposition from traditional elites, and each introduces new values that disturb
the otherwise peaceful functioning of traditional Ashkenazi Jewish society.
[Katz chooses to ignore the fact that the Hasidic revolution was subsequently
tamed and that Hasidism became one of the bulwarks of traditional Jewish
society in nineteenth- and twentieth-century Eastern Europe].

Despite its flaws, *Tradition and Crisis* was a major achievement. It made
innovative use of rabbinic responsa, as did his second book, *Exclusiveness and
Tolerance*, which focused on medieval Jewry.[11] (Interestingly, among Ben-
Sasson's major criticisms of *Tradition and Crisis* was Katz's interpretation of
responsa. This was the only part of the critique to which Katz felt compelled
to respond in the pages of *Tarbiẓ*). The book laid the ground for the acceptance of a social historical agenda among Jewish historians. Katz raised issues
that had not figured prominently in earlier scholarship. He was concerned

---

11. Jacob Katz, *Exclusiveness and Tolerance: Jewish-Gentile Relations in Medieval and
     Modern Times* (Oxford: Oxford University Press, 1961).

with such sociological categories as stratification and social mobility. He questioned the relations between religion and economics, a subject that he explored at greater length in *Exclusiveness and Tolerance*. His concept of institutions was broader than that of most historians. For example, he included the family and kinship structures as essential to an understanding of Ashkenazi society. In fact, his first historical article in Hebrew, published in *Zion* in 1944, was devoted, as its title indicates, to "Marriage and Sexual Life Among the Jews at the Close of the Middle Ages." This at a time when family history was scarcely recognized as a subject for inquiry, never mind a field. Throughout his career he looked at Jewish society through the social historian's lens, searching for overlooked details that might cast light on how the broader society functioned. His eye often fell on aspects of Jewish society that other scholars ignored, such as Orthodox Jews and their leadership, who annoyingly flouted the historians' conventional wisdom that they were always about to disappear, or the "Shabbes Goy," the Gentile who provided services forbidden to Jews to carry out on the Sabbath—an institution that no historian had thought worthy of consideration.[12] As Katz remarked in his memoir, "Topics rarely suggest themselves....Sometimes the historians' ability to discover that a phenomenon is worthy of research is his most important contribution."[13] Finally, at the end of *Tradition and Crisis*, in his discussion of the erosion of traditional Jewish society, Katz returned to the process of assimilation, which had been the subject of his doctoral dissertation in Germany, more than a quarter of a century earlier.[14]

The subject of Jewish assimilation was a natural one—though not a psychologically easy one—for a student of history with sociological inclinations to investigate in Germany of the 1930s, when the entire project of assimilation was under assault and its premises thoroughly undermined. In his dissertation [*Die Entstehung der Judenassimilation*; or The Origin of Jewish

---

12. See, for example, Jacob Katz, "Towards a Biography of the Ḥatam Sofer," in *From East and West: Jews in a Changing Europe, 1750–1870*, ed. Frances Malino and David Sorkin (Oxford: Oxford University Press, 1990), pp. 223–66. The essay was first published in Hebrew in 1967; Jacob Katz, *The "Shabbes Goy": A Study in Halakhic Flexibility*, trans. Yoel Lerner (Philadelphia: Jewish Publication Society, 1989). Under the title *Goy shel shabbat*, this appeared in Hebrew in 1984.

13. Jacob Katz, *With My Own Eyes*, p. 150.

14. Jacob Katz, *Die Entstehung der Judenassimilation und deren Ideologie* (Frankfurt: 1935). The completed work was submitted in 1934. It was reprinted in Jacob Katz, *Emancipation and Assimilation: Studies in Modern Jewish History* (Westmead, England: Gregg International Publishers, 1972).

Assimilation] Katz demonstrated the approach he would articulate fully two decades later in his theoretical article on social history. He shifted attention from single great intellectual figures of the general and Jewish Enlightenment to the processes of social and cultural change that would create the conditions necessary for a relatively large-scale change in attitude toward the larger society on the part of Jews. In Katz's view this change occurred when the formerly closed host society expressed its openness to Jews' participation in its cultural and socioeconomic life, and when the minority group was prepared to respond to the invitation.[15] Katz located the decisive moment in the development, and acceptance, of an ideology that promoted change and in the creation of turf on which social interaction could occur. He would return to these points in his subsequent work.

Perhaps Katz's most interesting and overlooked contribution to the social history of the process of Jewish assimilation in western and central Europe was a book that he regarded as an offshoot of his larger project on emancipation and assimilation. That was his study of Jews and Freemasons in Europe, published in 1970.[16] It is a model monograph for examining the institutional framework of Jewish integration in Europe. The significance of this book from the perspective of the social historian is that Katz was concerned not only with the ideas that fostered civic and (partial) social equality for Jews, but with the social spaces that served as sites for the integration of Jews within the larger society. As Katz wrote, "My…interest in this subject arose from studying the emergence of Jews into modern society, and my attempts to trace the routes by which these former ghetto-dwellers found their way into the social circles of their neighbors.[17] As in his dissertation, he was aware that assimilation required two elements—the desire of the minority to adopt aspects of the majority culture and the willingness of the larger society to absorb "the foreign body." This distinction was later elaborated by Todd Endelman, who labeled the two necessary but distinct forces as "acculturation" and "integration," and also by David Sorkin, who posited that German Jews did acculturate but were not successfully integrated. They therefore inadvertently created a distinct subculture because of the failure of German bourgeois to accept them into their social institutions.[18]

---

15. Jacob Katz, "Die Entstehung der Judenassimilation," pp. 201–2 and *passim*.

16. Jacob Katz, *Jews and Freemasons in Europe, 1723–1939*, trans. Leonard Oschry (Cambridge: Harvard University Press, 1970).

17. *Ibid.*, Preface and p. 1.

18. Todd Endelman, *The Jews of Georgian England: Tradition and Change in a Liberal Society* (Philadelphia: Jewish Publication Society, 1979), pp. 3–4, 7–9, 248 and

Masonic lodges were concrete examples of Katz's "neutral society," a term
he had used in *Tradition and Crisis*, or, in his revised formulation, the "semi-
neutral society" that began to appear ever so slowly under the impact of
Enlightenment ideals. In fact, the high level of resistance to Jews among some
Masonic lodges, especially in Prussia, was, as Katz himself acknowledges,[19] a
major factor in his modification of his assessment of the openness to Jews of
even the purportedly liberal elements in the larger society. Katz points out
that the association of Jews and Freemasons was a staple of anti-Semitic ideology. Much of the writing on the subject prior to his—whether polemical,
apologetic, or historical—explored an imaginary construction. As a social
historian, Katz could not be content with an exploration of the deployment
of the slogan alone, although he does address the slogan's historical development in the increasingly anti-Semitic climate of the late nineteenth century. And, as he writes in a chapter he entitles "Imaginary Relations," his
interpretation of the slogan in the latter part of the book "has dealt not with
the real position of the Jews in the Masonic movement but with the connections imagined to exist between the two."[20]

It is significant that Katz both introduces and concludes the book with an
ideological and political issue—the linkage of Freemasons and Jews—despite
his broader concerns with Masonic-Jewish relations in all their social ramifi-
cations. For much of Katz's work, as he expanded his depiction of emancipation and assimilation, was dominated by issues of intellectual and political,
rather than strictly social, history. Moreover, his sources, even in *Tradition and
Crisis*, were the stuff of intellectual history—primarily the writings of rabbis
in all their genres along with a smattering of works of Christian intellectuals
and maskilim. A handful of communal *pinkasim* was ancillary to his project.
When he wrote about the Ashkenazi family, his reliance on rabbinic responsa,
however innovative, provided only a partial view of family life, filtered
through the lens of *halakhah*. Katz was interested in how early modern rabbis
understood human sexuality rather than how ordinary Jews ordered their
marital lives and expressed their sexuality.

Out of the Ghetto, perhaps his most popular book in the United States and
the big project on which he was working when he happened upon the
Freemasons, was essentially a history of the elaboration of the *idea* of emancipation and its consequences in western and central Europe from the end of

---

David Sorkin, *The Transformation of German Jewry, 1780–1840* (Oxford University Press, 1987), especially pp. 99–103, 122–23, 173–78.

19. Katz, *Emancipation and Assimilation*, p. xii.

20. Katz, *Jews and Freemasons*, p. 219.

the eighteenth century through 1870.[21] Because of his focus on the idea, he
devoted most of the book to the first decades of the period, when different
visions of emancipation jostled each other in the public arena. Although he
followed his prior methodological strategy of generalization, Katz was far
more defensive about this posture than he had been in *Tradition and Crisis*.
"The presentation of Jewish emancipation in the West as a meaningful
whole," he noted, "is legitimate. For even if the results of the process differed
from place to place, the underlying forces effecting these changes were
identical."[22]

Katz traced these underlying forces and their ideational underpinnings in
developments in politics and the civic status of the Jews, rather than in
changed behavior among the masses. In fact, his interest lay with elites, both
Jewish and gentile, and their attitudes toward emancipation and assimilation.
Although he included some discussion of socioeconomic changes among the
Jews, his primary sources were legal and intellectual. He mined neither the
statistical data nor the qualitative sources of memoirs and letters that were
beginning to be used more frequently by social historians.

David Myers points to the "mix of social and intellectual change [that]
forms the background of... *Out of the Ghetto*," as its strength, and the strength
of his previous books as well.[23] According to Myers, Katz focused on the
interplay of shifting social conditions and cultural norms to explore the
precise relations of social change and ideological legitimation that characterized transitional periods. By including both intellectual and social forces,
he was able to present a multi-variable, dialectic view of social change.

However, in the interplay of the social and the intellectual, Katz privileged
the intellectual, although he recognized the dialectical relation between the
two. In the end, ideas engaged Katz's attention far more than human social
activity. That is, he considered that changes in behavior attained historical
significance only when they were intellectually (we might now say culturally)
legitimated. Katz made this clear in *Out of the Ghetto* but also in his articles
on Jewish nationalism and Zionism. Applying what he called a sociological
analysis to Jewish nationalism, Katz counted among its unusual features the
fact that the idea of nationalism, rooted in traditional messianism, preceded
any apparent social need. "Not the need created the idea but the idea created

21. Jacob Katz, *Out of the Ghetto: The Social Background of Jewish Emancipation, 1770–
    1870* (Cambridge: Harvard University Press, 1973).

22. *Ibid.*, p. 4.

23. David Myers, "Rebel in Frankfurt: The Scholarly Origins of Jacob Katz,"
    published in this volume.

the social unit," he concluded. "The common idea became a basis of social unity" among the first Nationalists.[24] Thus the idea sustained the forerunners of Zionism until political and economic conditions were propitious to find a receptive audience. But it was not sufficient alone to achieve its aims. For, Katz adds, "As our case in point demonstrates that ideas at times do appear in advance of their need, it conversely shows the limited power of any idea if it is not linked up with a social necessity."[25]

This stance toward the primacy of ideas in social change—even though ideas had to fill social needs—was also the source of Katz's critique of Azriel Shohat's Im Ḥilufei Tekufot (Beginnings of the Haskalah Among German Jewry).[26] He asserted that Shohat confused deviation from traditional patterns with conscious change. Deviation, which occurs regularly in traditional societies, has no lasting consequences (except possibly for the deviants), whereas conscious change challenges the legitimacy of, and ultimately undermines, the authority vested in traditional institutions. By focusing on cases of what Katz labeled deviation, Shohat wrongly (in Katz's view) pushed the beginning of change among German Jews back to the late seventeenth or the early eighteenth century. Katz asserted that ideologically conscious change was necessary to unleash "a new process that would lead ultimately to a new structure of society,"[27] and that such conscious change was evident in Jewish society only in the latter half of the eighteenth century.

This assertion of the need for ideological awareness in order for change to be significant is unusual in a self-proclaimed social historian, for social historians generally attempt to interpret behavior even when (perhaps I should say, especially when) it is not accompanied by a polished intellectual discourse. Todd Endelman, one of the preeminent representatives of the then younger generation of social historians of the Jews, made precisely that point in his study of eighteenth-century Jews in England.[28] In their casual attitude

---

24. Jacob Katz, "The Jewish National Movement: A Sociological Analysis," *Journal of World History*, Vol. 11, No. 1–2 (1968): 267–83, reprinted in *Emancipation and Assimilation*, pp. 129–45. The citation is found on p. 141. The article also appears in *Jewish Emancipation and Self-Emancipation* (Philadelphia: Jewish Publication Society, 1986), pp. 89–103.

25. "Jewish National Movement," p. 142.

26. Azriel Shohat, *Im Ḥilufei Tekufot* [With the Changing of Times, sometimes translated as Beginnings of the Haskalah among German Jewry] (Jerusalem: Mossad Bialik, 1960).

27. Katz, *Out of the Ghetto*, p. 35.

28. Endelman, *The Jews of Georgian England*.

toward traditional Jewish practice, English Jews of both the upper and lower classes indulged in behavior that represented a significant change from the forms of Jewish practice that were routinely displayed in Jewish communities on the continent. However, they articulated no ideological justification for their new behavior.

Perhaps because Katz deemed intellectual forces as central to all meaningful social change, he focused on the German-speaking lands in discussing emancipation and assimilation and its social foundations. The "typical" constellation of forces that promoted acculturation to secular thought, in his eyes, occurred in the German states and the German cultural orbit. To be sure, *Out of the Ghetto* made reference to the 1785 Metz Essay contest on the topic "Are There Means of Making the Jews Happy and More Useful in France?" and to the French Revolution as well. However, he saw the "literary discourse of Metz" as "clearly a continuation of what took place in Berlin a decade before" and the French Revolution as presenting "the forum where the ideas of reform could be put to the test.... The ideas of reform arose first in Germany but the impetus for their implementation came from France."[29] Revolutionary political change was ultimately less significant than ideological developments, sudden political spasms of less import than the gradual working out of new ideas. In taking account of the English experience, Katz noted, "Factual, non-reflective accommodation, as exemplified by the English experience, is by nature locale-bound. Studied and reasoned change is prone to be mobile" (and therefore was exported elsewhere).[30]

Because Germany was the home of studied change, Katz was eager to explore the impact of the German-Jewish experience of emancipation and assimilation on the Jews of western and central Europe and the United States. In convening a conference to address the question, and in publishing its results in book form (as *Toward Modernity: The European Jewish Model*), Katz provided one of the first examples of comparative modern Jewish history. Although he presumed the importance of the impact of the German model, he was sufficiently open to the participating scholars' findings to speak in the introduction to the book of the convergence of the impact of the German model with "the influence of local factors."[31] Critics of his Germanocentrism, like Pierre Birnbaum and Ira Katznelson,[32] both social scientists, often

---

29. Katz, *Out of the Ghetto*, pp. 73, 75.

30. Jacob Katz, *Toward Modernity: The European Jewish Model* (New Brunswick, N.J.: Transaction Books, 1987), p. 3.

31. *Ibid.*, p. 9.

32. Pierre Birnbaum and Ira Katznelson, "Emancipation and the Liberal Offer,"

fail to see his willingness to complicate his original project. They do acknowledge, however, that it is important "not to underestimate the profound [shared] qualities of emancipation that can get lost in an appreciation of variation....To the extent that emancipation conduced a redefinition of the relationship of Jews to the state," the variations in emancipation fall "within a more general story."[33] Yet they find that Katz's emphasis on "the shared aspects of Jewish emancipation in western and central Europe...pushes far too hard in the direction of singularity."[34] Still, their own project, a collective and comparative volume that grew out of two meetings in which the essayists together refined their subject, is hard to imagine without the precedence of Katz's pioneering effort.

Toward the end of his life Katz retreated from his earlier assertion that social history was ideally suited for the Jewish historian of the Diaspora. In a brief essay Katz noted the limitations of social history.[35] The social historical approach was justified only if the researcher made sure to include the political dimension of a society's experience. For Jewish historians that stipulation necessitated addressing not only the impact of external political power on Jewish life but also the internal political element within the Jewish community itself. Most importantly, social history could not provide explanations for phenomena that transcended specific times and locales, what he labeled the "supra-epochal" (his own version of the Annales' "longue durée"). Indeed, looking for social factors of causation in a particular case, when dealing with issues that developed over a long period of time, could lead the historian to offer misleading interpretations of specific events. As Katz put it, "there can be little doubt about the utility of a social history to comprehend and present an interconnected picture of all aspects in the life of a society *during a given epoch*. But such a method should not be elevated to the level of dogma."[36] As his case in point, Katz singled out the issue of anti-Semitism, which could be comprehended only as a supra-epochal phenomenon.

---

in their *Paths of Emancipation* (Princeton: Princeton University Press, 1995), pp. 1–36.

33. *Ibid.*, p. 16.

34. *Ibid.*, p. 17.

35. Jacob Katz, "On Jewish Social History: Epochal and Supra-Epochal Historiography," *Jewish History* VII, 1 (Spring 1993): 89–97. An earlier version of the article appeared as "Zur jüdischen Sozialgeschichte: epochale und überepochale Geschichtsschreibung," in *Tel Aviver Jahrbuch für deutsche Geschichte* 20 (1991): 429–36.

36. *Ibid.*, p. 94. The emphasis in italics is mine.

Katz's reconsideration of social history offered a defense of his own work. In *Tradition and Crisis* he limited himself to a defined epoch and locale, early modern Ashkenaz, recognizing that broad statements about the nature of the Jewish community required research into rabbinic literature from late antiquity through the Middle Ages. In presenting his account of Jewish experience with emancipation and acculturation in the modern West, he realized that modern anti-Semitism had to be treated in a separate and thorough study, which became his book *From Prejudice to Destruction*.[37]

Jacob Katz did not write a comprehensive social history of European Jewry, and his specific methodology has been superseded even for the many younger Jewish historians who see him as their intellectual mentor. Yet, I would evaluate him as one of the two most influential Jewish historians of the past century. He set the agenda for further scholarly research of a social historical bent. He alerted us to think big, beyond the monograph so beloved in our graduate education, and to explore institutions that earlier generations may have considered trivial. Because he studied in the yeshiva as well as the university and remained committed to traditional Jewish practice, he never treated religion in the modern period as simply a dependent variable of other social or ideological forces or as a reified object. He thought of categories as fluid, not as polar opposites. His own openness to new methodologies as well as his demonstration of their utility for the study of Jewish history continues to serve as a model for subsequent generations of scholars. More specifically, his combination of the social and the intellectual may have prepared the way for acceptance by Jewish social historians of the cultural turn in historiography. Even as two new generations of Jewish social historians explore new subjects with new perspectives, we continue to build on Jacob Katz's pioneering work.

---

37. Jacob Katz, *From Prejudice to Destruction: Antisemitism 1700–1933* (Cambridge: Harvard University Press, 1980).

JACOB KATZ ON THE ORIGINS AND DIMENSIONS OF JEWISH MODERNITY:
THE CENTRALITY OF THE GERMAN EXPERIENCE

David Ellenson

Hebrew Union College – Jewish Institute of Religion

The gifts Jacob Katz bestowed upon modern Jewish scholarship were by any standard immense. No one more brilliantly analyzed the course and complexity of modern European Jewish history than he did. In his landmark work, *Tradition and Crisis*, Katz fruitfully defined the motifs that were to mark a lifetime of scholarship. In its pages, he also employed a social-scientific methodology he had imbibed during his student years at the University of Frankfurt to illuminate the content and trajectory of the western European Jewish world as it confronted the ongoing challenges of adjusting Judaism to the demands of the modern world. Although he would later supplement that social scientific methodology with a more conventional narrative approach, Katz remained forever associated with the social scientific attitudes and concerns that informed his earliest books. This paper will focus on how Katz defined and investigated the demands that modernity placed upon Judaism and how he both distinguished the challenges and probed the adjustments that Judaism made to the realities of a modern setting through his seminal investigations of the nineteenth-century German Jewish community.

The first section of the paper will be devoted to an exposition of the sociological methods and concerns he employed as the framework for his initial forays into the field of German-Jewish history. For this framework was far from incidental to the historical claims he would ultimately make. Indeed, it helped to shape the conclusions at which he would arrive. His decision at that time to eschew the narrative mode of classical historiography in favor of a social-scientific lens permitted him to illuminate with unparalleled clarity what was at stake in the transition of Judaism from the medieval to the modern world. Consequently, an understanding of sociological tradition will help to emphasize the distinctiveness and direction that would always mark his scholarship. The conceptual sophistication he brought with him from the social sciences was instrumental in shaping the questions that would occupy his attention in his later books and essays as well, works that were marked by a narrative method of historical discourse.

Having outlined the disciplinary concerns and concepts that informed Katz, the essay will then turn to an examination of how he applied these concerns and concepts in the final chapters of his justly acclaimed *Tradition and Crisis*. In those last chapters, Katz focused on issues of enduring concern to students of Judaism in the modern setting. He provided a summary-analysis of the transition that marked German Judaism as it moved from the world of classical rabbinic traditionalism to the realm of emancipated pluralistic modern Judaism. Katz, in these pages, identified certain key issues that were crucial for an understanding of how this transition could be marked, as well as the vectors that would define the complex and uneven course of this transition. Through an examination of *Tradition and Crisis*, as well as several supplementary writings, these issues and vectors will become clear.

The third and concluding section of this paper will then investigate how the trajectory plotted by this scholarship found expression in major elements of his later narrative writings on German Judaism. Although a number of these writings will be presented, his widely heralded book, *A House Divided: Orthodoxy and Schism in Nineteenth-Century Central Europe*, first published in Hebrew 1995, will be highlighted. This work is a culminating achievement that goes far beyond its seemingly discrete subject matter, and it displays the concerns and conclusions that a mature Katz brought to this subject of Judaism and the Jewish response to the modern Occident. Here the thematic continuity that occupied his attention for a lifetime will be emphasized, and the precise manner in which he elucidated the Jewish response to the modern world through his work on the German Jewish community will be underscored. In so doing, this paper hopes to emphasize the enduring importance of his work for the scholarly reconstruction of the modern Jewish experience as well as the ongoing vitality his insights provide for comprehending the course of Jewish life in the modern West.

Sociological Frameworks and Concerns

Katz, in his 1934 doctoral dissertation, "*Die Entstehung der Judenassimilation in Deutschland und deren Ideologie*," already focused on the responses of Jews and Judaism as the people and the religion moved from the confines of a traditional society to the challenges of coping with a neutral one.[1] This motif was to occupy his attention throughout his scholarly career. The task that con-

---

1. This dissertation is reprinted in Jacob Katz, *Emancipation and Assimilation, Studies in Modern Jewish History* (Westmead, Farnborough: Gregg International, 1972).

fronted Katz in addressing this issue was how to define and measure this evolution, and to signify what this evolution meant for the beliefs of Judaism and the structure of Jewish life. The form of history that he ultimately felt to be most suitable to accomplish these goals was what he identified, somewhat idiosyncratically, as social history.[2] Social history, as Katz characterized it decades after his dissertation, "is concerned not with the single occurrence, but with the social reality at a given time....In other words, social history is concerned with describing institutions within the framework of...events."[3]

From the very outset of his career, Katz had been profoundly schooled in and influenced by the sociological works of men such as Weil, Mannheim, Weber, and Toennies. It is thus hardly surprising that Katz, in *Tradition and Crisis*, turned to the methodology of the ideal-type as well as the themes and concerns of contemporary sociology in order to illuminate and describe the movement of Judaism from the medieval to the modern world. The aim of the ideal-type was to isolate elements of social reality in order to explain their significance and importance. Katz deemed this theoretical construct appropriate for measuring the nature and institutions of Judaism and the Jewish community during the pre-modern period. He felt it could be employed to characterize the institutional and cultural reality of a nascent central European Jewish modernity as well. He therefore used the ideal-type to measure the adaptation and persistence that challenged and marked Jewish leaders and organizations as they coped with the onslaught brought on by this transformed setting. It was a method designed to focus on institutions, and it led Katz in *Tradition and Crisis* to emphasize how the structures of the Jewish community were altered by the encounter with the modern world, causing him thereby to eschew a narrative history.

In *Tradition and Crisis*, as well as elsewhere in his writings, Katz offered an overarching and insightful analysis of how modernity had destroyed the traditional parameters that had marked the Jewish community as a public corporation possessing legal authority over all its members. Instead, the modern world, by destroying communal legal bounds, had essentially defined Judaism in religious terms alone. In the process, it reduced Judaism to a largely voluntary association. As a result, Jewish pluralism became unavoidable, and in a country like the United States, voluntarism became virtually absolute.[4] The

---

2. For a comprehensive treatment of how Katz employed this term, see the analysis of Paula Hyman, "Jacob Katz as Social Historian," contained in this volume.

3. Jacob Katz, *Tradition and Crisis* (New York: Schocken, 1958), p. 5.

4. For Katz's point on this score, see his "Introduction," in Jacob Katz, ed., *Toward*

explanation Katz offered for this phenomenon was straightforward and
direct. As the modern state had dismantled the traditional political structure
of the community, no one group could any longer impose its definition of
proper Jewish practice and belief upon the entire Jewish community. Judaism
became a matter of assumed identity for many, and Jewish beliefs and practices, issues of negotiation and re-negotiation. The ideal-type allowed Katz
to highlight this. Katz was also able to turn to a broad sociological tradition
for an analysis of this situation precisely because this tradition centered large
parts of its discussion of the social trends that marked the modern West
around the theme of community and its political and cultural transformation.
From this perspective, it can be said that Katz simply applied the concerns and
questions of contemporary sociological discourse to the field of modern
European Jewish history.

This view of transformation in the ideal of community was best captured
in the writings of the famed German sociologist Ferdinand Toennies. Toennies saw the history of the West as marked by a move from the intimate face-
to-face personal relationship of the premodern *Gemeinschaft* to the rationally
ordered and bureaucratically dominated patterns of an impersonal *Gesellschaft*. In this transition from a folk to an urban society, traditional frameworks
for community—and the patterns of culture, religion, politics, and social
relations that supported them—were challenged and often collapsed.[5]

Katz was well versed in these themes and no Jewish historian-sociologist
has yet employed the framework this sociological tradition provided more
fruitfully and comprehensively than Jacob Katz did for understanding and
evaluating the impact these changes had upon the Jewish community. Katz
understood that this transition from *Gemeinschaft* to *Gesellschaft* was a result
of the secularization of life that came to dominate in the modern West. As
sociologists employ the term, secularization does not signify the disappearance of religion. Rather, it points toward the constriction of religion and
the compartmentalization of life. A distinction between public and private
spheres arises and religion becomes increasingly consigned to the private
realm. Religion no longer plays the role it previously did in informing the

---

Modernity: The European Jewish Model (New Brunswick and Oxford: Transaction Books, 1987), pp. 1–2. On p. 2, he observes, "Under the impact of
rationalization and enlightenment the state relinquished its claim to be directly
responsible for the religious conduct of the population. In the extreme case,
realized first in the United States, the state's disclaimer *became absolute*, leading to
the separation of church and state" (italics mine).

5. See Ferdinand Toennies, *Fundamental Concepts of Sociology*, trans. by Charles P.
Loomis (New York: American Book Company, 1940).

beliefs and guiding the activities of either persons or entire communities. Secularization brings in its wake a high degree of institutional differentiation that frequently consigns religion to the private realm. The structures that formerly supported and sustained religious organizations and beliefs are no longer diffused as organic elements throughout all the institutions of a given society. Instead, they are now shifted, as the sociologist Peter Berger has phrased it, "from society as a whole to much smaller groups of confirmatory individuals."[6] In the wake of such a process, traditional religious beliefs and structures sometimes collapse. However, as Katz realized, such beliefs and structures are at other times simply reformulated to accommodate and adapt to a novel reality.

In order to explain the situation that marked the Jewish community and its religion in modern Germany, Katz masterfully applied the sociological paradigm he had learned at Frankfurt to an analysis of the historical conditions of the Jews. Indeed, a great part of the genius that marked Katz was his realization that this model provided a framework for understanding the elements of continuity, as well as change, that marked Jews and Judaism as they entered into the modern setting. The social, educational, and religious institutions and patterns that informed Jewish life in the modern West were pluralistic and no longer exclusively Jewish. Consequently, the structures of modern European Jewish life could no longer foster and transmit the same unified notions of value, discipline, and conduct that they had during the Middle Ages. Jewish life was simply too open and diffuse. As a result, modern Jewish life could not reflect the homogeneity of its medieval antecedent.[7] Katz nevertheless insisted that this more open and pluralistic Jewish world could be comprehended, and he employed this notion of the "privatization of religion" to illuminate the process of change that defined modern Judaism as well as the diverse streams and institutions that were to flow from it.

This sociological sensibility and its attendant concerns allowed Katz to identify important themes for indicating how and why pluralism had come to flourish in the modern setting. As a result, Katz now possessed an apparatus for explaining how and why modern Jewish individuals were able to establish and choose discreet collectivities that could serve as mediating agencies for the promotion of particular ideologies and practices. His sociological acumen allowed him to delineate the adaptive mechanisms that marked Jews and the

---

6. Peter L. Berger, Brigette Berger, and Hansfried Kellner, *The Homeless Mind: Modernization and Consciousness* (New York: Random House, 1974), p. 80.

7. For the concise treatment Katz accorded this theme, see *Tradition and Crisis*, pp. 184–86.

Jewish community as they transitioned from the Middle Ages to modernity despite the fact that their identities were now forged from a heterogeneous variety of divergent ideological and religious sources. It provided a framework that could account for how traditional loyalties were simultaneously preserved *and* transformed as Jews and their communal structures confronted the modern situation. As Katz would put it, Judaism and the Jewish people did not simply collapse and expire when they faced the challenges of the modern world. They adjusted and responded to the reality of the modern world so as to counteract "the anticipation of an abruptly dissolving Jewish community."[8]

The utility of this sociological imagination for an assessment of Judaism in the modern era was self-evident to Katz. Armed with this methodology and cognizant of the themes and concepts identified by the sociological traditions that had informed him, Katz was now prepared to write *Tradition and Crisis*. In its pages, he would employ the concerns and the methods of this discipline to describe and analyze the transitions and adaptations that marked the Jewish group as it grappled with the test of the modern Occident.

Tradition and Crisis *and the Pursuits of a Career*

In the final chapters of *Tradition and Crisis*, Katz confronted what transpired in the inner intellectual processes of the Jews as well as the changes that marked the institutional structures of the Jewish polity as Jews and Judaism began their dialectical encounter with a nascent but insistent modernity. The motifs and concerns he addressed in these pages were to constitute more than mere touchstones in his work on German Judaism. They also defined the scholarly trajectory and agenda he would establish for others who would come to work in this field, for throughout his career Katz would place the history of the German Jewish community and its leadership at the center of modern Jewish historical scholarship. This community and these leaders consistently constituted a vanguard that stood at the cusp of modernity, and they therefore commanded the attention of scholars who would grasp the directions that Judaism would follow as the community and the religion would respond to the challenges imposed by the modern world. Katz, therefore, asserted that the history of this community possessed an importance for all modern Jews that extended far beyond its geographical confines. A summary of the final pages of *Tradition and Crisis* will indicate why this was so.

---

8. Jacob Katz, *Out of the Ghetto: The Social Background of Jewish Emancipation* (Cambridge, Mass.: Harvard University Press, 1973), p. 219.

At the end of *Tradition and Crisis*, Katz traced the way in which the Haskalah, not *Ḥasidut*, shattered the institutional and ideological foundations of traditional Jewish society. In speaking of *Ḥasidut*, he wrote appreciatively of its import. Nevertheless, Katz did not consider it decisive for establishing the course upon which Jewish life in Germany and modern Europe was about to embark. Katz wrote:

> Our analysis of Hasidism revealed the extent of the transformation that took place in traditional Jewish society during and after the days when that movement flourished. But all these changes applied only to the internal structure of the society—to the mode of organization, the sources of authority, and the criteria of stratification within society itself. In relation to the world outside, no change at all took place.[9]

Katz did not assess the impact of the Jewish Enlightenment in this manner. Instead, he affirmed that the Haskalah signaled a revolutionary change in the Jewish world. Katz claimed, "The social turning point to which we have alluded is revealed in the emergence of a new type, the *maskil*, who added to his knowledge of Torah a command of foreign languages, general erudition, and an interest in what was happening in the non-Jewish world."[10] The type of cultural change this embodied—the creation of a Jew who turned to the non-Jewish world for his intellectual values—was accompanied by other transformations in Jewish life. As Katz went on to observe, "After the emergence of the *maskilim*, new ideals pertaining to daily living, the organization and leadership of society, and the methods of education came to be formulated in a programmatic manner."[11] Katz was to devote considerable attention in his later works to a description of how far-reaching these changes in intellectual constructs and organizational frameworks were for the formation of a new type of Jew as well as a new kind of Jewish leader. Indeed, this focus upon cultural warrants and foundations would permit him to emphasize with great subtlety those elements of continuity between past and present that marked nineteenth-century central European Jewish society. At the same time, this concern permitted him to identify those components of discontinuity that emerged as both Jewish individuals and the Jewish community engaged in the challenges of adjusting to the modern condition.

Of course, in the last years of the eighteenth century, as the larger world moved the more personal realm of *Gemeinschaft* to the broader dimensions of *Gesellschaft*, it was not entirely clear how this process would evolve. As Katz

---

9. *Tradition and Crisis*, p. 245.

10. *Ibid.*, p. 246.

11. *Ibid.*

pointed out, a feeling emerged among many "that ultimately the utter eclipse of Jewish society would come about."[12] Nor were such sentiments completely unfounded. Processes of change in the larger world promoted the transformations that were about to take place in the political structure as well as the social boundaries of the community. The activities of the traditional kehillah—payment of taxes, liquidation of businesses due to bankruptcy, collection of promissory notes—were transferred to the state, and "direct means of compulsion, i.e., the *ḥerem*" were curtailed. In other words, Jewish political autonomy and the coercive communal legal authority that accompanied it were destroyed with the advent of the modern world. Nevertheless, Katz did not argue that modernity was, therefore, the absolute solvent in which the Jewish community dissolved. After all, if complete "withdrawal" from Jewish society were to have occurred, then "not only would the institutions [of that society have broken] down, but even their reconstruction would be renounced. The individuals in the Jewish society would then be absorbed by the surrounding society and their needs would be met through the institutions operating there. Jewish society...never went to that extreme."[13] Thus, Katz was to focus on the theme of Jewish reformulation, not dissolution, in his historiographic corpus.

As Katz explained, the changes produced by the modern world in no way compelled the Jew to abandon Jewish society, though many Jews did ultimately transfer their social-cultural goals "to the context of the surrounding non-Jewish cultural milieu." Echoing themes first discussed in his dissertation, Katz asserted that many Jews began to regard non-Jewish society "as a source of social gratification," and not just "as a framework for economic activity," for a non-Jewish class had emerged, one in "which the difference of religion had lost its circumscribing function."[14] This meant that elite elements in both the Christian world as well as the Jewish community could form a social and cultural order beyond their community of origin. As Katz phrased it, "The essence of the rationalists' social achievement lay precisely in their creation of a neutral basis above religious difference....From this point on, there was third sphere—the neutral, human one—to which members of both religions could belong."[15]

To be sure, for some of these Jewish rationalists, the creation of this "neutral sphere" did lead to the abandonment of Judaism. Yet, the emergence of

---

12. *Ibid.*

13. *Ibid.*

14. *Ibid.*, p. 251.

15. *Ibid.*, p. 255.

such a realm did not mean that most Jews followed this path. Indeed, the overwhelming majority of Jews continued to adhere in significant measure to Jewish society. Nor did the birth of this world mark the death-knell of Jewish communal structures. Rather, it meant, as Katz was to point out again and again in his *oeuvre*, that a reconfiguration of the structures of Jewish society and the aspirations of Jewish individuals was destined to take place. Indeed, what intrigued Katz was delineating how modernizing Jews such as Mendelssohn and his successors preserved their links to the Jewish community while reformulating their own values as well as the institutions of the community during their lengthy process of acculturation into the politics and norms of a broader German society.

Katz repeatedly emphasized that neither Jewish individuals nor the communal institutions of Jewish society atrophied and died with the advent of modernity. Instead, he indicated how Jews and both the Jewish community and Jewish religion were reconfigured and reinvented in light of a changed cultural, social, political, and religious order. Modernity did not simply foster assimilation. It also promoted an integration and adaptation that allowed Jews to create new ways—some more, some less successful—of being Jewish. In this sense, the German *maskilim* were harbingers of what was to come for virtually all western Jews.

After all, as Katz, quoting Gershom Scholem, correctly observed, numerous German Jews in the nineteenth century would discard "the burden of tradition, particularly in its normative halakhic form."[16] Yet, most of them did not leave Judaism, nor would they cast off their identity as Jews. Instead, modernity allowed them to claim "new sources of authority" informed by notions drawn from the surrounding culture that caused them to formulate principles that they claimed constituted sufficient grounds for "a renewal and reconstruction" of Jewish life apart from Jewish law.[17] Thus, the nineteenth century witnessed the birth of diverse Jewish responses to modernity. They ranged from a Reform Judaism that affirmed the Enlightenment axioms of historical evolution and philosophical-scientific-moral progress as the basis for charting a new course for Jewish existence, on one hand, to a Zionist movement that drew upon the contemporaneous Romantic ideal of *Volksgeist* to promote a renewal of the Jewish national ideal, on the other. Katz paid close attention to the different points on this continuum, and analyzed these and other trends in his academic corpus. At the end of *Tradition and Crisis* he

---

16. Jacob Katz, "The Suggested Relationship between Sabbatianism, Haskalah, and Reform," in Katz, *Divine Law in Human Hands: Case Studies in Halakhic Flexibility* (Jerusalem: The Magnes Press, 1998), p. 522.

17. *Ibid.*, p. 515.

took careful note of the factors that allowed these changes to emerge so that the Jewish community could reformulate and convert its institutions and cultural-religious patterns in order to accommodate the parameters that were fixed by a new era.

The key figure in his analysis was of course Moses Mendelssohn, for Mendelssohn established and embodied an ethos and sensibility that fostered and facilitated such transformation. Mendelssohn, Katz wrote, critiqued Jewish organizations "that continued to operate along traditional lines....In his opinion, all the powers of compulsion which the Jewish organizations had taken into their hands had come about through imitation of the Christian Church."[18] However historically questionable this Mendelssohnian assessment, it led to the position "that...only those Jewish organizations that were voluntary associations of individuals whose formation stemmed from the similarity of faith and ritual to which they adhered should be formed."[19] In putting forth this argument, Mendelssohn articulated a rationale that was congenial to the ethos that informed the modern West. It was also a rationale that Samson Raphael Hirsch would adopt and develop a century later in his struggle for Orthodox secession from the general Jewish community. Katz, by identifying it here, was to articulate a concern that would occupy his attention for the next several decades and that would culminate in *A House Divided*.

The alterations in the intellectual warrants that guided the Jewish Enlighteners, as well as the transformations that already reduced the political power and social functions of the kehillah, were signals that Jewish cultural and political life was already in the midst of being overhauled. Indeed, the description and analysis of the ways in which Jews engaged in the process of reconfiguring their institutions and reformulating their culture throughout the subsequent century would remain a matter of constant concern for Katz in his ongoing scholarship. From this perspective, there is a direct line from *Tradition and Crisis* in the 1950s and *Out of the Ghetto* in the 1970s to the 1995 *A House Divided*.

In *Tradition and Crisis*, Katz did not confine his analysis of the transformations that marked Jewish life to intellectual and political spheres alone. He also took note of allied educational and religious changes that came to mark the Jewish community at this time. He observed that educational institutions were created along rationalist lines, and he was keenly aware that in the sphere of religion a number of Jews began to insist that there could be a "harmonization" between the tradition and the values of the neutral society. Indeed,

---

18.   *Tradition and Crisis*, p. 263.

19.   *Ibid.*

a number of these people—forerunners of a position that was to characterize modern Orthodox Jews—even continued to accept its ritual "yoke in practice."[20] Finally, Katz pointed out that the synagogue was the least shaken and most adaptive of the traditional institutions, though its functions were curtailed. Increasingly, the synagogue was devoted to public prayer alone and a western aesthetic increasingly came to inform the external architecture of the synagogue as well as the form of ritual that took place there—the melodies, the style of the prayers, and the internal decor of the synagogue.[21] All these modifications in Jewish life would come to inform not only Liberal German Jews, but Orthodox ones such as S. R. Hirsch himself in the next century, albeit that the formal conservatism that guided the Orthodox would not allow them to change the wordings of the prayers themselves. However, given the definition of Judaism as a religion that would come to dominate in the modern setting, as well as the ubiquitous and unrelenting pressures the modern world would exert on occidental Jews, such reductions in organizational function and changes in cultural expression are hardly surprising.

Writing in *Toward Modernity* almost thirty years after *Tradition and Crisis*, Katz indicated precisely why the themes he had identified in *Tradition and Crisis* occupied his attention throughout his career, and why the German Jewish experience remained so vital a part of his concerns. In arguing for the seminal import of the *maskilim* and the German venue in the shaping of modern Jewish history, Katz wrote the following. Speaking of Moses Mendelssohn, he stated:

> Mendelssohn's contribution [in the shaping of the new trend in Jewish history] became of decisive importance; due to him Jewish aspirations to have access to non-Jewish society were not simply displayed in practice, as in England, but carried out under the cover of intellectual vindication. Jewish modernization in Germany turned articulate. The educational reform was in practice accepted by Austro-Hungarian Jewry out of the hands of the government, but its ideological exposition came from Berlin, from Naftali Herz Wessley.
>
> By virtue of intellectual articulation the German-Jewish social experiment became mobile, and that is why we find its influence in all the countries where similar experiments became the order of the day. The later stages of modernization, leading up to Reform, Wissenschaft des Judentums, and neo-Orthodoxy, came then simply as a continuation of the initial process. They too excelled in seeking literary expression of their tendencies, and due to it they became exemplary, to be

---

20. *Ibid.*, p. 269.

21. *Ibid.*, pp. 270–71.

emulated by their adherents and shunned and rejected by their adversaries.[22]

In assessing the themes and concerns that marked *Tradition and Crisis*, it is clear that Katz laid the foundations for understanding how Judaism reformulated itself intellectually and culturally and restructured itself organizationally and religiously in light of the impact of the modern world. The description and analysis Katz offered can thus be summarized in the following way. As Katz saw it, modernity dismantled the political structure of the traditional kehillah. At the same time, it promoted new ways for elements in the community to establish structures that would allow for the exercise of influential religious authority. Modernity fostered assimilation. Simultaneously, it allowed for the creation of new ways in which Jewish identity could be expressed. Modernity caused many Jews to abandon a traditional allegiance to halakhah and classical Jewish religious belief. Nevertheless, it permitted the rise of modern Jewish religious denominationalism that promoted novel ways of Jewish religious life and led to a nationalist Jewish expression that fostered a Zionist movement that culminated in the creation of the State of Israel. Katz identified all these directions in this early work. His subsequent writings on German Judaism and Jewish communal life would address precisely how these events and movements unfolded over the next century.

Secession and Modernity

The writings of Jacob Katz on the issues delineated above were legion, and a complete discussion and analysis of the attention he accorded all these topics in his many essays and books on Judaism and the Jews in Germany are beyond the scope of this or any single presentation. However, *A House Divided: Orthodoxy and Schism in Nineteenth-Century Central Europe*, clearly constitutes his culminating work on a number of these themes. For *A House Divided* not only brought together in narrative form many of the subjects that he addressed in his earlier work. It also allowed a fully mature Katz to offer a valedictory on a lifetime of scholarship. In this book, Katz did more than focus upon the struggle for secession that engaged large elements of the Orthodox Jewish community in Hungary and Germany during the nineteenth century —the ostensible subject of the book. He also allowed his reader to see how this struggle reflects upon the larger issues of political and religious-cultural transformations that marked the Jewish community in its encounter with and response to modernity.[23]

---

22. *Toward Modernity*, pp. 11–12.

23. Jacob Katz, *A House Divided: Orthodoxy and Schism in Nineteenth-Century Cen-*

In *Toward Modernity*, Katz had specifically observed that the challenge confronting the scholar in defining Jewish modernity was to determine the criteria whereby "the modern variation of" the Jewish community "could be differentiated from its predecessor, traditional Jewish society." And these criteria, he there pointed out, could be summed up as follows. He wrote, "In the latter the observance of the Jewish tradition could and would be enforced by the organs of the Jewish community. The authority to do so was conferred on the Jewish community by the state, and constituted a part of communal autonomy. There was also a measure of control over the spread of ideas.... The posttraditional Jewish community was denied the right to impose its will concerning *thought and action* on the individual."[24]

Hence, in Katz's schematization, modernity arose for the Jewish community when two factors were realized. First, modernity appeared when a limitation was imposed upon the political authority of the community. The organizational structures of the community were stripped of virtually all vestiges of legal power and Jewish institutional authorities could no longer employ coercion to impose their will upon Jewish persons. Secondly, modernity took place when the thought of large numbers of individual Jews no longer derived primarily, if at all, from the intellectual–legal–religious sources of Judaism. In such a setting, Jewish thought expanded beyond the parameters of Jewish tradition, and warrants for legitimating actions were routinely drawn from the surrounding culture. Katz, in *A House Divided*, centered his discussion on the question of Jewish communal schism in nineteenth-century central Europe around these two themes. In so doing, he elevated the significance of his discussion in this book beyond an analysis and presentation of the individual historical events themselves. Instead, he also demonstrated how the unfolding of this story cast light on the larger issue of how Jews and Judaism responded to the reality of a modern world.

In pointing to this larger theoretical concern, Katz emphasized here, as in past work, that the Jewish responses to the modern condition were multivalent and adaptive. Indeed, the German Jewish community did not disappear, nor did all its members abandon the tradition. In fact, as Katz indicated, there was even one element in this community that would ultimately identify itself and be identified by others as Orthodox that "continued to demand the observance of tradition in all its details." It was this group that occupied the great bulk of his attention in *A House Divided*, for these persons maintained

---

tral European Jewry, trans. by Ziporah Brody (Hanover and London: Brandeis University Press, 1998).

24. *Toward Modernity*, p. 1. Italics mine.

their fidelity to the ritual tradition "despite the changes in the status of the congregations (kehillot) and the abrogation by the secular authorities of their power of religious coercion." Furthermore, Katz noted that although Mendelssohn and others in Europe "imagined the Jewish congregations as voluntary frameworks," this vision, he maintained, was "slow to materialize [in reality]. The inclusion of Jews among the citizens of the state brought about the abrogation of many functions and powers of the kehillah, but not of the obligation of membership in it incumbent on all adherents of the Jewish religion. The requirement of membership in a congregation remained in force for most of the nineteenth century."[25] For, as Katz observed, the kehillah, "was [still] treated as the organizational framework of a religious community, like one of the Christian churches. Because of this formal classification, the kehillah could, with the help of authorities, obligate every Jew in its area of jurisdiction to be a member."[26] Jewish communities in America, "where no external forces impinged," were, in contrast to the German Jewish community of the 1800s, completely voluntary associations, where individual Jews were absolutely free "to organize around synagogues with different styles and prayer services [or not], according to their individual choice." The European situation was therefore distinct from the American one, and his study of how the German Orthodox reacted to this reality would both embody and illuminate the course of modern Jewish history. The demise of the absolute power the kehillah had enjoyed, as well as the emergence of religious pluralism in the modern situation, proved both challenging and problematic to all Jews. Indeed, in emphasizing this demise and in delineating the diverse ways in which both individual Jews as well as Jewish communal organizations responded and adapted to this demise, Katz provided the core narrative that has marked the study and teaching of all modern Jewish history. It is Jacob Katz who provided the conceptual framework that has dominated the writing of the modern Jewish experience.

For these reasons, Katz, as he wrote in another essay, turned to modern Orthodox Judaism as a, if not the, paradigmatic and instructive response to modernity. Orthodox Judaism, like every other stream of modern Judaism, arose in a specific historical context. It, like the more liberal branches and movements it ultimately would decry, did not arise in a vacuum. Orthodox Jews, no less than their non-Orthodox co-religionists, did not live in what Katz—following the insights that modern sociological tradition offered on this topic—labeled a "tradition-bound" society, one where "tradition was a

---

25. *A House Divided*, p. 7.

26. *Ibid.*, p. 9.

self-understood and uncontested guide to both religious observance and religious thought." Consequently, "The awareness of other Jews' rejection of tradition," Katz averred, "was…an essential and universal characteristic of all forms and variations of Orthodoxy." Orthodoxy, he concluded, was therefore a creation of the modern situation itself. It was "a method of confronting deviant trends, and of responding to the very same stimuli which produced these trends."[27]

Those Jews who perceived themselves as the guardians of an unbroken tradition had to confront the novel reality of a German world where the political functions of the community was severely curtailed and where shared religious values could no longer provide the ideological basis for communal unity. After all, Liberal Judaism promulgated principles and practices that many of these Orthodox Jews perceived as destructive to Judaism. The question of how to deal with these other Jews in the institutional structures of the community emerged as a focal point of debate and the issue of "organizational affiliation…became an important basis of modern Orthodoxy."[28]

As Katz traced the evolution and typology of Orthodox responses on this matter prior to *A House Divided*, he emphasized the centrality of Rabbi Moses Schreiber of Pressburg. In his opinion, the Hatam Sofer had articulated the first major Orthodox response that "grasped the full significance of the problem and took a principled, aggressive stance" toward it.[29] In a famous responsum to Rabbi Abraham Eliezer from Trieste on the membership of the Hamburg Reform Temple, the Hatam Sofer had written, "Were their sentence put in our hands, I would separate them from us, forbidding our sons to marry their daughters, so as not to be drawn after them, and their sect would be like that of Zadoq and Boethus, Anan and Saul, they following their ways, and we ours."[30] However, as Katz noted, the Hatam Sofer immediately

27. *Toward Modernity*, pp. 3–5. For parallels to this insight in modern sociological writing, see Berger, *The Heretical Imperative*, p. 29. There Berger describes the dilemma that the Orthodox of all faiths must confront when dealing with a modern pluralistic situation where empirical reality means that tradition no longer "has the quality of a taken for granted fact." Katz, in *Toward Modernity*, echoes the point made by Berger. Once more, his sociological sensibility is apparent.

28. *Ibid.*, p. 8.

29. Katz, "Towards a Biography of the Hatam Sofer," in *Divine Law in Human Hands*, p. 403.

30. *Responsa of the Hatam Sofer* 6:89. This responsum is cited by Katz in "The Controversy over the Temple in Hamburg," in *Divine Law in Human Hands*, p. 225.

added a disclaimer, for the Hatam Sofer wrote, "This is only in theory but
not in practice, for without the permission of the king...my words have no
authority." As a result, Sofer's words, in Katz's phrasing, were "reduced to
mere musings." The Hatam Sofer understood that the traditional authorities
had, "at this stage," already "lost their ability to enforce the observance of the
religious commandments. Individuals could violate the Sabbath in public and
commit any of the sins proscribed in the Bible, and the leadership of the
community, rabbinical and lay alike, had no means to force them to cease
their activities or to expel them from the community."[31] The problem that
now confronted these men was that "the functioning of the halakhah as a
judicial system" became contingent upon the "acceptance of its validity by
those involved [in it]," and such acceptance was precisely what the "trans-
gressors" refused to grant.[32]

By the onset of the nineteenth century, the political apparatus that had
marked the traditional medieval kehillah had been dismantled, and whatever
vestiges of coercive political authority that remained to the rabbinate were
soon destined to disappear. The rabbis were reduced to exercising "influential authority" alone. The genius of the Hatam Sofer was that he was the
first traditional rabbi to comprehend fully that the world had changed. Katz,
in analyzing his statements, was able to assert that rulings of the type issued
by the Hatam Sofer on such matters did not embody a genuine "halakhic
argument." Rather, in a world where the political power formerly enjoyed
by the rabbinate had been removed, the Hatam Sofer was compelled to face
the task of "weighing the advantages gained to the cause of religion by
[choosing among] various alternative steps." Hence, the Hatam Sofer engaged in what Katz labeled "religious policymaking."[33]

In offering this assessment of these writings, Katz was not dismissing the
importance of the stance the Hatam Sofer had adopted. Instead, he was
displaying an analytic clarity that would better elucidate the significance and
meaning of that stance. After all, legal philosophers have routinely indicated
that law often functions as what Ronald Dworkin has identified as a "policy."
Here the law aims imaginatively to express and preserve the community's
highest principles and ideals in the light of the limitations imposed by a
contemporary situation. A policy represents a broadly-based goal warranted
by the overarching spirit that animates the legal tradition, and it becomes
legally actionable as a guide that directs the community, or a segment of the

31. *Ibid.*

32. *Ibid.*, p. 228.

33. *Ibid.*, p. 229.

community, as its leaders attempt to construct its present and seek to shape its future.[34]

By employing this type of theoretical construct, Katz allowed his reader to understand that the particular events presented regarding one specific historical figure possessed a representative significance for comprehending the larger story of how Jews and Judaism responded to the modern world. The type of "prudential calculus" involved in "religious policymaking" as advanced in this instance by the Hatam Sofer, permitted Katz to emphasize the elements of commonality that Schreiber, despite his Hungarian setting, shared with both Mendelssohn, who preceded him, and Samson Raphael Hirsch, who rose to prominence after him. After all, the Mendelssohnian notion of "a voluntary community," as well as the "policy of secession" Hirsch was destined to advance, are highly reminiscent of Schreiber, and they reflect the reality of a central European Jewish world where secularization had made considerable inroads. The political unity of the Jewish community was splintered, and an attendant compartmentalization of Jewish life resulted, one that would have been impossible in a traditional setting. The description and analysis Katz offered through the utilization of this conceptual category highlighted this reality, for the "old rules" could no longer be applied in a direct manner. Instead, the new age required that "new policies" be formulated to cope with the demands of a changed setting.

At the same time, the focus Katz placed on modernization also allowed him to highlight the lines of distinction that separated these men. By paying careful attention to the intellectual grounds each man put forth to justify his policy on the political nature of the Jewish community in the modern situation, Katz was able to explore the ideological elements that distinguished these men from their medieval counterparts. Simultaneously, he provided a subtle description of the intellectual foundations that indicated how these men differed from one another as well.

In *A House Divided*, the reactions issued by the Orthodox rabbinate, in general, and Samson Raphael Hirsch, in particular, to the Reform Braunschweig Rabbinical Conference of 1844 constituted a key chapter in comprehending the course of the Jewish adaptation to modernity. In offering his description and evaluation of this event and these reactions, Katz noted that the overwhelming response of the Orthodox rabbis was a "dogmatic" one that reflected their inability to grasp the nature and enormity of the task the modern world had presented them. They put forth a furious attack against the Braunschweig Reformers and asserted rigidly, "Neither we nor anyone else

---

34. See Ronald Dworkin, "Is Law a System of Rules?", in R. M. Dworkin, ed., *The Philosophy of Law* (Oxford: Oxford University Press, 1977), p. 45.

has the authority to nullify even the least of the religious laws." Furthermore, they ascribed only the basest intentions to their opponents, claiming that "the motives of those who rid themselves of the burden of the commandments and customs is only 'the unrestrained pursuit of fame, wealth, and pleasure.'"[35]

Their fury was not difficult to comprehend. After all, the Reform Assembly, in the realm of ritual, abolished *Kol Nidre*,[36] and it discussed the abolition of *mezizah*. Moreover, in the realm of personal status, the Assembly addressed the issue of allowing marriage between Jews and non-Jews of monotheistic faiths. These matters, combined with a Reform posture that led to the removal of passages in the traditional prayer book that mentioned the return to Zion, the rebuilding of the Jerusalem Temple, and the renewal of sacrifices, justifiably aroused the ire of the Orthodox. Yet, Katz observed that the arguments put forth by most "Orthodox ideologues" against these deviations from the tradition reflected "their inability or unwillingness to deal with the intellectual arguments and the rational and historical critiques which...were set forth to justify throwing off the yoke of the commandments."[37] The polemics these rabbis issued were, of course, largely irrelevant to those Reform leaders whom they condemned, and Katz indicated, as stated above, that these traditional personages simply did not recognize the changed reality that they now had to face.

Despite this, some rabbis did recognize that a new situation obtained. Although they remained a minority at the beginning of the decade, Katz assigned these men, as he had the *maskilim* in the previous century, great historical significance. For these rabbis recognized, albeit regretfully, "that the government [was] no longer willing to serve as an intermediary to force others to observe the tradition as the rabbis [understood] it."[38] By the end of the 1840s, their perception became dominant in Orthodox circles, and "the idea of collective coercion" had vanished "from the minds of [even] the most conservative Jew."[39] The Orthodox no longer sought "to fence in the breaches in the lives of the community" by appealing to and to "govern-

---

35. *A House Divided*, p. 234.

36. Interestingly, Hirsch himself, in response to the same pressures that confronted the Liberals, once abolished the recitation of *Kol Nidre* early in his career at Oldenberg in 1839. See Mordecai Breuer, *Eidah v'diyukanah: ortodoksiya yehudit b'reich ha-germani 1871–1918* (Jerusalem: Merkaz Zalman Shazar, 5651), p. 44.

37. *Ibid.*

38. *Ibid.*, p. 240.

39. *Ibid.*

mental support."[40] Indeed, this was soon combined with a recognition that in Germany, by mid-century, "the abandonment of a traditional way of life [had become] a common phenomenon."[41] As Katz had already noted in *Out of the Ghetto*, this placed "conservatives (i.e., Orthodox leaders) in a quandary."[42] Excision of Liberal and secular Jews from the Jewish community was simply not feasible in a situation where the overwhelming majority of Jews had rejected fidelity to the halakhic tradition. Nor, in light of the commitment that the traditionalists had to Jewish law, could they ignore the fact that that same law stipulated that children born of Jewish mothers were marked by Jewish status. Nevertheless, what did emerge from all this, as Katz observed, was that the "[traditional] idea of mutual responsibility [*'areivut*]" that one Jew possessed for another did become attenuated as "the bonds of the traditional community" were removed or loosened.[43]

The question confronting the Orthodox remained one of deciding on an appropriate institutional response to this reality. The Hatam Sofer had already begun to formulate one response in his reaction to the Hamburg Temple Reformers two decades earlier. Yet, his was a "rejectionist Orthodoxy," one that eschewed the blandishments of modern culture. For, as Katz pointed, Moses Sofer believed "that reformulating Jewish tradition in a European idiom meant also exposing it to rationalistic examination. Thus tradition would be called before the tribunal of reason and called upon to vindicate its truths. It would have to be prepared then to accept the judgment of its investigators, whose method would lead to selective acceptance and rejection."[44]

This approach was not palatable to the German traditionalists, whose chief intellectual feature, like that of the liberals whom they frequently detested, was cultural integration into the surrounding milieu. For this reason, Katz, in *A House Divided*, turned his attention to Samson Raphael Hirsch. Katz correctly identified Hirsch as the central figure in the "neo-Orthodox" response to the modern situation, and he devoted considerable research to exploring the intellectual formulas and organizational solutions Hirsch proposed to meet the challenges of the modern world. He believed that Hirsch, more than any other Orthodox leader of the 1840s, correctly perceived, as the Hatam Sofer had two decades earlier in reaction to the Hamburg Reformers,

---

40. *Ibid.*, p. 241.

41. *Ibid.*, p. 254.

42. *Out of the Ghetto*, pp. 142–60.

43. *A House Divided*, p. 240.

44. *Out of the Ghetto*, p. 157.

the fact that a new reality obtained. Hirsch recognized "that reform was conceived as a reaction, albeit a misguided one, to the disintegration of traditional society." Reform "was not" condemned by Hirsch as "its cause." In offering this assessment of the situation, Hirsch, Katz pointed out, echoed the "ideas...expressed by [his teacher] R. [Jacob] Ettlinger." However, "in contrast to his teacher's despair of changing the situation," Hirsch, at this juncture in his career, believed that he had a program "to heal the breach." This program was one of educational adaptation to and cultural affirmation of the contours imposed by this new era. Later known by the slogan *Torah im derekh erez*, this type of Jewish Orthodoxy, in contrast to the "rejectionist Orthodoxy" advanced by the Hatam Sofer and his school, embraced the culture and social mores of the surrounding German society. Hirsch felt influential authority could be exercised by the Orthodox over the total Jewish community only if such adjustments were made by those loyal to the tradition.

In making these observations, Katz alerted his readers to the changes that had taken place in the Jewish world, including its traditional sector, in its encounter with modernity. After all, Hirsch represented "a new type" of Orthodox leader, one who affirmed the cultural worth of the modern world and who looked to intellectual warrants and cultural tropes drawn from figures ranging from Goethe to Kant to justify and bolster the position of the traditionalist camp. The attention Katz had devoted to identifying "new sources of authority" informed by notions taken from non-Jewish culture as a means for a measurement of the "renewal and reconstruction" that marked Jewish life in his previous historiography came to guide him here as well. This emphasis upon cultural warrants and intellectual formulations allowed Katz to underscore the critical role Hirsch played in the formation of a new variety of traditional Judaism.

However, Katz was not content to confine his analysis of Hirsch to the cultural realm alone. By continuing his focus upon organizational structures as well, Katz was able to point out how Hirsch's ideological commitments led him to advocate a novel political configuration for the Jewish community in the modern setting. For Hirsch, like his teacher Ettlinger, soon came to recognize that no program of cultural reconstruction could ultimately succeed in allowing the Orthodox to realize their hegemony over the entire community. Too much had changed. Therefore, as early as 1843, Hirsch, despite the cultural divide that separated him from the Hatam Sofer, began to echo Schreiber's thoughts on an organizational solution to this dilemma. Hirsch, as Katz put it, now started to toy seriously with "the idea of schism" as the one way to remedy the ills that confronted Judaism and Jewish people as Jewish traditionalists were compelled to grapple with the transformed reality of the modern era.[45] The solution that occurred to Hirsch, as Katz put it, was "the establishment of separate communities, composed exclusively of those loyal to Torah, which would divorce themselves from the overall organization encompassing all the Jews of a place."[46]

The very contemplation of such a proposal indicated, according to Katz, that Hirsch had already begun by the 1840s to arrive at the conclusion that there was no overarching remedy for the afflictions of widespread non-observance and unbelief that marked modern central European Jewish life. Only a novel institutional structure could provide a cure for the burdens secularization had imposed upon the Jewish world. Although the focus here was upon the Orthodox, Katz remained aware that this Orthodox response was of historical significance precisely because it was representative of a broader array of Jewish reactions—traditional and liberal alike—to the conditions imposed by modernity. It was a "test case" of the Jewish responses to the modern setting, and it reflected how Judaism, including its most traditional sectors, was affected, though not abnegated, by the modern world. The proposed creation of a separatist Orthodox community along the lines of a modern congregational model only testified to the inroads modernization had made in Jewish life, and foreshadowed a growing trend toward Jewish religious denominationalism that would increasingly come to divide the modern Jewish world. Katz was able to analyze its origins in this episode in modern Jewish history in light of the larger intellectual and political circumstances that modernity had unleashed. Here there is once again a direct line between the methodology and concerns of social history articulated by Katz in *Tradition and Crisis* and his lifelong project in this area.

Indeed, the historical importance Katz attached to this development is evidenced in the considerable attention he devoted to a description of its content and to an analysis of its meaning. The establishment of a separatist Orthodox community as a way to cope with the challenges of a modern world involved no "mere distancing oneself from an individual who is suspected of one or another transgression." Rather, it required "isolation from a community that has abandoned one of the principles of faith, the subservience to the authority of the Talmud," which alone could serve "as a basis for unity."[47] As a result of Hirsch's efforts, "the idea of separation already began to glimmer in the eyes of the faithful" by the 1840s as a solution to the crisis engendered by the reality of church–state separation.[48]

45. *Ibid.*, p. 244.
46. *Ibid.*, p. 243.
47. *Ibid.*, p. 244.
48. *Ibid.*, p. 17.

However, it would take two decades before this policy would fully crystal-
lize. Katz engaged in a meticulous description of the historical factors that
promoted this crystallization, and crafted a comprehensive analysis of the
arguments Hirsch had put forth on this matter during the late 1860s and
throughout the 1870s. He pointed out that Hirsch had wanted "absolute
organizational independence" for the Orthodox by this point in time.[49] In
presenting his case for this notion before the gentile authorities of the day,
Hirsch acknowledged that the law now granted Orthodox Jews the right to
erect separatist congregations apart from the general community. Nevertheless, he complained that despite this privilege, the Orthodox were still
compelled to pay taxes to a general kehillah that was generally dominated by
Reform elements, and he "considered this unfair and a miscarriage of justice."[50] Hirsch claimed that in the pre-modern world the laity and the rabbinate possessed a shared ideological commitment to Jewish law. For this reason,
common Jews obeyed the religious strictures promulgated by the religious
leadership of the community. Compulsion, claimed Hirsch, played no role
in promoting such observance. Indeed, Hirsch went beyond the position
Mendelssohn had advanced on this topic[51] by denying "the very existence of
such coercive measures." As Katz indicated, Hirsch maintained that "the
traditional congregation was an institution founded entirely on the will of
individuals to observe the *halakhah*; only a community founded on this
principle should be recognized as a legitimate congregation."[52] Of course, as
Katz pointed out, this contention was historically unfounded, for, "despite
general identification with its values, the leadership did resort to compulsion,
the most obvious of which was the ban."[53] Katz concluded from this that
Hirsch, in making this claim, had put forth a definition of Judaism that both
reduced its traditional parameters and emphasized its religious character in a
manner that was in keeping with the ethos of a Protestant-dominated western
world that increasingly privatized religious life by removing it from the political arena.

Nevertheless, Katz demonstrated that this portrait that Hirsch had constructed regarding the relationship that obtained between pre-modern rabbinic authorities and the Jewish laity—however historically questionable—
was of considerable utility for achieving his political goal of separatist Ortho-

---

49. *Ibid.*, p. 237.

50. *Ibid.*, p. 238.

51. See p. 13 above.

52. *A House Divided*, p. 239.

53. *Ibid.*

dox congregations. Hirsch had argued that if the Orthodox were compelled by law to continue to pay taxes to the general Jewish *Gemeinde*, it would make it appear as if "Judaism equally grants the right to exist to those who deny religious law and to those who sanctify it."[54] Yet, as Hirsch, writing in 1873 on behalf of a proposed *Austrittsgesetz*, stated, Orthodox Jews "accepted religious customs as the products of revelation, and as Divine Laws," whereas Reform Jews denied this. Consequently, "The differences between the various Christian denominations are no deeper than the differences between Reform Judaism and Orthodox Judaism."[55] Therefore, Hirsch concluded that the State ought to extend the same privilege to Jews that it bestowed upon Christians, and allow Jews, just as it permitted Christians, to leave their religious community if they ceased to identify with its principles.[56] Hirsch thus grounded his argument on behalf of Orthodox institutional autonomy on a modern warrant embedded in western liberal political theory—the notion of "freedom of conscience." Hirsch, forged as he was by western as well as traditional Jewish culture, may well have actually affirmed this value as worthy in its own right. However, Katz emphasized that what was of special historical note in this episode was that an ideal drawn from the larger culture was assimilated into the consciousness of a modern traditionalist and employed by that figure to serve the cause of tradition in the modern setting. In so doing, Katz illuminated the larger dynamic of how a traditional religion can reach out to a broader intellectual universe and adapt and reformulate itself—its arguments and ideology—so as to cope with the demands of an evolving world.

Of course, here, as elsewhere, Katz was attuned to the subtle dialectics that mark all traditional religious readers, and he did not ignore the role that the religious tradition itself played in the mind of Hirsch as the entire process unfolded. Indeed, Katz offered a minute and characteristically sensitive exposition of the halakhic debate that obtained between Samson Raphael Hirsch and his antagonist Seligmann Baer Bamberger, the *Wurzbuerger rav*, over the issue of Orthodox secession from the Frankfurt Jewish community during 1877–1878. Hirsch had maintained that wherever possible Jewish law demanded Orthodox secession from any Jewish community under non-Orthodox domination. *Contra* Hirsch, Bamberger had argued that Jewish law did not mandate Orthodox secession from a general Jewish communal structure under Liberal control in instances where the community provided financial

---

54. *Ibid.*, p. 239.

55. *Ibid.*, p. 242.

56. *Ibid.*

support for and autonomy to Orthodox institutions. He based this in part on a legal position that maintained that such Reform Jews fell under the Jewish legal rubric of "*mumarim l'hach'is* – principled apostates," and not under the category of "*mumarim l'teiavon* – apostates for convenience." The latter category, although serious, did not carry the gravity of the former grouping. By drawing upon these Jewish legal categories and in applying them as he did, Katz was able to show that Bamberger reasoned that the rebellion these Reform Jews displayed against traditional Judaism resulted from human frailty and appetite alone. Their rebellion, so construed, did not constitute a dogmatic rejection of classical rabbinic authority. There was no ideological dimension to their non-observance. However incorrect he actually was in applying this typology to the ideology that many of the Reformers in Frankfurt actually championed, the typology itself permitted Bamberger to rule that Jewish law did not proscribe association with such Jews in instances where they supplied for the needs of the Orthodox.

Hirsch responded to this argument by saying, in effect, that this point was completely irrelevant to the case at hand. In fact, Hirsch stated that he in no way prohibited association with Reform Jews as individuals. Indeed, he maintained that in issuing his ruling he did not speak of Reform Jews at all. Rather, he was describing their communities. This distinction was a vital one for Hirsch, for he wrote, "I deliberately use these abstract concepts which refer to the system and not to the people."[57] Indeed, Hirsch engaged here in what legal scholars would label "purposive interpretation" and claimed that the proscriptions found "in earlier sources regarding idolaters, sectarians, and heretics" did not apply to individual persons *per se*, but to "an ideological essence" of heresy. This intellectual construct, as Katz viewed it, meant that Hirsch had no need to apply these sources to "the sectarians and heretics themselves, who no longer exist[ed], but to their spirit, which ha[d] a place of honor in the Reform community."[58] The "burden of the commandments" was now placed on the public, not the individual Jew.[59] In Katz's opinion, "Hirsch's distinction between sectarians and apostates, as opposed to heresy and apostasy, created an unprecedented situation, for which no direct proofs could be found in the sources."[60]

In making this claim, Katz once more revealed his keen sociological-historical awareness and sensitivity. He had learned from his training in

---

57. *Ibid.*, p. 265.

58. *Ibid.*

59. *Ibid.*, p. 275.

60. *Ibid.*, p. 271.

history and in the sociology of knowledge that the critical variable involved in an analysis of a legal holding was not determining whether that decision had a precedent. Katz knew that the author of such a ruling frequently had a welter of rules and principles that were capable of providing guidance in a given case. Rather, the point was to focus on the contextual factors that led an author to select one precedent over another, or to indicate what the concerns were that caused that author to reformulate precedents in a novel way. In this instance, Katz emphasized the innovative Hirsch drew upon to combine precedents and contemporary language to reconfigure the tradition. He was thereby able, through this narration of a discrete historical episode, to highlight the more general process of how religious leaders recontextualize the past in light of the needs of the present as well as to underscore the irony inherent in the decision Hirsch rendered on this matter. The desire the Frankfurt rabbi had to preserve the Jewish religious tradition drove him to adopt a novel Jewish legal stance unknown to the tradition itself. Through this presentation and analysis of the position advanced by Hirsch, Katz was able to demonstrate the accuracy of the contention he had put forth earlier, that Orthodoxy itself was a creation of the modern world, a self-conscious "method of confronting deviant trends." The consistency of his project and his ability to define the significant from amidst a mass of details is once more apparent.

Katz's work in *A House Divided* can be seen as the finale of a lifetime of coherent thematic and methodological concerns. He indicated how his lifelong preoccupation with the issue of Jewish continuity and reconfiguration in the face of the challenges imposed by the modern condition played itself out in this instance. In *Tradition and Crisis* and *Out of the Ghetto* Katz had observed that the early opponents of *Haskalah* had feared the mission of extricating "Jewish society from its cultural isolation by reformulating Jewish teachings in the idiom of the European Enlightenment" that the Jewish Enlighteners had assigned themselves.[61] They were convinced that such embrace of modern culture would mark the end of Jewish life. Yet, the bulk of the Jewish people remained "linked by deep emotional ties" to their identity as Jews and they insisted on remaining part of the Jewish community.[62] The history Katz offered in *A House Divided* thus confirmed an observation he had made years before in an article entitled, "Judaism and Christianity against the Backdrop of Modern Secularism." There he had observed that "history and many other branches of knowledge teach us that

---

61. *Out of the Ghetto*, p. 157.

62. *A House Divided*, p. 266.

the source of religious commitments lies deeply embedded in the nature of man and that its rational justification is a secondary phenomenon....This is why religion retains much of its power even in the face of" secularism and massive change.[63]

In *A House Divided*, as in *Out of the Ghetto* and many other essays and books, Katz not only related the way in which neo-traditional German Jewish leaders like Hirsch embraced this cultural change. He also analyzed how the defenders of Jewish tradition, despite such change, refused to allow the Jewish community and its institutions to dissolve. The culture and institutions of the Jewish community did not disintegrate. They were maintained and rebuilt. By emphasizing and illuminating the process and mechanics of this reconstruction, Katz was able to show that such change, "by its very nature, generated the forces that halted and reversed the tide of dissolution" in both the political and cultural realms.[64] The themes of cultural integration and political reorganization that marked his early writings found expression in his later works as well. They have left us with a portrait of the German Jewish response to the modern world that is dynamic and sophisticated. As such, the legacy of Jacob Katz is enduring and he has defined an agenda that later generations of scholars will explore for years to come.

Jacob Katz, in his autobiography, *With My Own Eyes: The Autobiography of an Historian*, observed that Yitzhak Baer had once told him "that the only proof of the validity of a historical method is its ability to describe historical processes in a convincing manner."[65] This essay has attempted to indicate how the studies of Jacob Katz on the historical processes that define the origins and explain the dimensions and directions of Jewish modernity have been convincingly illuminated by his investigations on the German Jewish experience. The work of Jacob Katz provides an invaluable intellectual legacy for those of us who follow.

The ancient rabbis, in a commentary on Song of Songs 7:10, spoke lovingly of the eternal instruction and guidance that *talmidei ḥakhamim* offer their disciples. In commenting upon the words, "moving gently the lips of those that are asleep—*doveiv siftei y'sheinim*," these rabbis said of such scholars, "Even when they are dead, their lips quiver in the grave—*siftoteihem dovavot*

---

63. Jacob Katz, "Judaism and Christianity Against the Backdrop of Modern Secularism," in Katz, *Jewish Emancipation and Self-Emancipation* (Philadelphia: Jewish Publication Society, 1986), p. 47.

64. *Out of the Ghetto*, p. 124.

65. Jacob Katz, *With My Own Eyes: The Autobiography of an Historian* (Hanover: Brandeis University Press, 1995), p. 168.

ba-qaver." In reviewing his teachings here as well as elsewhere in this volume, we see that Jacob Katz's lips move from the place of his eternal rest and continue to provide us with knowledge and insight. May they continue to do so for generations to come.

How Central Was Anti-Semitism to the Historical Writing of Jacob Katz

Richard I. Cohen

The Hebrew University, Jerusalem

For many Jacob Katz is associated with his untiring efforts to uncover the ways in which traditional Judaism maintained itself, faced the development of Kabbalah, and encountered the threat to its existence in the modern period.[1] For others he is known for his seminal studies on the precursors of Zionism and some of their religious figures, notably Rabbis Zvi Hirsch Kalischer and Yehuda Alkalay, and his more programmatic essays on the nature of the movement and its evolution. Another aspect of Katz's historical involvement was related to his inquiries into the failure of Jewish integration into German society, the recurrent appearance of anti-Jewish attitudes, and the ultimate tragedy of European Jewry during World War II. Though all regions of Jewish history engaged his interest and research, German-Jewish history in medieval and modern times lay at the center of his professional involvement, in no small measure due to the events of World War II. Indeed, one is struck, in reviewing Katz's work, by the contrasting temperament that reigned over his oeuvre. Alongside the optimistic and open nature of the man as an individual and an historian, there lies the pessimism of the European Jew of the previous generation, who was forever grappling with the implications and meaning of the Holocaust and the enduring generations of anti-Semitism. As he wrote in *Commentary* in 1975: "Whatever subsequent generations will make of it, for the generation that lived through it the Holocaust can only be characterized as a trauma, a wounding experience beyond the reach of intellectual conceptualization."[2] Yet, he could not relinquish his search for an historical understanding. Similar to historians of his generation of the likes of Léon

---

1. For an updated biography of Katz's writings, see the appendix to *Zion* 63, 4 (1998): 39–61, "In Memory of Jacob Katz" (Hebrew).

2. Jacob Katz, "Was the Holocaust Predictable?" *Commentary* LIX, 5 (May, 1975): 45. For versions of this article in other languages, see *ibid.*, no. 144, p. 49.

Poliakov, Jacob Talmon, and Shmuel Ettinger, Katz did not accept a "lachrymose conception" of Jewish history, but was motivated, as they were, to
uncover the ultimate reasons and sources of the tragedy of European Jewry.[3]
This essay will argue that though Katz never researched directly the Holocaust *per se*, many of his studies—far removed from the Holocaust at face
value—were informed by a profound drive to explain why the Jews, and not
any other people, were the victims of this event in history. Put differently,
how the ultimate tragedy of the Jews relates to their previous history and
cannot be simply confined to the historical events of the years 1933–45. This
argument requires a preliminary methodological comment.

In 1958, the same year that Jacob Katz published his classic work *Tradition
and Crisis*, Fernand Braudel published in *Annales* his conceptual presentation
of time-frames in history, in particular his programmatic study of the "*longue
durée.*" Braudel argued that mentalities of individuals and collectives—their
values, beliefs, rituals, customs, and norms—are shaped by developments that
are not apparent to all but have a definite impact on historical development.
Moreover, Braudel was concerned with the interaction of a large network of
structures, be they society, culture, politics, environment, or economics.
Change within these structures evolves slowly and can be evaluated, at times,
within the perspective of short, medium, and long time-periods, though
Braudel advocated more and more the "*longue durée*" as the necessary tool for
the historian.[4] *Tradition and Crisis*, I would argue, did just that, choosing the
long-frame of history, although Katz at that period was hardly aware of the
development in French historiography from the early days of the *Annales*.
Katz's presentation in *Tradition and Crisis* posited the centrality of the evolution of the Jewish "organic" unity from the Talmudic period until the late
eighteenth century. This unity determined, to a very significant measure, the
ways Jewish society preserved its uniqueness, developed remarkable internal
resiliency, countered non-Jewish figures, structured its laws of organization
and inter-family relations, and so on. What was central to Katz's argument
was also at the root of the Braudelian notion of *longue durée*: actions taken by
Jews at different moments of the post-Talmudic period, even centuries later,
were, to a significant degree, influenced by this mentality. Interestingly, it

---

3. On the lachrymose conception of Jewish history, see Robert Liberles, *Salo
    Wittmayer Baron. Architect of Jewish History* (New York and London: 1995), pp.
    338–59.

4. Fernand Braudel, "Histoire et sciences sociales: la longue durée," *Annales:
    économies, sociétés, civilisations* IV (1958): 725–53; an abbreviated English version
    of the article was published in F. Braudel, *On History*, trans. Sarah Matthews
    (Chicago and London: 1980), pp. 25–54.

was only in the last decade of his life—as far as I have been able to trace—that Katz commented on the notions of the French orientation. He did so critically in his essay "On Jewish Social History" (1991),[5] claiming that "short" and "long" "are relative terms that say nothing about the characteristic features of the specific time-periods being examined" while suggesting a different characterization. He proposed using the terms "epochal" and "supra-epochal"—adding his definition: "A period of time that can be characterized in terms of constant features is epochal, while a phenomenon whose impact stretches over several individual periods or epochs is supra-epochal."[6] The supra-epochal nature becomes apparent through analysis of a specific historic problem. Yet his dismissal of the French terminology did not persist. Several years later, in his *A Time for Inquiry – A Time for Reflection*—published shortly after his death—Katz reversed his earlier objection to the notion of *longue durée*. He now saw its value as an important principle, as it makes one aware that a contemporary event has its source "deep in the far past...(influenced by) factors that act in a hidden manner over a long period."[7] This reevaluation appears in the central chapter of the book, entitled, quite significantly though uncharacteristically for Katz, "The Course of Jewish History in the Shadow of Christianity" (בצלה של הנצרות מהלך ההיסטוריה היהודית).[8]

---

5. "On Jewish Social History: Epochal and Supra-Epochal Historiography," *Jewish History* 7 (Spring, 1993): 92ff. The essay was originally published in the Toury Festschrift in 1991 in German; see Katz bibliography (n. 1, above, no. 274).

6. *Ibid.*, p. 93.

7. Although this is the only reference to *longue durée*, it is meaningful coming when it does in the context of his discussion of anti-Semitism, Jewish nationalism, and their historical outcome. See Jacob Katz, *A Time for Inquiry—A Time for Reflection. A Historical Essay on Israel through the Ages* [in Hebrew] (Jerusalem: 1998/99), p. 47. This remains the only untranslated book by Katz, yet it contains some illuminating perspectives on his historical writing. The first chapter, entitled "History and the Historians, New and Old," was translated by Ada Rapoport-Albert and published as a special booklet by The Institute of Jewish Studies, University College, London, 1999 with a short appreciation of Katz and his writings by Chimen Abramsky and Rapoport-Albert. This booklet is absent from the Katz bibliography (see n. 1, above).

8. Katz had originally called the chapter "Between Strangeness and Integration" (בין זרות להשתלבות); however, after the book was edited, he changed the title to the above. This was his own suggestion and not that of the editor, Mr. Yehezkel Hovav of The Zalman Shazar Center for Jewish History in Jerusalem. I thank Mr. Hovav for providing me with a photocopy with Katz's handwritten correction.

The intersection of modern situations or events with the historical trends he detected was at the heart of much of Katz's work. This was the essence of his studies on various halakhic concepts, as can be seen in his history of *The 'Shabbes Goy': A Study in Halakhic Flexibility* and in his collected case studies *Divine Law in Human Hands* and also in his understanding of Jewish-Christian relationships, anti-Semitism, and the Holocaust.[9] Indeed, in the above-mentioned chapter of his last book, Katz argued that the negative Christian attitudes to Jews and Judaism and the desire of Jews to redeem themselves from the Christian environment stand out as the two phenomena that illuminate the value of the historical framework of *longue durée*. These two inter-related currents had, in his mind, a "significant role" in the Holocaust and the creation of the State of Israel. By asserting his affirmation of the long time-frame, Katz came full circle with his initial pre-occupation with the fate of German Jewry in his 1934 dissertation, which dealt with German-Jewish assimilation and its ideology.[10] For the nexus of this issue to the historical fate of the Jews in World War II remained a persistent concern of Katz that brought him to inquire again and again into the intricate relationships between Jews and Christians over the centuries. Forever troubled by these historical implications, Katz could not be satisfied by an historical interpretation that placed the onus for these events solely on the years 1933–45. As he himself summarized his position in an international conference on "Judaism and Christianity under the Impact of National Socialism, 1919–1945" in Jerusalem in 1982:

> The key to the understanding of what happened in the 19th and 20th century in Jewish-Gentile relations, including its catastrophic climax in the Holocaust, is not to be found in the immediate past but in the course of Jewish history, at least since its entanglement with the history of Christianity. It was the tragic mistake of the 19th century enthusiasts to believe that the traces of such deep-seated antagonism could be eliminated simply be declaring it unreasonable or unfounded.[11]

---

9. *The 'Shabbes Goy': A Study in Halakhic Flexibility* (Philadelphia: 1989); *Divine Law in Human Hands. Case Studies in Halakhic Flexibility* (Jerusalem: 1998).

10. Jacob Katz, *Die Entstehung der Judenassimilation in Deutschland und deren Ideologie* (Frankfurt: 1935); reprinted in *idem, Emancipation and Assimilation. Studies in Modern Jewish History* (Westmead: 1972), pp. 195–276.

11. *Idem*, "Christian-Jewish Antagonism on the Eve of the Modern Era," *Judaism and Christianity under the Impact of National-Socialism*, ed. Otto Dov Kulka and Paul R. Mendes-Flohr (Jerusalem: 1987), p. 34.

The contrary was also true. The Holocaust enabled one to understand events in European Jewry even several generations removed from it. Thus, in seeking a perspective to understand the roots of the cataclysmic period, Katz came to reject not only psychological or ideological explanations but also the viability of the social-historical methodology he had advocated in the 1950s.[12] He argued in the early 1990s that "the history of anti-Semitism is thus one example illustrating my thesis that the social-historical approach cannot do justice to the entire array of questions raised in historiographical research. Alongside this perspective, there is ample justification for tracing events and processes within a longer time frame."[13]

The longer time frame—the supra-ephocal or *longue durée*—for Katz meant in this regard the life of Jews "in the shadow of Christianity." The shadow of Christianity had different implications for Katz, ranging from the way the political and social status of the Jews was determined to its existential implications for the future of Jewish uniqueness. Particular historical events could not be completely disassociated from the framework that dominated the relationship between Judaism and Christianity, so with regard to specific cases of Jewish-Christian friction or localized outbursts of anti-Jewish sentiment. For Katz, neither the arguments raised during the Hep Hep controversy of 1819 nor the opposition of certain Freemason societies to allow Jews entry into their lodges, could, for example, be fully understood solely from within their immediate prism. They needed to be viewed within the traditional anti-Jewish prejudices that surfaced with the appearance of Christianity. Similar to James Parkes and Jules Isaac, and foreshadowing Gavin Langmuir, Katz saw the conflict between Jews and Christians within the religious sphere, granting minimal relevance to pre-Christian attitudes to Jews and Judaism, in contradistinction to two of his Jerusalem colleagues, Menachem Stern and Shmuel Ettinger.[14] As he saw this supra-epochal conflict in religious terms in which Christian animosity to Jews and Judaism was met by

---

12. Jacob Katz, "The Concept of Social History and Its Possible Use in Jewish Historical Research," *Scripta Hierosolymitana* III (1956): 292–312.

13. Katz, "On Jewish Social History," p. 96.

14. I have mentioned only several scholars in order to situate Katz's writing, although many more writers and scholars have addressed this issue in one manner or another. For several helpful surveys of some of this literature, see John Gager, *The Origins of Antisemitism. Attitudes toward Judaism in Pagan and Christian Antiquity* (New York and Oxford: 1983); Robert A. Everett, *Christianity without Antisemitism. James Parkes and the Jewish-Christian Encounter* (Oxford, New York and Seoul: 1993), esp. pp. 189–277; Peter Schaefer, *Judeophobia. Attitudes toward the Jews in the Ancient World* (Cambridge, Mass.: 1997).

Jewish separateness and steadfastness, Katz tried to "unpack" how this confrontation played itself out in the modern period, that is, how Christian attitudes were reworked or transformed, and how Jews in a new setting reconfigured their separateness or strangeness. The interplay between the two vantage points—anti-Jewish attitudes and Jewish separateness—was constant and had a seminal role on the development of Jewish history. Thus Katz strongly rejected the notion that anti-Judaism or anti-Semitism had no place in Jewish history.[15] To disregard anti-Semitism or to claim that it was only a phenomenon relating to the history of the country wherein it transpired was to minimize its consequences for Jewish relations with others and to overlook the role Jews played in this configuration. On the contrary, for Katz and for leading figures in the "Jerusalem school of history," anti-Semitism was part and parcel of the twists and turns in the unfolding relationship between the Jews and European society.[16] This grand scheme, which Katz seems to have formulated early on in his career, accounts for his extensive studies into a wide realm of issues that were intrinsic to the historical encounter between Jews and Christians. Yet, I should add that, even as Katz asserted the relevance of history to the modern event studied, he cautioned the historian time and again not to project knowledge of the events on the consciousness of contemporaries who had no notion of the future developments. History—including the history of European Jewry—was not predetermined and the Holocaust not "predictable."[17]

In opting for the *longue durée* as a necessary category for comprehending the Holocaust or by placing the modern conflict on the back of the medieval

15. This emerges from various essays and books. See in particular, Jacob Katz, "Misreadings of Anti-Semitism," *Commentary* LXXVI, 1 (1983): 39–44; *idem*, "World War I—A Crossroads in the History of European Jewry," *Yad Vashem Studies* XXVII (ed. David Silberklang; Jerusalem: 1999): 11–21. This essay was published after the appearance of the Katz bibliography (above n. 1) and is not mentioned there. See also *idem*, *A Time for Inquiry*, ch. 2.

16. Clearly, individuals within the "Jerusalem school" harbored different views on the centrality and persistence of anti-Semitism over time. For example, David N. Myers has argued that Yitzhak Baer continued to uphold the "lachrymose conception" of Jewish history. See *Re-Inventing the Jewish Past. European Jewish Intellectuals and the Zionist Return to History* (New York and Oxford: 1995), p. 120; Israel Jacob Yuval, "Yitzhak Baer and the Search for Authentic Judaism," *The Jewish Past Revisited: Reflections on Modern Jewish Historians*, ed. David N. Myers and David B. Ruderman (New Haven and London: 1998), pp. 77–87. The attitude of the "Jerusalem school" to anti-Semitism deserves a special study.

17. *Inter alia*, Katz, "Was the Holocaust Predictable?" pp. 41–48.

legacy, Katz lent support to those schools of thought that argued for a certain degree of continuity between traditional and modern anti-Semitism. Coming from different backgrounds and scholarly approaches but sharing a common belief that traditional/Christian anti-Jewish teachings remained the bedrock of modern anti-Semitism and could very easily be reasserted in a modern context, these scholars were far from united on their connection to and influence on Nazi anti-Semitism.[18] Probably the most significant voice to be added to the school came from Gavin Langmuir, who, in his *History, Religion, and Antisemitism*, delved deeply into the Christian sources and pinpointed events in the twelfth century as a critical turning point in the history of anti-Semitism. Though Langmuir perceived strong associations between Christian and Nazi anti-Semitism, emphasizing many parallels between their ideologies, he refrained from asserting a direct link between them. Irrational projections dominated the minds of medieval Christians and Hitler, but their solutions differed.[19] Recently, Jonathan Frankel in his monumental study of the Damascus Affair has intimated that the nineteenth century's preoccupation with Jewish ritual murder affirms the claim that the medieval Christian tradition continued to have a profound resonance in modern anti-Semitism. The attacks on the Talmud during the Affair, the irrational attempts by liberal society to support classical anti-Jewish canards on the sacrifice of humans by Jews and the use of blood to make *maẓot* asserted the perseverance of the medieval Christian tradition.[20] In pursuing this direction, the continuity of anti-Jewish themes (the *longue durée*), Katz did not merely adopt the classical Zionist notion of Judeophobia but confronted a recurrent factor in the history of Jewish society. In his quest to penetrate its aberration in the twentieth century, Katz concentrated on the attitudes of

---

18. My special thanks to Marc Saperstein of George Washington University for his comments on the oral presentation of this paper on May 16, 2000. He has also generously shared with me a paper in progress that deals with the theme of continuity and discontinuity in anti-Semitism. Temporarily entitled "Christian Doctrine and the 'Final Solution': The State of the Question," the paper maps out a variety of opinions on the connections between Christian anti-Jewish attitudes and those of the Nazis on the Final Solution. For a different survey and focus, see Steven E. Aschheim, "Small Forays, Grand Theories and Deep Origins: Current Trends in the Historiography of the Holocaust," *Studies in Contemporary Jewry* 10 (ed. Jonathan Frankel; 1994): 139–63.

19. Gavin Langmuir, *History, Religion, and Antisemitism* (Berkeley, Los Angeles, Oxford: 1990).

20. Jonathan Frankel, *The Damascus Affair. "Ritual Murder," Politics, and the Jews in 1840* (Cambridge: 1997).

European society to the Jews in the modern period, accepting the overpow-
ering, formative nature of the medieval position. Indeed, as David Berger
shows in this volume, Katz relied to a great extent on previous studies and
received wisdom and did not do basic research into the Jewish-Christian
polemic of the period.[21] Katz approached the *legacy* of the Jewish-Christian
medieval tradition, wondering how the modern period negotiated with its
past traditions and preoccupations.

Katz's study, in the 1960s, on the Freemasons and Jews provided him an
excellent framework with which to analyze the resilience of traditional
views.[22] Freemasonry posited a universalistic, humanistic ideology, openness
to all peoples, a voluntaristic society without the cudgels of tradition. Moreover, as we now know more from the studies of Margaret Jacobs and others,
the Freemasons often housed, especially in the eighteenth century, some of
the most radical enlightened thought and in some lodges were clearly at odds
with all forms of organized religion.[23] Such radicalism neatly corresponded
to the emerging notions of integration that began to surface in Jewish society
in different countries, creating a perfect test case for Katz's inquiry into the
process of acceptance of Jews into European society. His painstaking research
into the problems Jews encountered in entering into Freemason lodges,
especially in Germany, revealed both the staying power of Christian symbols,
dogmas, and rituals, and a certain social and political reticence to allowing
Jews to become an integral part of the lodges. As social equality was not taken
for granted in the nineteenth century, the desire of Jews to join the lodges
in large numbers was commonly stymied. This process of rejection mush-
roomed in Weimar Germany when even Jews who had been members of the
lodges were now pushed out in significant numbers. In this development it
was the inability of Freemasonry to create within a growing secular world a
wholly new tradition, free from Christian sources, that drew Katz's special
attention:

> Since there was no binding local tradition in the other countries, it was
> relatively simple to adopt ideas and symbols from any source that ap-

---

21. See above, David Berger, "Jacob Katz on Jews and Christians in the Middle
    Ages," pp. 41–63.

22. Jacob Katz, *Jews and Freemasons in Europe 1723–1939*, trans. Leonard Oschry
    (Cambridge, Mass.: 1970), originally published in Hebrew in 1968 with a
    somewhat different title: *Freemasons and Jews. Real and Imaginary Connections*.

23. Margaret C. Jacob, *Living the Enlightenment. Freemasonry and Politics in Eight-
    eenth-Century Europe* (New York: 1991); *idem*, *The Radical Enlightenment.
    Pantheists, Freemasons and Republicans* (London: 1981).

pealed to the mood and fancy of the members of each particular lodge, and among them were those predisposed to mystic and mystifying doctrines. This type certainly did not abjure any Christian concepts and symbols but even presumed to lead the Masons, in the higher degrees, to the revelation of profound Christian mysteries.[24]

The fact that the Freemasons were unable to create a setting for integration was the clearest affirmation for Katz that "the idea of total emancipation was only an unattainable Utopia,"[25] a formulation he returned to on various occasions and that was clearly influenced by Mannheim's classic *Ideology and Utopia. Jews and Freemasons*. Yet, it had disturbing implications as it "exemplifies the difficulties encountered by Jews in becoming absorbed in Germany" (p. 8). Katz cautioned, at the outset of the work, against reading later conclusions into earlier developments. Integration was not achieved in many lodges as one continued to view the world in one sense or another through the prism of religion. For Katz this was an affirmation that, alongside its cohesive nature, religion had a very divisive role in modern secular society.[26] As long as the burden of Christian tradition was present and impacted on society, as it did, complete integration of Jews was mere utopia.

The inability to integrate fully was further enunciated in *Out of the Ghetto*, where Katz returned to his 1934 dissertation and to the period in which he so often traveled, 1770–1870. Here Katz shows that the failure to integrate had, of course, two sides—that of European society and that of the Jews. European society's ambivalence toward the Jews manifested itself in the eighteenth-century Enlightenment. It both endeavored to emancipate the Jews but also hoped to see the gradual dissolution of the Jews, their unique qualities and social framework. Katz was in full agreement with much of Arthur Hertzberg's argument in *The French Enlightenment and the Jews* (1968), which utilized Jacob Talmon's thesis on totalitarian democracy and applied it to the Jewish context—specifically, that the Enlightenment vision was driven by a totalitarian mindset, paving the way to the disasters of the twenti-

---

24. Katz, *Jews and Freemasons*, p. 207; see also *ibid.*, pp. 197–206.

25. Jacob Katz, "The German-Jewish Utopia of Social Emancipation," *Studies of the Leo Baeck Institute*, ed. Max Kreutzberger (New York: 1967), p. 80. This essay, to my mind, represents most succinctly Katz's perspective on the issues of integration. Originally published in an abbreviated form in Dutch (1963/64), {Katz bibliography, no. 89}, the essay was reproduced in several of his collected papers.

26. *Idem*, "Religion as a Uniting and Dividing Force in Modern Jewish History," *The Role of Religion in Modern Jewish History*, ed. Jacob Katz (Cambridge, Mass.: 1975), pp. 1–17.

eth century. Though Katz shied away from such a sharp formulation and took issue with Hertzberg's extreme categorization of Voltaire, he was clearly in agreement with his interpretation of the "bargain of emancipation."[27] Hertzberg's critical assessment of the underlying motivation of the proponents of Emancipation sat well with Katz's evaluation of the false utopian belief in Jewish integration, mentioned above. Thus, Katz's shift from the phrase "neutral society" in *Tradition and Crisis* to describe the Berlin milieu in which Moses Mendelssohn lived in the eighteenth century to "semi-neutral society" in *Out of the Ghetto* was not mere cosmetics. The former phrase was already present in the 1934 dissertation and withstood the intermediary historical events. Rather, the shift was occasioned by research Katz himself pursued between these works, first and foremost on the Jews and the Freemasons, but also on the background to Mendelssohn's *Jerusalem*.[28] This change in emphasis indicates a certain turn to a more pessimistic reading of the past. In a sense it was Katz's recognition that even the hallowed friendship between Mendelssohn and Lessing was but a glimpse into an imaginary world that would never materialize in European society. It was a growing affirmation that few elements in European society, supporters of emancipation and its opponents, were able to overcome a basic desire for the demise of Judaism. Katz was not the first to make this claim, but he now advanced it with considerable vigor, bringing to bear more and more examples of this mindset. The positions taken on the "Jewish Question" by Fichte at the beginning of the nineteenth century and by Mommsen in the controversy over Treitschke loomed larger and larger in Katz's historiographical scheme as representatives of both sides of the divide.[29] In essence, they reflected the pre-racial dream of seeing Jews voluntarily terminate their existence. Notwithstanding the strides Jews had taken to penetrate European society and to refashion their Jewish identity, Jews continued to be considered a collective ("a state within a state")[30] that would not or could not divest itself

---

27. Review of Arthur Hertzberg, *The French Enlightenment and the Jews* (New York: 1968), *Commentary* XLVI (Oct. 1968): 94–96.

28. "To Whom Did Mendelssohn Reply in His 'Jerusalem'?" *Scripta Hierosolymitana* XXIII (1972): 214–43; originally published in *Zion* 29 (1963).

29. See, *inter alia*, Jacob Katz, "The Turning Point of Modern Jewish History: The Eighteenth Century," *Vision Confronts Reality*, ed. Ruth Kozodoy (New York: 1989), pp. 40–55; *idem*, "Leaving the Ghetto," *Commentary* 101 (1996): 29–33. Similar discussions appear in other works as well.

30. *Idem*, "A State within a State. The History of an Anti-Semitic Slogan," *The Israel Academy of Sciences and Humanities Proceedings* IV (Jerusalem: 1969/70), pp. 29–58.

of its cohesive nature. In *Out of the Ghetto* we are presented with a bleak appraisal of the one hundred years of Jewish entry into European society—though Katz is specifically concerned with the integration into Germany, a fact that has engendered certain criticism.[31] The social situation was magnified by the inability of European society to shed its stereotypical views of the Jew, the legacy of the medieval tradition that reverberated over and over in the arguments on integrating, emancipating, or accepting the Jews.

Why was European society unable to free itself from the past as it emerged into an age of rationality? This was the historical issue that engaged Katz in two other book-length studies in the 1980s. *From Prejudice to Destruction. Anti-Semitism, 1700–1933* brought together Katz's various forays into the changing terrain of Jewish-Christian relations in the modern period. Beginning with Johannes Eisenmenger's study of Judaism in the eighteenth century, through the writings of Deists, Voltaire, and various thinkers of the nineteenth century, and culminating with racial theory, Katz pursued the interaction between ideas and social developments. He showed how certain expressions of anti-Jewish animus continued to gain public support in the modern period, as the process of Jewish integration intensified. Moreover, rationalist thinking was not able to erase completely the negative Christian tradition and, though latent, it remained a significant factor in the reception of anti-Semitic ideas and movements in the late nineteenth century. Even secular arguments, advanced by such thinkers as Voltaire, Bruno Bauer, and Eugen Dühring minimized Judaism as opposed to the Christianity they rejected. One figure who attracted a special study, Richard Wagner, and who has often been aligned with racial thinking is seen in a less dramatic manner than often portrayed. Wagner in Katz's interpretation epitomizes the merger of social conflict and latent anti-Jewish animus. In encountering certain obstacles in his career in which Jews were involved, Wagner enunciated strong anti-Jewish pronouncements that had clear Christian roots. Jews remained, in his eyes, a separate entity and thus the only solution to their integration was by going asunder, by a process of de-Judaization. This was not a break with anti-Semitic tradition but rather a reformulation of a long line of anti-Semitic thinking. In casting Wagner in this manner, Katz reduced the onus of future events on the composer, but furthered his own understanding of the ways in which anti-Semitic thought continued to persist in an age of reduced Christian influence.[32] Such an approach did not detract from the importance of

---

31. See, e.g., Pierre Birnbaum and Ira Katznelson, "Emancipation and the Liberal Offer," *Paths of Emancipation. Jews, States, and Citizenship*, ed. P. Birnbaum and I. Katznelson (Princeton: 1995), pp. 3–36, esp. 15–24.

32. Jacob Katz, *The Darker Side of Genius. Richard Wagner's Anti-Semitism* (Hanover

racial thinking. This form of anti-Semitic argument raised the stakes in the Jewish-Christian imbroglio, but still did not reduce the power of traditional views. According to Katz's understanding of modern anti-Semitism, "even if they negated the Christian motives responsible for the creation of the situation, anti-Semites still took it as the basis of their operation. There is a patent historical continuity between the two phases of the Jewish predicament."[33] Certainly solutions were not of the same order and possibilities of escape from Christian pressure were radically simpler than from the racial vise, but this did not loosen the hold of the pre-modern arguments and images on the modern anti-Semitic thinkers.

As mentioned above, there were two sides to the failure of integration. The other side, the bright one—from Katz's point of view—was the Jewish one. Integration was also doomed, so to speak, since Jews were unwilling to completely forego their attachment to Jewish particularity as was envisaged by Enlightenment and emancipation thinkers from the end of the eighteenth century. *Out of the Ghetto* brought to light the persistence of Jews to maintain a sense of connection, what I prefer to call a feeling of belonging. Though the "state within a state"—Jewish autonomous existence—which assumed such excessive attention at the turn of the nineteenth century was clearly dissipated, many Jews continued to show an inclination to maintain some semblance of identification with other Jews and the Jewish past. Leaving the ghetto did not terminate Jewish existence, but refashioned it in forms that were uniquely theirs. Even as they emphatically desired integration, they developed an intricate web of associations and contacts that formed a kind of subgroup in society. This notion was later developed by David Sorkin, who saw this evolution as being connected with the overall burgeoning of the Jewish community.[34] Sorkin brought to bear a host of examples to illuminate this transformation that affirmed integration and concepts of *Bildung* yet consciously or subconsciously generated greater association with Jewish particularism. Jews did not simply accept the mold that had been shaped for them. They wanted new associations, new involvements, and even new appearances, but not necessarily a total "face lift." Katz viewed this development as the persistence of Jews to remain a defined subgroup in society, an indication of their "atavistic" response, "represented (by) an adherence to

---

and London: 1986).

33. *Idem, From Prejudice to Destruction. Anti-Semitism, 1700–1933* (Cambridge, Mass.: 1980), p. 321.

34. David Sorkin, *The Transformation of German Jewry, 1780–1840* (New York and Oxford: 1987).

a pattern of behavior after the reason for it had disappeared," a sign that residues of the past were still very much at work.[35] This position foreshadowed a change in orientation of historical writing on the nineteenth century in the last generation, what Jonathan Frankel has called the "re-mapping of modern Jewish history."[36] Yet for Katz this process was inherently related to his tremendous concern with the acceptance or lack of acceptance of the Jews by European society. As he later wrote in his *From Prejudice to Destruction*, "this very guarantee of their survival elicited or intensified a peculiar brand of social animosity." That survival was facilitated by Jewish "social cohesion and compactness," which activated "the complex of imaginary notions about the Jewish mentality and other characteristics."[37] Interestingly, the younger generation of scholars involved in this "re-mapping" has relegated anti-Semitism to a less central place in its historical understanding. This may be attributed to the impact of a more optimistic outlook on life, generated in some cases by the American context of some of these writers, as Todd Endelman has argued,[38] and/or to the greater engagement with more contemporary issues, such as gender, spirituality, memory, and community.

Katz's depiction of the resilience of Jewish society in the nineteenth century, buttressed by the anti-Jewish animus, echoes his earlier concerns with Jewish attitudes to Christian society in earlier periods. Whereas in modern times the utopian vision of the Enlightenment that anticipated a dissipated Jewry, totally atomized in its economic, social, and cultural profile, encountered a remarkable Jewish persistence to survive, so Christian perspectives in the medieval period faced Jews, who were far from submissive ideologically. Already in *Tradition and Crisis* but even more pronounced in *Exclusiveness and Tolerance* and in *Shabbes Goy* and numerous classic essays, such as בין תתנ"ו לת"ח-ת"ט,[39] Katz endeavored to show how Jewish mental-

---

35. Jacob Katz, *Out of the Ghetto. The Social Background of Jewish Emancipation, 1770–1870* (Cambridge, Mass.: 1973), p. 205; similarly in other places, see, e.g., "Religion as a Uniting and Dividing Force," pp. 1–17.

36. Jonathan Frankel, "Assimilation and the Jews in Nineteenth-Century Europe: Towards a New Historiography?" *Assimilation and Community. The Jews in Nineteenth-Century Europe,* ed. Jonathan Frankel and Steven J. Zipperstein (Cambridge and New York: 1992), p. 1.

37. Katz, *From Prejudice to Destruction*, p. 323.

38. Todd M. Endelman, "The Legitimization of the Diaspora Experience in Recent Jewish Historiography," *Modern Judaism* 11, 2 (1991): 195–209.

39. Published originally in Hebrew in the Baer Festschrift (Jerusalem: 1961), pp. 318–37. For its reissue in Hebrew, see Katz bibliography, no. 216. Katz re-

ity in Christian Europe maintained itself as a minority religion vis-à-vis the
majority religion. Jews were always active agents in their fate but "never
masters of their own destiny."[40] Katz showed the theological and social
mechanisms at work that guaranteed the minority's steadfastness in the face
of adversity—what he later called מעשה הירואי עליון (a supreme heroic act)
or in other contexts "the audacious Jews."[41] Christian notions of supremacy
were met with Jewish notions of spiritual supremacy and only gradually did
these yield to less conflicting attitudes. That is, the difficult predicaments in
which Jews found themselves, in the "shadow of Christianity," both in the
medieval and modern periods, sharpened for Katz his perception of the
Jewish situation.

If the failure of integration was a result of the interplay between European
reticence to accept the Jew and Jewish singularity, did this imply that eventually Jews were in some sense responsible for anti-Semitism and ultimately the
outcome of the events in World War II? As was commonly argued in European discussions on anti-Semitism—Émile Zola and Jean-Paul Sartre, to
name two of the most prominent writers—had Jews fully assimilated they
could have minimized anti-Semitic outbursts. The converse could also be
claimed and has been, that had Jews not left traditional society and entered
into the modern realm they could have prevented the onslaught against them.
Others still, like Theodor Herzl, believed that anti-Semitism was borne of the
friction caused by the penetration of Jews into European society and their
clash with parallel non-Jewish elements. Katz, as far as I understand him,
walked a tightrope amidst these various hypotheses, coming very close to
intimating that Jewish behavior was, in some way, a cause, but not responsible
for anti-Semitic activity. He, who accepted "Jewish vulnerability...to be the
unavoidable legacy of the Jewish past,"[42] viewed Jewish solidarity as a thorn
in the eyes of non-Jewish society, and upheld modernity even though it
ruptured the seams of tradition. Asking rhetorically, he wrote:

> Yet who among us, even knowing what finally lay in store for them,
> can blame them for having seized the modern opportunity, or for hav-
> ing imagined that it spelled the end of their historic tribulations? Who

---

turned to the theme of Jewish response to martyrdom in ages of diversity in his
controversy with Edward Fram. See J. Katz, "More on 'Between 1096 and
1648–1649'," [Hebrew] *Zion* LXII, 1 (1997): 23–29.

40. Katz, "Leaving the Ghetto," p. 33.

41. *Idem, A Time of Inquiry*, p. 56.

42. *Idem*, "Misreadings of Anti-Semitism," p. 44.

among us, desirous of honoring their memory, would dare to judge their long and ardent struggle against the vise of circumstance?[43]

In his discussion of the utopian vision of integration maintained by various Jewish figures, and first and foremost by Moses Mendelssohn, Katz had only the highest regard: "His vision served for generations to come as an ideal toward which to strive. Despite its failure to materialize...Mendelssohn's noble dream thus fulfilled a worthy function, and even our own disillusioned generation cannot, with propriety, treat it with disdain."[44] Katz was certainly aware of the fine line he had drawn, praising Jewish modernity in its visionary scheme, extolling Jewish solidarity, but also uncovering various negative attitudes Jews had harbored toward Christians and Christianity during the Middle Ages. Did he think that these negative depictions influenced Christian behavior toward the Jews? Katz is not explicit on this seminal issue, but he seems to imply that, on some level, it had a consequence. He concluded *Exclusiveness and Tolerance* with the remark that it is only "a later generation—our own—(that is able) to lay aside the notions of static doctrine and teachings, and courageously to trace the true development of ideas and practices down the centuries."[45] This is a surprising remark coming so soon after the Holocaust. Who in "that generation"—in the late fifties—was willing to call a spade a spade and "reveal" some of the harsher arguments Jewish thinkers harbored toward their Christian neighbors?

It was the Zionist in Katz that feared not the repercussions of his research. It was in the spirit of Gershom Scholem's call for a Jewish historiography free from the apologetics of *Wissenschaft* and in line with Katz's own understanding of the remarkable contribution of Zionism to Jewish self-dignity. But years later, in his autobiography, Katz recalled the reticence of Alexander Altmann, the editor of the proposed volume *Exclusiveness and Tolerance*, to publish the book as it "might provide ammunition for the enemies of the Jewish people."[46] Katz, as I have mentioned above, was not very clear on what he thought about the relationship between Jewish attitudes to Christianity and Christian responses to them, even though he claimed that their relationship was a "reciprocal one."[47] But, if he thought Jewish attitudes were

---

43. *Idem,* "Leaving the Ghetto," p. 33.

44. *Idem, Exclusiveness and Tolerance,* pp. 180–81.

45. *Ibid.,* p. 196.

46. *Idem, With My Own Eyes. The Autobiography of an Historian,* trans. Ann Brenner and Zipora Brody (Hanover and London: 1995), p. 147.

47. Katz, *Exclusiveness and Tolerance,* p. 3. Katz claims there: "The behaviour of the

a definite factor in the rise of modern anti-Semitism, one could have expected more specific attention to these opinions in the most obvious place—his synthetic study *From Persecution to Destruction,* where they are indeed totally absent. Though one could also claim that they had no role in such a discussion, since Katz believed that in the modern period Jewish attitudes to Christianity had moved away from their exclusive and contrary stand to a more tolerant and utopic one, as seen in the writings of Mendelssohn or the decisions of the Paris Sandhedrin. Katz, it would appear, was more engaged in understanding how Jews reckoned with the majority religion than how their behavior and attitudes affected its attitude to them. Though Jews could never become "masters of their own fate" in the European setting, through their organistic and atavistic behavior they preserved a certain particularism and were thus doomed to resentment. Particularism was not *the* cause of anti-Semitism, but it did arouse opposition and the traditional voices of discontent. These needed little to be triggered as they lay deep in the foundations of Christian society. Katz seems to have accepted a time-honored Zionist view, akin to the Pinskerian notion of Judeophobia. The Zionist answer is fully upheld in reality and historically. It enabled Jews to reassert their self-image, "regain their balance and freedom," and possibly reduce the tension between Jews and Gentiles.

In conclusion, according to Katz, living in the shadow of Christianity for generations had its impact on all aspects of Jewish life and self-image. Together with the enduring rabbinical tradition and its method of interpretation of daily life, Jews forged an assertive, instrumental manner of dealing with the majority world. Halakhah and theology seemed to be shaped by these premises. As traditional life modified itself dramatically, replaced by a Utopian vision best enunciated by Moses Mendelssohn, Jews believed that they could change themselves, or better, regenerate themselves, but not always in the guise desired by the non-Jew. Thus, regeneration could not be realized, as the dormant tradition of Christian animosity was not able to live with the atavistic nature of Jewish society that could not totally dissolve. The *longue durée* of deep-seated Jewish separateness, honed and sharpened over time, remained forever at odds with Christian-European society and, in reality, no utopian image could ever overcome that shadow. Therein lay to my mind an overarching thesis of Jacob Katz that penetrated, overtly and covertly, consciously and subconsciously, so much of his lucid and pathbreaking historical research from his first foray into the study of German-Jewish assimilation in 1934.

Jews towards their neighbours is conditioned by the behaviour of the latter towards them, and vice versa."

A Hungarian Rhapsody in Blue:
Jacob Katz's Tardy Surrender to Hagar's Allure*

Michael K. Silber
The Hebrew University, Jerusalem

I.

Jacob Katz came late in life to chronicle his native Jewry, but when he did, his contribution to the history of Hungarian Jewry was substantial and lasting. It is the Hungarian dimension in Jacob Katz's historiography that I wish to explore here.

We may begin by posing what might be a contrived question: Why this tardy surrender to the allure of Hungarian Jewish history? One may be tempted to dismiss this question outright—after all, why should a historian of Katz's caliber and catholic interests, one who roamed the length and breadth of Jewish history with sovereign assurance, limit his compass to the Pannonian hills? There is much to commend this point. Indeed, Katz never became a historian of Hungarian Jewry in the sense of those "national" Jewish historians who adopted the nation-state as the primary framework of their analysis. Nevertheless, Katz did devote considerable time in his later years to the field, enriching it immeasurably. First, his biographical study of the *Hatam Sofer* in 1967 brought new understanding to the personality who more than any other shaped the course of Hungarian Jewish history. His monograph on the Orthodox secession, *A House Divided,* published almost three decades later in 1994, recounted and analyzed one of the pivotal episodes in the historical narrative of Hungarian Jewry, a turning point that sealed its fate and determined its unique character as the most polarized of modern Jewish communities. In between, he published a series of case studies on what he called "halakhic flexibility," where the discerning reader cannot but note that among the various "national" styles of halakhic deliberations and decisions, the tenor set by the Hungarians proved to be the most strident, stringent, and intractable (a source no doubt of perverse national pride to some Hungarian Jews).

---

* Hagar is an archaic Hebrew term for Hungary [ed.].

In what follows, I will trace the Hungarian component of his career in the hope that exploring his contributions to Hungarian Jewish history will also shed some light on larger issues of his historiography.

II.

The notion that the young Katz (and as he was wont to say, his academic age was a generation younger than his biological one) would try his hand exploring the history of his native Jewry seems less farfetched on second thought. In fact, early in his academic career, he was in close contact with a younger colleague in the Department of Sociology at Hebrew University who did just that. Like Katz, Joseph Ben-David came from a Hungarian Orthodox background; in fact, he was born and raised in Győr, the native town of Katz's mother, the community where his uncle had served as rabbi. Ben-David left Hungary to study history and sociology in Jerusalem and London in the 1940s, and went on to lead a distinguished career as one of the leading figures in the sociology of science. It was an historical study, however, that marked his academic debut: an article on the beginnings of modern Jewish society in Hungary. Although it was to be a onetime foray into Hungarian Jewish history, the article hinted at what was to become Ben-David's lifelong interest in the role of the intellectual in society.

It is worthwhile to digress here to review this pioneering work, which only recently has been translated into English.[1] The article makes us aware of the options available to Katz in employing the methods of historical sociology that characterized the finest work of the first decade of his career. The two men were intellectually close and Ben-David cited Katz's 1945 article on marriage and sexual life,[2] and, in turn, Katz singled out Ben-David, along

---

1. Originally published in *Zion* 17 (1952): 101–28, it has recently been translated into English as Joseph Ben-David, "The Beginnings of Modern Jewish Society in Hungary in the First Half of the Nineteenth Century," *Jewish History* 11 (1997): 57–97. This translation is now prefaced by an abstract that Ben-David prepared for his M.A. thesis submitted to Ben-Zion Dinur in 1950, which had first appeared in the English summaries section in *Zion* 17 (1952): vi–viii. In a preface to the notes, Ben-David states that the article "summarizes the sociological conclusions" of his M.A. thesis. From what I have heard, the M.A. thesis, now lost, was identical to the article. It seems to me that this phrase probably referred to the English abstract that does contain important sociological formulations that are not found in the article itself.

2. See Ben-David's notes 12, 14, 17 and 22. Katz's and S. N. Eisenstadt's early work on immigrants and generational change are the only works not directly related to Hungarian Jewry that Ben-David cites more than once.

with S. N. Eisenstadt and Yonina Talmon, as the colleagues who read and critiqued the manuscript of *Tradition and Crisis*.[3] Ben-David's study on Hungarian Jewry is important in that it foreshadowed some of the methods and concerns that Katz was to address in *Tradition and Crisis* and later studies. The proximity, the shared origin, education and interests of the two men, their mutual respect, might also explain why the younger man's treatment of Hungarian Jewry's "tradition and crisis" may have satisfied by proxy whatever intellectual compulsion (and perhaps commemorative obligation during those years so close upon the Holocaust) that may have otherwise impelled Katz to study Hungarian Jewry.

In his study of modernization (a term that does not appear yet in the vocabulary of this 1952 study), Ben-David casts his analytical web wide, adopting an ambitious systemic approach that embraces such varied aspects of Hungarian Jewry as demography, economy, society, and culture. However, Ben-David purposely eschewed a comprehensive exploration of the numerous economic, social, and cultural processes involved in the modernization of Hungarian Jewry, concentrating instead on the analysis of a number of limited facets of its social structure.

It is structures, above all, that drew his analytical gaze. It allowed Ben-David to narrow his focus, reduce and simplify his units of analysis. He argued that a surrogate could be found for the multiplicity of factors involved in modernization, one that would illustrate the complex process of change by condensing it into relatively few, manageable components.

The structural transformation of elite relations was where Ben-David proposed to locate this convenient proxy. This is the major methodological contribution of the article and its analytical axis. Ben-David views continuity and change from the perspective of the leadership stratum, concentrating upon three key elements or patterns of relations: the collective ends and values embodied by the elites; the interaction between the leading elites, in this case, the wealthy and the learned; and finally, their contact with the masses. As a general rule, he argues, societies tend to be stable as long as their elites continue to embody collective values, closely interact with each other, and maintain contact with the masses. When these relations are disrupted, the social equilibrium of the system is upset.

It is around this sociological framework that Ben-David weaves his analysis of the history of Hungarian Jewry in the early nineteenth century and in the

---

3. See the 1957 preface to *Tradition and Crisis: Jewish Society at the End of the Middle Ages,* translated and with an Afterword and Bibliography by Bernard Dov Cooperman (New York: New York University Press, 1993), p. xiv. Katz joined the Department of Sociology at Hebrew University in 1953.

article we encounter many of the classic themes of Weberian and Durk-heimian sociology, with more than a dash of the then-novel structuralist-functionalism of Talcott Parsons and Robert Merton.

What happens to a society whose leaders become alienated from their con-stituency and its collective values? When customary sources of cohesion prove inadequate to the task, alternative modes of solidarity emerge. Ben-David suggests that these conditions are particularly conducive to the emer-gence of youth movements. It is his functionalist-structural approach that leads to the insight that the appearance of the radical revolutionary youth of 1848 and the students of the Pressburg yeshiva are but obverse sides of the same coin. Both are (youthful) manifestations of an intellectual elite increas-ingly detached from the wealthy lay leadership and the broad masses. Both challenge the authority of the establishment and flout society's conventions.

It is under these unstable circumstances that charismatic leadership tends to emerge. Thus paradoxically, that very bastion of conservatism, the Press-burg yeshiva of the Hatam Sofer, in fact, embodied two innovations—the charisma of its founder and the counterculture of its students. Anticipating the findings on fundamentalist movements a generation later, Ben-David dis-cerned that there was a perspective from which Pressburg Orthodoxy could be viewed as a new and innovative phenomenon, part and parcel of the process of modernization, rather than simply going against its grain.

Although the innovative energies of the Hatam Sofer's yeshiva harbored the potential to threaten the establishment along the lines of the Hasidic movement, these charismatic forces were deliberately contained and har-nessed to revitalize tradition. "The unique social phenomenon that interests us here is the consolidation of part of a crumbling community into a group with a charismatic leadership, a process in which the conscious exploitation of charisma as a means of social consolidation was accompanied by opposition to the institutionalization of the charismatic group."[4] The Orthodox sector of Hungarian Jewish society emerged from the crisis with its cohesion recon-stituted, but henceforth, cemented by new bonds. It is from a position of strength that the scholarly elites reoccupied their roles as leaders of the Ortho-dox community, restoring the ruptured breach between the rich and the learned. But the balance between the two elites, concludes Ben-David, was now clearly tipped in favor of the latter.

I need not belabor here some of the themes shared by the two men as they worked their way through what in retrospect seems the stillborn field of Jewish historical sociology. Both sought to present, in Katz's words, "a total-izing comprehensive social history," a complex "interconnected picture of

---

4. Ben-David, p. 89.

all aspects in the life of a society during a given epoch." They both began with a "momentary snapshot" of traditional Jewish society in a "quasi-static state," analyzing its structures and functions, as well as their complex linkages, by means of Weberian ideal-types. Although this synchronic snapshot of "before" was quite thoroughgoing, it was followed by a more sketchy diachronic analysis of the transition to a new state of "after."

It is the emphasis on structure and Weberian ideal-types that lead both men to discern underlying similarities in phenomena that, on the surface, have little in common. Both see the challenge to traditional Jewish society mounted in tandem by two movements diametrically opposed to each other: Ben-David by the newly secularized lay and intellectual elites, and the yeshiva of the charismatic Hatam Sofer in nineteenth-century Hungary; Katz five years later in *Tradition and Crisis*, by the rationalism of the Haskalah and the charisma of the Hasidism in the framework of Ashkenazi Jewry in the eighteenth century. A consequence of their systemic approach was that no sector of society was neglected; both Orthodoxy and Hasidism were incorporated into the narrative of modern Jewish history. And although there had been previous attempts to view Hasidism as a modern phenomenon (albeit for reasons other than those advanced by Katz), Ben-David undoubtedly deserves to be singled out as the first to insist that Orthodoxy also merited analysis within the framework of modernization.

There are, of course, significant differences between the two scholars. We may note, for instance, that Ben-David's analysis focused almost exclusively on the institutional sphere, on leadership, its norms and values defined rather abstractly as wealth and learning, but eschewed any attempt to analyze ideology, whether of Orthodoxy or of its opponents. In fact, the leitmotif of Ben-David's article might well be disengagement and indifference, rather than conflict and *Kulturkampf*, which was to mark Katz's later work. Still there are striking similarities in the work of the two men and any analysis of *Tradition and Crisis* would benefit from a closer reading of Ben-David's article. For our purpose, it does shed light on Katz's subsequent work related to Hungary, the Hatam Sofer, and Orthodoxy.

Here is what Katz himself wrote in a postscript to the translation of Ben-David's article:

> What was innovative and surprising in Ben-David's paper?...[It] showed that the conservative elements in Jewish society changed no less fundamentally than its other parts....I had myself been in close contact with Ben-David and have always felt indebted to our exchange of ideas which was motivated by similar methodological intentions. (This holds particularly of my *Tradition and Crisis*.) ...It is ...a confirmation of his insightfulness that those who studied the same period more extensively

have endorsed his analyses …The same applies to my own study of the
life of the Hatam Sofer, which built upon Ben-David's work without
modifying its conclusions.[5]

III.

In time, Katz did come to study Hungarian Jewry, but only after many years
had passed. One reason may have been that his conception of social history
tended to transcend national borders. If in his later work his net was never
cast quite as wide as the pan-Ashkenazi sweep of *Tradition and Crisis*, nevertheless, he seldom limited himself to any one nation-state, even Germany,
preferring instead a broad regional terrain, often vaguely defined as central
Europe, stretching from France to Hungary. In the last two decades, he came
under criticism for obscuring national variations.[6] But in fact, he quite will-
ingly conceded that "there is such a thing as the collective identity of Jewry
of every country and these communities are variegated especially in modern
times…" noting in the case of Hungarian Jews that they "possess particular
features as a collective."[7] After all, years before he had written a "think piece"
entitled "The Uniqueness of Hungarian Jewry" and much earlier, in his
dissertation, he had observed that national variations in social structure
created divergent paths of emancipation.[8]

---

5. Jacob Katz, "Postscript: Ben-David's Study Forty-Five Years Later," *Jewish History* 11 (Spring 1997): 99–100.

6. See in particular Todd Endelman, "The Englishness of Jewish Modernity in England," in *Toward Modernity: The European Jewish Model*, edited by Jacob Katz (New Brunswick and London: Transaction Books, 1987). (The subtitle of the collection was a clear departure from the "German Jewish Model" that had been initially the focus of the conference.) and Pierre Birnbaum and Ira Katznelson, "Emancipation and the Liberal Offer," in *idem*, eds., *Paths of Emancipation: Jews, States and Citizenship* (Princeton: 1995), pp. 15–17.

7. "The Identity of Post-Emancipatory Hungarian Jewry," in *A Social and Economic History of Central European Jewry*, edited by Yehuda Don and Victor Karady (New Brunswick and London: Transaction Books, 1990), p. 15.

8. Katz had remarked that Jews did not assimilate into *the* German people, but rather into a specific stratum, the newly constituted middle class. Emancipation coincided with the emergence of this new middle class. Hence, he endorsed Gabriel Riesser's insight that, where such bourgeoisie failed to develop as in Russia, Jewish emancipation would not be achieved. See *Die Entstehung der Judenassimilation in Deutschland und deren Ideologie* (Frankfurt: 1935) reprinted in Jacob Katz, *Emancipation and Assimilation: Studies in Modern Jewish History* (Westmead, England: Gregg International, 1972), p. 226, n. 70. The comments

Katz had the opportunity to reflect upon the evident preference of historians for the history of one particular Jewry in another essay that underscored uniqueness, only now the subject matter was not Hungarian Jewry, but rather the object of his passion over many decades, the history of German Jewry. From his dissertation in the thirties through the major and minor studies of the sixties, seventies and eighties, such as *Freemasons and Jews, Out of the Ghetto,* and *From Prejudice to Destruction,* the substantive bulk of his work on modern Jewish history was, in fact, preoccupied with German Jewry even though he permitted himself to stray into other countries in "central Europe" whenever he felt it necessary. As his wont, he tended to understand his own obsessions within a broader context that served as the title of his essay, "The Unique Fascination of German-Jewish History."[9] Here he noted the overwhelming superiority of the historical research and presentation concerning German Jewry in contrast to Polish, Hungarian, or even Dutch and French counterparts, not only with regard to quantity but also to quality, concluding with the assessment that "German Jewry stands apart from its counterparts."

In trying to answer "What has engendered this abundance?" Katz drew a distinction that provides us with a key toward understanding his perception of Hungarian Jewish history. There are differences, he argued, between the way descendants of Eastern European Jewry, on the one hand, and German Jewry, on the other, chose to identify with past generations. The former attached themselves to certain elements of the Eastern European past, perpetuating its memory by means of emotive acts and emblems." By contrast (if we are permitted to recast Katz's argument somewhat), the German Jewish past was addressed as history, not as memory. Whereas collective memory is by its very nature parochial, he argued, history proves to be universally accessible. Hence, not only descendants of German Jews but others, Jews and non-Jews as well, could view the historical experience of German Jewry as a uniquely instructive guide for Jewish modernity.

Not only the contrast between memory and history provides the rationale for the unique fascination of German Jewish history, narrativity is also enlisted to argue the case. "Contrary to other Jewish communities the history of which would be cultivated only to keep alive the memory of the past, the study of German-Jewish history has the additional motivation [that it holds

---

on Hungarian Jewry appeared in a Hebrew essay in *Hanhagat Yehudei Hungaria be-Mivḥan ha-Shoah* (Jerusalem: 1976), pp. 13–24, translated into English as "The Uniqueness of Hungarian Jewry," *Forum* (1977): 45–53.

9. "The Unique Fascination of German-Jewish History," *Modern Judaism* 9,2 (May 1989): 141–42.

the] possible explanation of the community's doom....In this instance one could apply the phrase 'The Rise and Fall of German Jewry,' which is not so in connection with any of the other communities where the fall is in no way related to the preceding rise." Other national narratives such as of Polish and Hungarian Jewry were cut short by the outside intervention of Nazi Germany. In contrast, German Jewish history has an uninterrupted narrative that possesses autonomy and closure, lending itself to a metahistorical interpretation.[10] The genre into which Katz casts German Jewish history is predictably tragedy. "The tragic figure," writes Katz, "...commits a minor sin, the consequences lead, in an uninterrupted chain of events, to his downfall." What makes for tragedy is "the victims's own unintended participation in their destruction." The tragic flaw of German Jewry was an overzealous pursuit of integration that only aggravated the hostility of the host society. "This tragic feature of their history may be an additional reason for its unique attraction."[11]

In time, Katz came to recast the past of his native Jewish community in a not too dissimilar mode. He found its tragic flaw and the perspective from which the past of Hungarian Jewry could be approached as a history, universally accessible and interesting, transcending the narrow parochialism of its emotive memory. He found the unique fascination of Hungarian Jewry in the history of Hungarian Orthodoxy.

IV.

Ostensibly, nothing could have been more natural than that Jacob Katz should turn his attention to the phenomenon of Orthodoxy. His unique combination of rabbinic training and sociology seems to have almost predestined him for the task. After all, his arrival in Frankfurt coincided with the recent publication of two path-breaking studies in the sociology of knowledge by his future mentor Karl Mannheim: *Ideology and Utopia* and an extensive essay entitled "Conservative Thought." One would have thought that a Jewish version of the latter was naturally called for, but, in fact, intensive engagement in the study of Orthodox Jewry, which today is seen as one of the important fields that Katz pioneered, would have to wait almost another forty years.

---

10. See also "Reflecting on German-Jewish History," in *In and Out of the Ghetto: Jewish-Gentile Relations in Late Medieval and Early Modern Germany*, edited by R. Po-Chia Hsia and Harmut Lehmann (Cambridge: 1995), p. 1.

11. "The Unique Fascination of German-Jewish History," 149–50.

It was only toward the end of the 1960s and the early 1970s, that he began to publish his first articles on the theme—a biography of the Hatam Sofer (to which we will return), a chapter in *Out of the Ghetto*, and a paper on "Religion as a Unifying or Dividing Force in Judaism." In the 1980s, having completed his book on anti-Semitism and a monograph on Richard Wagner, he returned to a number of case studies in the history of halakhah that culminated in the collection *Halakha ve-Qabbala* and *The Shabbes Goy*. It was here that he came to see his unique contribution to the field.

> Of course, other historians have occasionally observed the changes that occurred in halakhic theory and practice under the influence of changing reality, but I do not think that anyone has formulated the fundamental question as a basic guideline for future research. I may be permitted to claim the credit for doing so, and in this way opening a new avenue for critical insights into an important branch of Jewish historical reality.[12]

What is important to note is that Katz's focus before 1984, the year that both *Halakha ve-Qabbala* and *The Shabbes Goy* appeared, was largely confined (the final chapters of the latter work excepted) to the pre-modern period. It was as an octogenarian that Katz turned to the study of Orthodoxy in modern times as a field of its own. Perusing his published lecture notes and readers of his seminars in the late fifties and early sixties, one gets the clear impression that not unlike his colleagues, he, too, was focused on the modernist movements, and even when he touched on religious trends, his primary interest lay with religious reform with only a passing glance at the Orthodox.[13] It seems

---

12. Preface to Jacob Katz, *Divine Law in Human Hands: Case Studies in Halakhic Flexibility* (Jerusalem: Magnes Press, 1998), p. 7

13. This can be seen in a variety of semi-academic publications. The tenth lecture in his 1958 course *Western European Jewry in the Nineteenth Century,* addressed religious change, but made little mention of Orthodoxy. See *Yahadut ma'arav eiropa be-meah ha–19…le-fi hartzaotav shel Prof. Ya'akov Katz* (Jerusalem: 1958). A collection of sources prepared for a seminar entirely devoted to religious change in nineteenth-century Western Europe concentrated overwhelmingly on Reform. Only three of the twenty-two documents treat Orthodoxy, one of which is predictably written by Samson Raphael Hirsch, the one Orthodox figure that even mainstream historians did not fail to mention. *Ba'ayot datiyot be-yahadut ma'arav eiropa be-mea ha–19* (Jerusalem: Department of Sociology, 1961). The other two documents are the Hatam Sofer's response to the Hamburg *bet-din* in *Ele Divrei ha-Brit* and Zvi Hirsch Kalischer's letter to Rothschild. The same emphasis is also apparent in the textbook he prepared for high school: *Yisrael veha-'Amim* (Jerusalem: Tarshish, 1957), part III, Book 2, ch 36: "The Reform Movement and its Opponents."

that only in the sixties did he begin to grow increasingly interested in the problem of Orthodoxy. Over the next two decades, he supervised a number of dissertations that dealt with the response of traditional Jewry to the various challenges of modernity and began to conduct seminars on the theme toward the end of his teaching career.

His turn to the study of Orthodoxy began, more or less, with the publication of his biographical study of R. Moses Sofer, the Hatam Sofer, first published in 1967 in the Gershom Scholem jubilee volume.[14] At first glance, biography seems to be a surprising departure for one who had made his name as a social historian and had insisted on the validity of approaching the past through Weberian ideal-types instead of the particulars of history. Indeed, later he was to remark that when he wrote his biography of the Hatam Sofer "there my sociology did not help me."[15] In divorcing the two disciplines he seems to be echoing unwittingly a passage from Ben-David's concluding section. "In theory, the Talmudic elite could have joined Hasidism, crumbled, or degenerated while preserving what existed. The path it actually chose rested on an ideology propounded by the Hatam Sofer, who had himself elaborated it as a response to his biographical experiences. (The latter are a matter for biographical study and do not enter within the confines of sociological analysis.)"[16]

Protestations to the contrary, Katz had actually ventured into both biography and sociology early in his career, and had found the combination of the two genres mutually enhancing. His first methodological essay, on the precursors of Zionism, was informed by two biographical studies of rabbis Kalischer and Alkalay.[17] Whereas these articles were mainly excursions into intellectual history, his study of the Hatam Sofer was to revel in the minutiae of biographical reconstruction.

---

14. Translated as "Towards a Biography of the Hatam Sofer," in *Divine Law in Human Hands,* pp. 403–43. Of course, we can assume that the article was preceded by years of research.

15. "An Interview with Jacob Katz," *JSS* 1, 2 (Winter, 1995): 70.

16. Ben-David, p. 89.

17. "Le-virur ha-musag 'mevasrei ha-tziyonut'," *Shivat Zion* 2–3 (1949/50): 91–105; "Demuto ha-historit shel ha-rav Zvi Hirsh Kalischer," *Shivat Zion* 2–3 (1951/52): 26–41 and "Meshihiyut ve-leumiyut bemishnato shel ha-rav Alkalay," *Shivat Zion* 4 (1955/56): 9–41. Two other methodological essays appeared those very years: "He'arot sotziologiyot le-sefer histori," *Behinot* 2 (1951/52): 69–73 and his classic statement, "The Concept of Social History and Its Possible Use in Jewish Historical Research," *Scripta Hierosolymitana* 3 (1956), 292–312.

In fact, it is the Weberian notion of charismatic authority that girds the infrastructure of Katz's sensitive portrait of the Hatam Sofer. Katz reconstructs in a most convincing manner the psychological profile of the young Hatam Sofer, delineating both the youth's troubled relations with his parents and his unquestioning, total commitment to his charismatic mentor, Rabbi Nathan Adler. Katz demonstrated that the tradition-bound figure of the Hatam Sofer, who, in his mature years was to coin the famous slogan "*Hehadash asur min ha-Torah*" ("the new is forbidden by the Torah"), had, in fact, belonged during his youth in Frankfurt to a sectarian group clustered around Rabbi Nathan, repeatedly excommunicated by the scandalized community. This was the key to the religious psychology of the Hatam Sofer, a man who felt that he himself had "attained his master's quality of charisma. In blending charisma with several other qualities, however, he not only concealed it, but also used it to develop a much greater sphere of influence than his master had vouchsafed for him."[18] Charisma restrained, a leitmotif made familiar by Ben-David, is the hallmark of the Hatam Sofer. When unbridled, as in the case of Nathan Adler and Hasidism, charisma can be destructive to tradition, but when sublimated and channeled by the Hatam Sofer, it could revitalize traditional society in Hungary.

Katz's essay is not quite a full-blown biography of the Hatam Sofer. It concentrates on his youth, marriage, and early career, but stops in mid-life, just after he arrives at Pressburg and begins to formulate his conservative ideology. Katz reconstructs the outlines of his thought by delving primarily into the Hatam Sofer's sermons; very little analysis is devoted to the Hatam Sofer's responsa and halakhic method. This lacuna, so striking in light of his later emphases, is explained by Katz himself: that very year his student Moshe Samet had completed his dissertation, *Halakha ve-Reforma*, which traced the encounter of halakhah with early modernity from the time of Ezekiel Landau to the conflict of the Hatam Sofer with Reform; consequently Katz felt exempt from pursuing the subject. He did however take it up later in a series of case studies on halakhic flexibility, in which, of course, the Hatam Sofer continued to play a central role.[19]

If Katz's essay begins with the problem of charisma, it also concludes the way Max Weber predicts charisma usually comes to an end—it becomes routinized. The concluding section is devoted to a detailed reconstruction of

---

18. "Contributions," p. 247.

19. See "An Unclarified Episode in the Life of the Hatam Sofer: The Alexandersohn Affair," *Zion* 55 (1990): 93–126, translated into English along with the other studies in *Divine Law in Human Hands*.

the last days of the Hatam Sofer and the succession of his son to the charismatic father's office. But in a sense, this routinization is also manifested in the transformation of the entire Hungarian rabbinate. For not only does the Hatam Sofer leave behind an intellectual legacy of conservativism, his very charisma becomes institutionalized in a newly revitalized and militant rabbinate.

V.

By the time Katz turned seriously to the study of Orthodoxy in the 1980s, the case study had become his favored medium. These were, for the most part, of article length, though rather long articles at that, a unit that most clearly suited an octogenarian who always set out to complete what he began and had a realistic notion of his time horizon. This mode also had a clear methodological advantage, for by narrowing his focus to one problem at a time rather than a broad history of Orthodoxy, he was able to trace changes that were subtle and nuanced, often not apparent to both the adherents of Orthodoxy and its opponents. He had done a certain type of *Begriffsgeschichte* in the past, whether tracing apologetic phrases in the Middle Ages or the terms emancipation and the state within a state in the modern era. And his students Moshe Samet and Hayim Soloveitchik had demonstrated in their dissertations just how fruitful the case study genre was when applied to the history of the halakhah.

If Katz had begun his *Shabbes Goy* as an exercise in the history of halakhah from the time of the Sages through the Middle Ages up until modern times, with the completion of the book, he began to devote himself entirely to case studies of issues set in modern times and related to the rise of religious reform. Here, too, Katz drew a nuanced picture of generations and regional variations. Here, too, Hungarian Orthodoxy adopted a clearly defined posture that often set it apart, one based upon the stringent methods and means formulated by the Hatam Sofer, but often fully realized only in subsequent generations.

One should not assume that Hungarian authorities were monolithic; in fact, there were discernible differences between moderates and zealots. Nevertheless, Katz drew an instructive contrast between Galicia, where tradition was not yet unduly threatened and the halakhic process could proceed in a more or less organic fashion, and Hungary, where tradition emerged tempered in the crucible of the *Kulturkampf* and the formal halakhic process was often subordinated to broader ideological considerations.

Interestingly, it is in a work devoted to a case study in halakhic flexibility that Katz shows himself sensitive to what we can only call "national" variations—that very heterogeneity that Katz was repeatedly criticized for having ignored in his *Tradition and Crisis* and *Out of the Ghetto*. The very chapter headings of the work bespeak variety: of Poland, Russia, Germany, and Hungary. Katz's work on halakhah and Orthodoxy suggests how we can begin to explore the emergence of readily identifiable and clearly differentiated national styles even among the most traditional segments. This process was most rapid and quickly produced national enclaves with local rabbinic literature developing for the most part in splendid isolation from each other.

But in time he began to chaff with the restrictions the case study format imposed upon his writing. As he drew close to his ninetieth year, he expressed more than once his desire to write an old fashioned narrative, fast-paced and exciting. He realized that a change in form also implied a change in method. So when asked in 1994 whether he still viewed himself as social historian, there came a surprising answer:

> As far as my work touches upon certain themes, then I certainly left the fold of social history. My forthcoming book, on the divisions between Orthodoxy and [Reform in Hungary and Germany] is a case study and certainly a social history…I think, though, that these religious divisions cannot be explained in terms of social context, but rather as a political event, especially in Hungary…In taking up the subject of the schism, then, I certainly have left the realm of social history.[20]

Ha-Qera she-lo Nitaḥa, recently translated as *A House Divided*[21] is just such a fast-paced narrative, interlaced, of course, with the sharp analytical insights that one has come to expect from Jacob Katz. Going over some old, but mainly new ground, he turned to chronicle the secession of the Orthodox in Germany and Hungary.

VI.

"An almost personal connection exists between the topic of this book and someone like myself" begins the introduction to *A House Divided*. Indeed, as he informs us, his biography linked him to the two architects of schism in Hungary and Germany: on his mother's side he was related to the Maharam Schick, one of the great luminaries of the Hungarian rabbinate, whereas as a young man he spent many years in Frankfurt in the household of the champion of secession in Germany, Rabbi Samson Raphael Hirsch.

The theme of the book seems tailor-made for Katz, an opportunity to bring together the two Jewries that played such an important role in his life.

---

20. "An Interview with Jacob Katz," p. 73.

21. Jacob Katz, *A House Divided: Orthodoxy and Schism in Nineteenth-Century Central European Jewry,* translated by Ziporah Brody (Hanover and London: Brandeis University Press, 1998).

Of course, the history of the schism could have been written in the context of separate Hungarian and German histories. Previous histories did just that. Yet in *A House Divided* Katz eschews the hermetically sealed national narratives of the schism and instead opts to weave German and Hungarian history into one narrative. As far as Hungarian Jewish history is concerned, this is perhaps less surprising because the German-Jewish model of modernization was an unavoidable paradigm that could be shunned or imitated, but certainly not ignored. Indeed, it would be difficult to write almost any episode of Hungarian Jewish history in the age of emancipation without reference to developments in Germany. On the other hand, as a glance through the index of any major work on German Jewry quickly reveals, the converse is not true. Even Katz who had distinguished himself earlier as one of a few historians who made reference to Hungary in his analyses of what he called "central European Jewry," invariably assigned Hungarian Jewry a role that was largely marginal to the main narrative, dictated primarily by German developments. One of the novelties of *A House Divided* is that, for once, it reverses the traditional roles of these two Jewries (if only for a brief period in the 1860s and 1870s), to offer a fresh vista on German Jewish history from the vantage point of Hungary. In fact, it is Hungarian Jewry that provides the narrative backbone of the book with introductory and concluding chapters on Germany serving modestly to bracket the main story line.[22]

I cannot explore this wonderfully nuanced work in such short time. Suffice it to say that the historical reconstruction is exemplary and in many ways groundbreaking. Even more impressive are the carefully weighted, judicious characterizations of the protagonists and their actions. This, in particular, is the enduring facet of Katz's contribution that I doubt will be superseded. The superb sensitivity to nuances and distinctions, a near perfect pitch if you will, is something that at least one historian of Hungarian Jewry readily concedes is beyond his grasp.

I say "near perfect," for no laudatory critique will convince an audience without some criticism, so here are some of my brief comments.

One can begin by noting that this is a one-sided story in the sense that the reform opposition, the Neologs, rarely make their appearance on the stage and the focus is almost exclusively on the Orthodox as the subtitle of the book clearly states. Elsewhere Katz had often remarked that the historian is sover-

---

22. Recognizing this, the original title of the work in Hebrew reserved pride of place for Hungary: *Ha-Qera she-lo Nitaḥa: Prishat ha-Orthodoxim mi-khlal ha-qehilot be-Hungaria uve-Germania* (Jerusalem: Merkaz Zalman Shazar, 1995). The subtitle of the English translation, however, subsumes Hungary under the comprehensive "Central Europe."

eign to define his field of inquiry; clearly here he did not feel compelled to
provide an analysis of both sides. How distant this is from the systemic total-
izing approach of *Tradition of Crisis* that sought to accommodate all sides to
the transformation between two book covers![23]

Of the parties to the clash, Katz sees the Orthodox as clearly the more interesting, and even more important, the more dynamic. It is not only their ideology that draws his attention, but rather their actions or what he terms their
politics. Here then is a "political history" that precedes conventional periodization or understanding of Jewish politics; a site that is not the conventional one of Eastern Europe and protagonists that are not the conventional
allies of modernity.

There is yet another departure from convention, a surprising one especially to those who are acquainted with the history of the schism. For conven-
tionally, the leading Orthodox roles of the drama in Hungary are assigned to
the neo-Orthodox Rabbi Esriel Hildesheimer and the zealot ultra-Orthodox, R. Hillel Lichtenstein, R. Ḥaim Sofer, and Akiva Yosef Schlesinger.[24]
It is startling to see how Katz has reshuffled the heroes of the Hungarian
conflict and cast R. Samson Raphael Hirsch and R. Moses Schick, the
Maharam Schick, as the leading men.[25] At times, the evidence that he adduces
to this effect is pretty thin. Especially puzzling is his certitude that no one but
Schick or Hirsch was capable of formulating what proved to be decisive

---

23. See Jacob Katz, "On Jewish Social History: Epochal and Supra-Epochal
    Historiography," *Jewish History* 7 (1993): 89–97, and especially 91.

24. Previous studies included Nathaniel Katzburg, "The Jewish Congress of Hun-
    gary 1868–1869," in: *Hungarian Jewish Studies*, vol. 2, ed. R. L. Braham (New
    York: 1969) and *idem*, "The Rabbinical Decision of Michalowce in 1865"
    [Hebrew] in *Studies in the History of Jewish Society in the Middle Ages and in the
    Modern Period Presented to Professor Jacob Katz on his Seventy-Fifth Birthday by his
    Students and Friends,* edited by Emanuel Etkes and Yosef Salmon (Jerusalem:
    1980), pp. 273–86; Mordekhai Eliav, "Rabbi Esriel Hildesheimer and his
    Influence on Hungarian Jewry" [Hebrew], *Zion* 27 (1962): 59–86; *idem*, "*Torah
    im Derekh Erez* in Hungary" [Hebrew], *Sinai* 51 (1962): 127–42; and *idem*, ed.,
    Rabbiner Esriel Hildesheimer Briefe (Jerusalem: 1965); David Ellenson, *Rabbi
    Esriel Hildesheimer and the Creation of a Modern Jewish Orthodoxy* (Tuscaloosa,
    Ala.: 1990); and Michael K. Silber, "The Emergence of Ultra-Orthodoxy: The
    Invention of a Tradition," in *The Uses of Tradition: Jewish Continuity since Eman-
    cipation,* ed., Jack Wertheimer (New York-Jerusalem: JTS distributed by Har-
    vard University Press, 1992), pp. 23–84.

25. Although it is true that Y. Y. Grünwald did cast Schick in such a role. See his
    *Le-Toldot ha-Reformatzion ha-datit be-Germania uve-Ungaria: Ha-Maharam Schick
    u-zmano* (reprinted; Jerusalem: 1972).

strategic moves. Unfortunately, the surviving paper trail, especially of private correspondence, is so thin, that even the publication of one new document can change the accepted picture of the past. Consequently, I was struck, and I must say impressed, by Katz's bold assurance. At other times my instinct told me that a sneaking identification with his distinguished great-great-uncle, the Maharam Schick—both were men who bloomed late in life and were marginal to the centers of power until they were catapulted into the limelight in their sixties—perhaps tended to skew his judgment somewhat.

VII.

What "lessons" did Katz think could be found in his work? How did his own *Weltanschauung* as a religious Jew affect his work? In a recent interview he remarked:

> Renan said that the study of religion can only be undertaken by one who was once religious and then left the fold. It is true that a certain distance is necessary to study religion. But I would add that those who abandon religion altogether to the point where they are totally alienated from it, they too are incapable of studying it.[26]

Katz took religion and the study of religion seriously. He contrasted his own position with that of Ben-Zion Dinur. Although Dinur came from a religious background,

> once he left the fold...he devoted little scholarly attention to religion, with the exception of Hasidism. But even Hasidism was examined by him and many others not because of its intrinsic religious relevance, but rather as a social force, a way out of tradition. Their commitment to the new trends in Jewish life shaped their scholarly directions. Well this is one possible perspective on Jewish history. My own contribution was that I maintained that Orthodoxy too is something new, and that variations within the continuing tradition are worthwhile looking into, no less than what led out of tradition entirely. Perhaps my own religious perspective is responsible for this approach.[27]

On more than one occasion, Katz went on to protest that there were no unambiguous lessons to be drawn from his work.

> What conclusion concerning the continuing relevance of halakhah can be drawn from the historical analysis? It is beyond the capacity or

---

26. Interview held in the fall of 1997, broadcast 11 June, 1998 in the Open University series on Jewish Studies conducted by Moshe Halberthal.

27. "An Interview with Jacob Katz," pp. 72–73.

authority of the historian to answer this question. Historical inquiry can lead to contradictory conclusions. For some people, the observable changes in halakhah during the course of history will support the negation of its eternal validity. For others, its adaptability to changing conditions will guarantee its continued preservation.[28]

With the rise of an increasingly militant Orthodoxy, Katz could not resist enlisting his academic work to combat some of the unhappy developments in Israel and America. He exposed the limits of halakhah to provide adequate guidelines for a *medinat halakhah*, something he termed as an empty slogan, but one with increasing power to undermine the very foundations of the state. In his article on *Da'at Torah*, he tried to show how this unprecedented, unqualified authority claimed for halakhists was a recent phenomenon and grew out of a concrete historical situation. "Though a historian should never try to prophesy, this does not prevent him or her from hoping that what has emerged in the course of history may also vanish in the course of time."[29]

How did he assess the schism? And what lessons if any could be learned from the chronicle of Hungarian Jewry that he had so deftly sketched? Here I think we should distinguish between the actual history of the schism and what he termed in the introduction to the book as its sad consequences. The traditional Orthodox narrative had celebrated the schism as the triumph of an embattled minority against overwhelming odds. That it was achieved unexpectedly at the very last minute made for a tense plot; that a key event coincided with Purim, provided sure evidence of providential intervention. The moderate Orthodox historian Yekutiel Yehuda Grünwald concluded his account of the schism in just such a celebratory vein. The last sixty years, he wrote in 1929, only confirmed the wisdom of Hungarian Orthodoxy in splitting off from the Neologs. Had they been forced to stay in a unified framework, "not one Orthodox *minyan* would be found within the boundaries of Hungary today." Instead, Hungarian Orthodoxy maintained its integrity and enjoyed an unprecedented efflorescence, whereas the Neologs, cut off from the nourishing springs of a traditional source, withered away.[30]

Katz, it seems to me, evinces more than a measure of sympathy for this view. He cannot but silently cheer the Orthodox underdogs as they outmaneuver the smug patronizing Neolog bullies. The very mode he employs to tell the story, a political history, makes sense only if Orthodox actions are

---

28. Preface to *Divine Law in Human Hands,* p. 8.

29. "*Da'at Torah*—The Unqualified Authority Claimed for Halakhists," *Jewish History* 11 (1997): 49.

30. *Li-flagot Yisrael be-Ungaria* (Devo, Romania: 1929), p. 82.

deemed worthy of serious consideration, rather than dismissed as *shtibel* politics. Katz can appreciate the Orthodox triumph. He points an accusing finger at the condescending Neologs, who, by their intolerance, played no small part in painting the Orthodox into a corner where the only viable strategic option that remained was secession.

Unfortunately, Hungarian Jewry bequeathed a legacy of divisiveness that well outlasted the place and time of its inception. "Even the two major trials that the Jewish nation has since undergone then, the horrors of the Holocaust and the experience of the establishment of the State of Israel, ostensibly watershed events, were not sufficient grounds for second thoughts. The breach that was created with the secession of the Orthodox did not heal; it has likely even widened and deepened in Orthodox ideology of all types."[31]

At the conclusion of his work, he addresses the advocates of "isolationist concepts among the Orthodox of our day," asking whether they are cognizant of the singular historical constellation that "served as the background to their deeds and decisions"? The secession was conditioned by specific circumstances and what was understandable and perhaps even justified in the specific context of Hungary and Germany in the immediate post-emancipatory years, became years later "anachronistic."[32]

Just how many years later, Katz informs us in a "think piece" on the Jewish community in the age of emancipation that appeared posthumously.[33] At the conclusion of the essay, Katz ventures "a hypothetical question which has often intrigued me" and although "fully aware that such questions are unanswerable and they should perhaps be anathema to the historian...," nevertheless he does not think that "pondering such questions is an entirely futile exercise."

The question relates to the timing of the secession in both Hungary and Germany and whether it was in fact unavoidable. The schism came about in the years immediately after emancipation was achieved in both countries. It was a time when Jewish integration seemed assured a smooth course and threats to the community from without seemed to be at their nadir. When menaced in the past, the community had shored up its walls and closed ranks;

---

31. *A House Divided*, p. 278.

32. The phrase appears in "The Uniqueness of Hungarian Jewry," p. 52.

33. "Ideological Differences Over the Status of the Kehilla: The Jewish Community in the Age of Emancipation," in *Perspectives on Jewish Thought and Mysticism ...dedicated to...Alexander Altmann*, edited by Alfred L. Ivry, Elliot R. Wolfson and Allan Arkush (Australia, etc.: Harwood, 1999). The paper was first delivered in a conference the very year that his book on the schism was published, 1994. It does not appear in the bibliography of his publications.

now the security created by the prevailing liberal temper had undermined the age-old cohesion. This diminished solidarity proved incapable of withstanding the centrifugal forces unleashed by the *Kulturkampf.*

But what if the conflict had been postponed by even a few years, would the schism still have taken place under greatly transformed conditions? Within a decade, modern anti-Semitism created an entirely different climate both without and within the Jewish community. Presumably, anti-Semitism would have so enhanced Jewish cohesiveness that schism would no longer have been contemplated. If we follow this hypothetical reasoning, then the "window of opportunity" of the schism was, in fact, very narrow indeed, for the first signs of anti-Semitism actual appeared just before the Prussian *Landtag* decided in favor of Jewish secession in 1876.

Hence, one could plausibly speculate that the schism could well have been avoided. Understanding the contingent nature of the secession, its genesis at a peculiar, fleeting moment marked by "exceptional openness of Gentiles toward Jews" would be to recognize that the breach was the product of an uncharacteristic lapse in the history of Hungarian and German Jewry and its persistence beyond the vanished era of liberalism, nothing but a tragic anachronism.

"I do not believe that any historical investigation can provide answers to contemporary problems," he had cautioned long ago at the beginning of his career, "but history can help us understand the background to the situation we face today."[34] Assuming the role of the therapist, Katz the historian unveils the etiology of secession in the hesitant hope that knowledge might begin a process of understanding and healing.

Here then is a Hungarian Jewish history with appeal, a subject matter of more than parochial importance, a challenging historical problem that resonates with relevance, a story line that perhaps rivals the German Jewish narrative. The added element of tragedy, no doubt, enhances its attractiveness. The tragic hero adopts extreme measures in an emergency situation that perhaps are the only means available; his flaw lies in the inability to recognize that whatever merit such actions may have had in the past, they become all too soon a bizarre holdover of an irrelevant past.

On an elegiac note, Katz concluded his essay on the uniqueness of Hungarian Jewry with an uncharacteristic, lyric passage:

> In the concentration camps and the extermination transports, individuals and groups who never imagined that they had anything in common came together. This was also true of the victims from other coun-

---

34. See the preface of *Tradition and Crisis*, pp. xiv–xv.

tries, but among the Jews of Hungary this was far more acute. The religious, cultural and social polarization that developed in the course of the formation of modern Hungarian Jewry accompanied it to its destruction. With trembling and humility we can express what they could only dimly feel, that they were united in the fate of a people singular in its suffering and unique in the mystery of its existence.[35]

VIII.

Preparing this paper afforded me yet one more opportunity to glance over Jacob Katz's oeuvre. The experience would be humbling for most, but for one like me, whose work has evolved in close proximity to his, it is also a daunting task, fraught with a healthy "fear of influence." I am struck that hard-won insights that I thought were my own had been anticipated years before, neatly spelled out with that deceptive simplicity that many have come to see as the hallmark of Jacob Katz. I hazard that I share with others this sentiment. His unique presence of discerning insight and wisdom will long continue to be felt our field.

Jacob Katz's book *A House Divided*, is entitled in Hebrew *Ha-qera she-lo nitaha*. The phrase that inspired a rabbinic pun on the rift with the Karaites[36] derives from a famous biblical passage that depicts the parting moment of the prophet Elijah.

> When the Lord was about to take Elijah up to heaven in a whirlwind... Elijah said to Elisha, Tell me, what can I do for you before I am taken from you? Elisha answered, Let a double portion of your spirit pass on to me. You have asked a difficult thing, he said. If you see me as I am being taken from you, this will be granted to you; if not, it will not. As they kept on walking and talking, a fiery chariot with fiery horses suddenly appeared and separated one from the other; and Elijah went up to heaven in a whirlwind.
>
> Elisha saw it, and he cried out, Oh father, father! Israel's chariots and horsemen! When he could no longer see him, he grasped his garments and rent them in two. *Va-yehazeq bivgadav va-yaqriem lishnayim qeraim.* (II Kings 2:1, 9–12)

---

35. "The Uniqueness of Hungarian Jewry," pp. 52–53.

36. *'Im ha-qaraim einan mitahin le-'olam* "with the Karaites, one must never unite [in marriage]." See, for example, Eliezer Judah Waldenberg, *Responsa Ziz Eliezer*, pt. 12, no. 66.

It is from this verse that the Sages learned that one must rend his garments on the death of a teacher who has taught him wisdom.

Over the years many have learned wisdom from our mentor and master, Jacob Katz. May those who aspire to his mantle, to merit a portion of his spirit, rend in mourning the passing of a great scholar and teacher as is proper: *Elu qra'in she-ein mitaḥin, ha-qorea…al rabo she-limdo ḥokhma…ha-qer'a eino mitaḥa le-'olam.*[37]

---

37. Radaq's commentary on II Kings 2.12 after Moed Qatan 26a. The Talmud speaks of *rabo shelimdo Torah*; Radaq, however, has *rabo shelimdo ḥokhma*.

JACOB KATZ ON HALAKHAH, ORTHODOXY, AND HISTORY

Moshe Halbertal
The Hebrew University, Jerusalem

Jacob Katz's research touched upon patterns of continuity and change in central domains of Jewish history. He investigated medieval Jewish society's attitude toward its Christian environment and its transformation when Jews began to integrate into European society from the late eighteenth through the nineteenth centuries. He examined the internal structure of traditional Jewish society in Central and Eastern Europe and its disruption with the rise of Hasidism and the *Haskalah*. And last, but not least, he analyzed the emergence of Orthodoxy as a response to the crisis of traditional society, and the advent of Jewish nationalism in the modern age.

Beyond his major achievements in these areas, Jacob Katz made a unique methodological contribution to social history. He taught us to think not only about events and people, but also about structures and patterns. His writings on these varied subjects exhibit a marvelous and unique sense of language— clear, penetrating, and restrained. His writing neither praises exorbitantly nor condemns ruthlessly. His sentences are careful, considered, and economical. This restraint is manifest in his work even when he discusses complex subjects, such as relations between Jews and non-Jews or the rise of Orthodoxy, subjects that invite the scholar to involve himself, to appraise different positions, and to render a verdict. Katz analyzes these subjects in detail and in a most incisive way, but he abstains from expressing a position and from making value judgments.

Yet, after many years of scholarship, Jacob Katz broke his silence and took a stand. With the dedicated help of Emanuel Etkes, Katz prepared his last book, *'Et Laḥkor ve-'Et Lehitbonen* ("A Time to Study and a Time to Reflect"), which not only crystallizes his position on methodological issues in history, but also reflects his views on Israeli society—its hopes and predicaments. The fact that this time of reflection came in his later years, as his final bequest, means that this book has the quality of a will and testament. It is a fascinating personal verdict, which demands the special attention of his students and readers. My essay, which concentrates on Jacob Katz's last book, is, therefore, not devoted to a detailed analysis of one of the many subjects with which he dealt as an historian. My aim is to explicate his value stance, to address how Katz used historical investigation to shape and support such a stance, and how, in turn, his position may have shaped his direction as an historian. I shall focus on the connection between Katz's great historical and structural analysis of the rise of Orthodoxy and his judgment and assessment of its role in modern-day Israel.

Katz articulated his principled value stance with a two-front polemic: his response to the critique of Zionism as advanced by the "new historians" and his reservations concerning the attitude of the State of Israel toward Orthodox Judaism, in both varieties, the Haredi or ultra-Orthodox and Religious Zionism. Although, on the face of it, these are two entirely different issues, a unifying concept lies behind Katz's response. He makes a methodical defense of classical Zionism based on a clear-headed view of national sovereignty—the sovereign government, in Weber's definition, has a monopoly on the legitimate use of force, and a sovereign power is judged on the basis of whether it uses too much or too little coercion.[1]

In contrast to the critical attitude of the "new historians," Katz identifies entirely with the decisions made by the Yishuv leadership during the Holocaust. Since Ben-Gurion understood that the Yishuv was powerless to do anything to change the fate of European Jewry, he refrained from investing resources in that direction. An investment of resources in a lost cause, when those same resources were critical for the future struggle for national independence, was for Ben-Gurion a luxury that the Yishuv could not afford. Ben-Gurion rejected his critics' contention that such an investment would fulfill a sentimental moral obligation. Ben-Gurion acted as a statesman, and his greatness lay in not allowing his emotional instincts to determine his political decisions.[2]

Katz makes a similar argument about the creation of the Palestinian refugee problem. When the War of Independence began, Ben-Gurion believed that the Yishuv would not be able to survive without a Jewish majority and a broad territory. His critics err in assuming that the outcome of the struggle was clear from the start. Yet this was not how it looked to those who held

---

1. "A state whether Jewish or not Jewish can't give up the use of force…. It will sin in diverting from the right course in both directions: either in using force when it was not necessary, or in avoiding using force when it was necessary." J. Katz, 'Et Laḥkor ve-'Et le-Hitobonen (Jerusalem: 1998), p. 134.

2. See ibid., pp. 124–28.

the political and existential fate of the Yishuv in their hands. In a state of existential danger a state can permit itself exceptional, painful measures.[3] In both these matters Ben-Gurion acted as a pragmatic politician and used force justifiably. In Katz's opinion, the "new historians" display a great deal of the wisdom of hindsight and very little political sense.

According to Katz, Israel failed the test of sovereignty on the other front, the religious public. Orthodox Judaism produced two ideologies with opposite attitudes toward the state. One, the Religious Zionist movement, viewed the state as part of a messianic process. It, therefore, attempted to impose upon the state political positions that accorded with its messianic theology.

The second movement, the Haredim, was non-Zionist. It viewed the state as a continuation of the Exile. Its attitude was, thus, one of passivity, non-involvement, and opposition, even as it became more and more financially dependent upon the state for its existence and growth. According to Katz, the state failed by not asserting its sovereignty against Religious Zionism and the Haredim. The government of Prime Minister Levi Eshkol should have prevented national-religious Jews from establishing wildcat settlements in the territories. It made no difference whether the government favored or opposed establishing Israeli settlements in the West Bank and the Gaza Strip. In either case, the decision should have been made only by the state. By abstaining from exerting its authority, the state displayed weakness and opened the door to attempts by messianic groups to control the state's policy and character.[4]

So too, the state failed as a sovereign power in its attitude to Haredi society. A national state does not fund the educational system of communities that oppose its very existence and that evade bearing the common burden shared by all other citizens. On this, Katz is adamant:

> There is nothing like this in any properly-run country. When the state imposes mandatory general education it also supervises that education to ensure that it is compatible with its needs, which are the society's needs. Only the State of Israel allows itself the luxury of bringing up under its own sponsorship—and to a large extent at its own expense— a generation that is directed a priori to not recognizing it and to not shouldering the obligations imposed on the rest of its citizens. This phenomenon indeed corrodes the rule of the state in the name of reli-

---

3. See *ibid.*, pp. 131ff.

4. "To the fault of the government, which didn't fulfill its role and didn't not annul the deed (the settlements) that was done against its order had far reaching implications. The state gave away its sovereignty in regards to its citizens in a sensitive domain of its foreign relationship" (*ibid.*, p. 137).

gious ideology, with the tacit, and even more than tacit, consent of the state.[5]

Katz's assessment of the State of Israel's treatment of entirely different groups reveals him to be an *étatist*. He judges a state by how it exercises its prerogative and sovereignty. Zionism's mission is to establish a sovereign entity that will improve the political position of the Jewish people. Ahad Ha'am's belief that Zionism's principal role was to create a cultural center for the Jewish people is foreign to him. A political framework does not produce a cultural renaissance; it is meant to fulfill its role as sovereign faithfully and consistently. This is the test of its achievements and failures. There is great force in Katz's historical temperament and in his defense of pragmatic state Zionism. History, according to Katz, is not a dramatic arena that swings its subjects from the depths of despair to the heights of redemption. Jacob Katz was a historian with no predilection whatsoever for romantic and metaphysical concepts of history as the manifestation of a great transcendent spirit.

I do not want, in this limited framework, to address the various facets of Katz's accounting with and reflection on Israeli society. I am interested in focusing on that dimension that touches on his previous historical scholarship. Neither the Yishuv's attitude on the Holocaust nor the history of the Jewish-Palestinian struggle were ever subjects of his scholarship. He responded to them as one who participated in these events and as an experienced historian. However, his response to Orthodoxy's attitudes toward the state is anchored deeply in his previous work. I am interested in examining the relationship between Katz's historical studies on the history of Orthodox religious law and his acerbic and critical reaction to the rabbinical leadership's attitude toward the State of Israel. After examining this link I shall relate my findings to the great methodological questions that Katz posed in the first chapter of his book on the study of history. First, however, I must present Katz's position on the history of the halakhah and the growth of Orthodoxy.

Jacob Katz dealt with the history of the halakhah largely during periods of change and crisis. Beyond his contribution to clarifying specific issues in the history of the halakhah, he made a huge contribution to understanding basic patterns of the crystallization of the halakhah and the creation of structures of halakhic authority. His work on how the halakhah reacts to periods of change and transformation reveals a fixed pattern. The community, facing a change in its circumstances, creates norms that are based not necessarily on halakhic sources but on what Katz calls "the community's ritual instinct." The community creates such norms organically, without negotiation with a

---

5. *Ibid.*, p. 177.

rabbinical authority, and, sometimes, on the basis of advice received from educated dilettantes who have not attained the status required to rule authoritatively on legal questions. After the norms have become rooted, halakhic authorities examine them in light of legal sources. Sometimes they consent to the norms *ex post facto*; sometimes they reject them; and sometimes they reinterpret the halakhic sources to make them fit the norms that have been created. Katz noted this pattern in his analysis of a number of historical situations.

In his book *Exclusiveness and Tolerance*, Katz casts light on the evolution of the halakhah, exemplified in the following two historical situations. At the beginning of Jewish settlement in Ashkenaz, small Jewish communities created norms of their own to govern commercial relations with Christians. These norms accorded with the economic and political pressures faced by the communities and with their understanding of what was fitting or forbidden in contacts with Christians. In many cases these norms were not consistent with the halakhah as formulated in authoritative sources. The final crystallization of Ashkenazi halakhah on these matters was a product of attempts made by halakhic authorities to bridge the gap between the norms created organically by these communities and the norms dictated by the Talmud. Katz investigated in depth a similar halakhic process, that of the "Shabbes goy," the non-Jew hired to perform acts forbidden to Jews on the Sabbath. When Jewish economic activity expanded into new realms, such as renting estates and running factories, a complex web of norms emerged that were shaped without direct consultation with halakhic authorities. In some cases the community's ritual instinct led it in stricter, rather than more lenient, directions.

Katz's analysis of the crystallization of the halakhah in situations of change demonstrates that the halakhah is not solely the product of encounters among legal authorities, circumstances, and the halakhah's authoritative texts. In situations of change and transformation the halakhah is often a product of a normative response that comes from below. Halakhic authorities establish their position, then, through confrontation with that response.

Katz made another profound contribution to the history of the halakhah by analyzing the response of traditional society to situations of crisis. Situations of crisis differ from situations of change in that the framework conditions and rules are modified. The regular operation of casuistic halakhic thinking, which ostensibly proceeds step by step, from precedent to resolution of the problem at hand, does not function in a state of crisis. In times of crisis, the fixed background conditions that allow the movement from precedent to current problem do not exist. It was in this context of traditional society's response to crisis that Katz analyzed the rise of Orthodoxy.

By the end of the eighteenth century, with the rise of the centralized state, Jewish communities had lost their autonomy and their coercive power. Loyalty to the halakhah by members of the community could no longer be taken for granted. Orthodoxy appeared as a response to this crisis. One of its constitutive characteristics was the expansion of the purview of halakhic authorities to all areas of policy and life. Katz noted the paradoxical phenomenon that, as the community's commitment to the halakhah shrank, the power of the halakhic authority over those who remained in the framework expanded. The challenge to tradition created a more profound dependence by the community's members on the rabbi, who, in this period, became Judaism's central mediator. Moreover, since the power of the halakhic authority became restricted to those who had survived the crisis, the rabbi no longer had to compromise with other powers functioning alongside him.[6]

Beyond the expansion of the power of the halakhic authority, Orthodoxy is characterized by a "prohibition upgrade." The legal distinctions between custom and law, between non-mandatory strictness and the norm, disappear, and every attempt at change is interpreted as a challenge to an equally important norm. Katz took note of this, for example, in his discussion of the debate over the location of the *bima* in the synagogue, and over the second day of holiday added outside the Land of Israel. Katz showed that the authority structure of Orthodox society differed from traditional medieval society. In traditional society the rabbi recognized the broad authority of the public and community leadership. The medieval rabbis dealt largely with manifestly halakhic issues and supported their positions by adhering closely to halakhic categories. In contrast, the Orthodox concept of *da'at Torah* granted Orthodox halakhic authorities broad, ranging powers, without requiring that they be grounded within the familiar lines of Jewish law. Orthodoxy, like its rivals, is a non-traditional modern phenomenon. It is a product of the response of halakhic authorities to a crisis in which they lost the guaranteed allegiance of members of the community to the halakhah, as well as their means of coercing obedience.[7]

The crisis created by modernity, which gave rise to Orthodoxy, was followed by a subsequent crisis to tradition—the establishment of a sovereign Jewish state. The State of Israel faces tradition with a crisis no less profound, because it, too, radically changes the rules. The Zionist revolution presented traditional Judaism with a twofold dilemma. The Zionist movement established a Jewish state that was neither exile nor redemption. This state, which

---

6. See J. Katz, *Ha-Halakhah ba-Meitzar* (Jerusalem: 1992), pp. 18–20.

7. See *ibid.*, pp. 11–20.

was supposed to come into being through methodical human effort, broke the fundamental historical picture of Judaism, which saw the Jewish people moving between the two poles of exile and redemption with no intermediate ground. An additional and much more serious problem was that Zionism offered a national, secular alternative to Jewish identity, which had previously been defined, for devout Jews, in terms of faithfulness to the Torah and its commandments. The appearance of a Jewish collective that did not identify itself in halakhic terms yet was interested in preserving a basic particular Jewish identity was an utter innovation to halakhic authorities. They had been accustomed to ranging themselves against the assimilationists and adaptationists, who had become a powerful force in Europe in the nineteenth century. The accepted categories of *mumar*, *meshumad*, and *min*, which denote a Jew who has converted to another religion or changed his national identification, were useless for coping with members of a new nationalist movement that had thrown off the yoke of the commandments. Furthermore— and this is of central importance—a sovereign Jewish state faces the halakhic authorities in a situation opposite to that of the crisis of the nineteenth century. At the beginning of the nineteenth century the community's means of coercion were taken from it. Now it was being given, via the centralized Jewish state, coercive powers far beyond what the autonomous medieval Jewish community had ever exercised. The fact that the community faced the crisis of Zionism after it had organized its authority structure in reaction to modernity is of great importance. Katz points to the contemporary halakhic authorities' refusal to recognize the legitimacy of the state's secular legislative and judicial institutions.

Katz's great contribution to our understanding of the relations between religion and the State of Israel is contained in the following argument. Traditional medieval halakhic authorities did not hesitate to grant legitimacy to institutions of authority that were not based in the halakhah. For example, they understood that the procedures and rules of evidence that the halakhah requires, such as two witnesses and advance admonition against committing the offense, turn the halakhah into an utterly ineffective system for maintaining social order. Rashba, Ran, and other authorities recognized, alongside the halakhah, a framework of legislation, adjudication, and punishment that operates according to its own rules of evidence. Therefore, according to Katz, when an important modern halakhic authority declared, in effect, that the halakhah does not permit evidence provided by a suspect who has been promised immunity or a lighter sentence, he was saying something that would have seemed absurd to those traditional medieval authorities who accepted the community's judicial powers. Traditional halakhic authorities recognized that without extra-halakhic rules of evidence no person could ever be convicted. When Rashba authorized community leaders to sit in judgment on cases of injury as they see fit, he stated, "monetary fine or physical punishment, since if all must be done according to the laws stated in the Torah the world will be destroyed." According to Katz, from the point of view of traditional halakhah, a halakhic state is an empty slogan, and the current involvement of halakhic authorities in matters of politics is an unprecedented extension of the halakhists' traditional authority.[8]

Halakhic authorities find it difficult to defer to the state and its institutions precisely because they arrived at this crisis subsequent to the creation of Orthodoxy, which itself emerged from the crisis faced by traditional society. The Orthodox authority structure that took form in the nineteenth century, which granted exclusive and all-encompassing power to the halakhic scholar, paralyzes tradition when it confronts the secular state. The fact that there is no contemporary halakhic authority of the highest echelon who grants legitimacy to the secular judicial system shows to what extent religious society is trapped by the paradigm of the Orthodox power structure. Had the state been founded in the context of traditional society, there would have been much less tension between religion and state than there is in the confrontation between Orthodoxy and the state. Although Katz might be sympathetic to the rise of Orthodoxy as a successful strategy for confronting assimilation in Central Europe, he is hostile to its presence under the new conditions of a sovereign Jewish state. In the nineteenth century the all-encompassing claim for rabbinic authority lacked any access to state power. Israel has given rabbinic authority potential state power. In this way, Katz expresses his anxiety concerning the application of the Orthodox authority structure in this new situation:

> It is a direct danger to the religious community and indirectly to the whole state. There is a reason to be concerned that the community who sees itself as loyal to halakhah will lose its freedom of thought and judgment in political and national issues which it is asked to adjudicate in a democratic process.[9]

Note that the question of the legitimacy of the non-halakhic governing and legislative systems, and the idea of the halakhic state that Katz confronts in his book, have become much more central than they have ever been. The reason lies in processes that have accelerated since his book was written. Ḥaredi society is undergoing profound processes of integration into the state. Its economic dependence on the state's resources is an influence in this direc-

---

8. See ʿEt Laḥkor ve-ʿEt le-Hitbonen, pp. 169–78.

9. Ibid., p. 178.

tion. Furthermore, it is especially hard for Ḥaredi society to internalize, over a long period of time, a consciousness of exile within a sovereign Jewish state. The Ḥaredi public, perhaps to the chagrin of its leadership, sees Israel as its home, and identifies with the most nationalist elements of the Zionist movement. Jewish nationalism is, after all, very tempting. So long as the Ḥaredi public saw the state as a foreign power, it had no interest in affecting the state's institutions of government and justice. Did the Ḥaredi Agudat Yisrael party ever try to make Poland over into a halakhic state? Now that there is identification with and involvement in the state, the judicial system has taken the state's place as the ideological enemy. The question of a Jewish state did not concern the Ḥaredi leadership because it opposed the very idea of a state. With the decline of opposition to and apathy toward the state, legislative and judicial questions have become the focal point of the confrontation. Zionism may, thus, find itself the victim of its own success.

An opposite process, but one with similar implications, is taking place in the Religious Zionist camp. As long as this public and its leadership saw the state as "the inception of redemption," the focus of the state's religious significance was the political/diplomatic arena, which created the messianic drama. Contemporary judicial and legal arrangements were seen as temporary matters that would pass with the progress of the dialectic messianic process. In recent years the internal energy of the messianic conception has eroded. Secular Zionism is not playing the dialectic role assigned to it in Rabbi Kook's scheme, and the messianic structure has lost much of its force. For both the Ḥaredim and the Religious Zionists, the State of Israel is coming to be perceived as a homeland of neither exile nor redemption. As a result, the dividing lines within this public are changing and new coalitions are being formed. The distinction between Zionist and non-Zionist Orthodoxy is a thing of the past. There will be a different fault line in the religious public; it will not separate Zionist from non-Zionist. Instead, on one side will be those observant Jews who accept the legitimacy of the country's secular institutions of government. On the other side will be those, among them the Religious Zionist rabbinical leadership, who grant broad, absolute powers to halakhic authorities.

With his sharp observation of Israeli society, Jacob Katz became one of the great defenders of statism (*mamlakhtiyut*) versus the "new historians" and one of the most forceful critics of Orthodox policy in Israel. As an active participant in the Zionist experience and an historian, Katz was a concerned observer of the process by which the state was falling apart and no longer constituted a general sovereign framework. This dissolution derived, among other things, from the failure of the Orthodox leadership to respond to the new conditions presented by Zionism. As Katz states:

It could be said that two new Jewish religious streams were established within the State of Israel. One demands authority over the political leadership, whether because of its messianic beliefs or because of its understanding of certain sections of the halakha. This is an activist stream, manifestly different from the passive attitude of the traditional Judaism of the Exile, which avoided any planning of the future, placing its fate in the hands of heaven. The second stream went a similar but opposite distance. It flees accepting any responsibility for planning the future, even after becoming part of the state, whose glory lies in that its citizens themselves decide the questions that determine its fate. The members of both streams weigh down on the country's life. Far be it from me to tempt fate and state what this burden can lead to if the situation is not mended.

In his previous scholarly work on Orthodoxy, Jacob Katz always refrained from taking a position. In this book, however, he reveals himself to be a sharp critic of the Orthodox authority structure, of the concept of a halakhic state, and of the idea of *da'at Torah*. On this issue, unlike his response to the "new historians," Katz's criticism is based squarely on the conclusions he reached as an historian. Katz uses the discontinuity between traditional and Orthodox society that he pointed out in his scholarly work to attack the Orthodox rabbinical leadership's demand for excessive powers. Since the foundation of Orthodox authority is tradition, the claim that Orthodoxy itself is an innovation has far-reaching ideological implications. Katz argues that the Orthodox claim is based upon a mythologized conception of the past and, when the facts are presented, the claim no longer is valid. Katz's critique of Orthodoxy echoes earlier scholarly use of historical investigation to lay the foundation for a demand for change. But Katz, unlike Geiger, is not interested in reforming ritual; nor does he argue that ancient prayer practices can be unearthed to serve as legitimization for challenging existing practices. But he makes the same move with regard to the Orthodox authority structure. In the book before us, written toward the end of his life, Jacob Katz made his views on central issues known. He also has made it possible for us to see one of the aspects that motivated his studies on the consolidation of Orthodoxy. It will be interesting to investigate whether Katz's sophisticated polemical use of his scholarly achievements fits with his positivist methodological approach outlined in the first part of the book. This issue must await another essay.

Jacob Katz as a Dissertation Advisor

Immanuel Etkes

The Hebrew University, Jerusalem

I think we all agree that directing doctoral students is the highest level of academic instruction. Nevertheless, as far as I know, there is no set of regulations or code to define the task and duties of the advisor. Although universities show considerable activism in creating regulations and instructions regarding the duties of research students, they do not publicize precisely what they expect from the teachers guiding research students. Moreover, whereas many aspects of a professor's work are exposed to the public eye and subject to criticism, the advising of doctoral students takes place in the intimate setting of teacher and student.

Questions arise about the task of the advisor: What considerations should guide a professor in deciding to take on a certain student? Should the advisor suggest that the student write about a subject close to his or her own field of research, or is it better to draw clear boundaries between one's own research and that of one's students? How should guidance be expressed in the course of the writing? How much should the advisor influence the conclusions of the research? There are no obvious answers to questions like these.

As is only natural, since there is no clear doctrine regarding the task of the advisor, every advisor works in his or her own way. A professor's personal style as an advisor is, of course, connected closely to his personal style as a scholar and teacher. Hence, when we try to explain the sort of advisor that Jacob Katz was, we open a window through which we may observe Katz the scholar and teacher, and, indeed, Katz the human being.

In his autobiography, Katz addressed some of the questions raised above:

> The greatest reward for the academic scholar lies in the guidance of talented students, the scholars and teachers of the next generation. Such satisfaction, however, is dependent on two conditions: (a) that the teacher carefully choose the candidates and subjects of their research and (b) that he not be stingy with his time and guidance. As is well

known, not all university instructors fulfill these conditions. University folklore the world over is full of stories of students who followed in their teacher's shadow for years without having a well-defined topic of research or ever finishing their project. Other tales are told of mutual recriminations between teacher and student, of accusations of purloined information, and of jealousy and intrigue that threaten to topple the ivory tower of academe. I was saved from all of these.

Katz clearly regarded the guidance of doctoral students as a great privilege, a serious and highly responsible task. The advisor bears responsibility for seeing that the adventure known as "writing a dissertation" is successfully completed. A necessary precondition for this is willingness to invest the requisite time and attention. Another precondition is to insist upon accepting only capable students. On that matter, Katz wrote:

> My major rule of thumb was not to accept a research student without having first seen a written example of his ability to deal with a scholarly topic similar to that which he planned to write under my guidance. If he had not already done so, I asked him to do so. Only after I was convinced that he had the ability to understand the sources and apply them to historical research would I agree to accept the student.

Katz's view regarding the advisor's responsibility led him to another conclusion: it was not enough to test the student's scholarly skills; his scholarly bent also had to be compatible with that of the advisor:

> My criteria were not only the talents of a given candidate. A student might show ability to interpret the sources, but his inclination was methodological-philosophical and not historical-genetic. When this happened, I would advise the student to find another mentor from whose guidance he was likely to profit.

More than anything else, Katz was apprehensive about becoming involved with a student who dragged the writing of his dissertation on for years and years, never managing to complete it. There is no lack of such instances. Thus, it is not surprising that Katz, who usually was extremely modest, wrote:

> I was fortunate enough to have avoided all such mishaps. All my students succeeded, sooner or later, in completing their work.

For that reason Katz was scrupulous not to accept new doctoral students after he reached the age of eighty. He was afraid he would not live long enough to finish the task he had taken on.

So far, I have dwelled upon two conditions that Katz set: the scholarly skills of the student and the advisor's willingness to carry out his task faithfully.

Another condition whose importance Katz frequently emphasized was what he called "the viability of the project."

> An important condition for the success of any research is the viability of the project, and the responsibility for determining this falls on the advisor. A professor is free to grope for answers to a question that may prove to be unanswerable by the sources at hand. He is not free to assign a topic to a student without being reasonably certain that it can be done. For the same reason the subject must be carefully defined. Scouring the sources in the hope that a subject will take shape is not a profitable venture. Of course, a mature and independent scholar who peruses the sources is likely to find evidence for any number of issues. The beginning researcher, however, should focus his attention on proving the theses he has formulated.

The sharp distinction between the risks that an established scholar might take upon himself and those he may impose upon his students is typical of Katz's approach and expresses his view of the advisor's responsibility toward his student.

So far, we have presented Katz's own words about the dissertation advisor's task. Now let's look at the memories and impressions he left with his students in this capacity. The following remarks are based on conversations with Mordecai Breuer, Henry Wasserman, Michael Silber, Moshe Samet, Menahem Friedman, Benyamin Kedar, Sylvia Shinkolvski, Yosef Salmon, and Shaul Stampfer, as well as calling upon my own memories. Naturally this testimony is partial and suffers from the flaws typical of all personal memories of the distant past. Nevertheless, it seems to me that, taken together, it provides a reliable picture of Jacob Katz, the advisor.

Katz did not like holding abstract conversations with his students about their work. It is a fine thing to toss lovely ideas out into the air, but the true test of a young scholar is the text he produces. Katz always preferred to discuss a written chapter. Did the young scholar interpret the sources correctly? Did he get all he could out of them? Were his insights and conclusions convincing?

Katz was a very serious and systematic reader. He was attentive both to generalizations and to details, even marginal ones. His reading included examination of the primary sources upon which the writer based his work. The comments that he wrote in the margins of the work—usually in a handwriting that he, himself, found difficult to read—served as the basis for discussion. During that discussion Katz placed his skill as a reader of the sources and his methodological judgment at the student's disposal. Nevertheless, his readiness to help the student never involved an effort to intervene or to impose his own ideas or directions of thought on the student, against the student's own inclinations; Katz honored the student's autonomy.

Katz attributed a great deal of importance to the structure of the argument. He did not hesitate to ask a student to rewrite a chapter because it was poorly constructed. Style was another aspect to which Katz attributed great importance. He expected things to be written in a cautious and restrained style. Moshe Samet recalls that Katz asked him to rewrite some chapters because they were written in a rabbinical style. Samet adds that he had the impression that Katz was proud of having freed himself from rabbinical style and having achieved an academic style. In any event, the advisor and his student toasted the agreement to rewrite the chapters with a glass of brandy. Later we shall return to the role played by Jacob Katz's liquor cabinet.

Another flaw for which Katz would ask a student to rewrite a chapter was the exaggerated use of sociological jargon. This happened to Shaul Stampfer when he submitted the first chapter of his dissertation on the Yeshivot of Lithuania. Katz told him that if he really had something to say, he should say it in simple words; high-flown language was liable to make the content shallow. Menachem Friedman had received a similar comment several years earlier. In the course of a conversation with Katz about a certain scholarly issue, Menachem had used pompous sociological language. Katz responded by saying that if it was possible to explain things in human speech, there was no reason for using high-flown language. That response, Friedman says, has stayed with him to this day.

Thus, Katz was an exacting teacher. The demands he made of his students were similar to those he made of himself. However, his exacting nature never went so far as to create tension between the student and him or to insult the student. Mordecai Breuer seems to have hit the mark when he characterizes Katz as being able to balance strictness with cordiality toward his students.

Katz's main contribution as an advisor lay in the methodological judgment that he placed at the student's disposal. His systematic manner of thinking, his common sense, his controlled and cautious use of abstract concepts, his ability to see an individual case as the point of departure for a comprehensive and fundamental insight—all the traits that characterized his work as a scholar—were expressed also in his activity as an advisor. He was very helpful to a student even when the subject of the student's research was far from his own areas of specialization, for that same faculty of judgment and that systematic manner of thinking is applicable to any subject. This was the experience of Sylvia Shkolavsky, who, under Katz's guidance, wrote about the Zionist Movement in Argentina.

Michael Silber recalls that Katz wrote few comments in the margins of the chapters he had submitted to him. Nevertheless, Silber was deeply influenced by Katz, both by reading Katz's writings and from attending his classes. In this context Silber refers to a section of Katz's autobiography with which he identified. There Katz describes his first encounter with Karl Mannheim, when he was a student at the University of Frankfurt:

> Even while I was hearing the very first of his lectures, I sensed and decided that he was the man from whom I would be able to learn more than from any other person. Years later I realized that I was not the only one to whom this had happened.

What happened to Katz with Mannheim and to Silber with Katz also happened to other students of Katz's. By that I mean that they received the essence of their training in historical research from his seminars.

Katz's MA seminars were an inspiring experience. First of all, it was evident that its participants were usually the best students from the departments of Jewish history and sociology. Many would become prominent scholars, each in his or her own field. The high level of the participants ensured a high level of discussion, which centered on the historical issues that Katz, himself, was grappling with at the time. He never doubted the students' ability to approach these subjects and, in a certain sense, he made them partners in his research. Of course, the discussion centered on the historical interpretation of texts. Katz did not lecture. Rather, he encouraged discussion and motivated the students to think. After asking several members of the seminar for their opinions, he would summarize the discussion, making use of all that had been said. Nevertheless, his summaries always included something new and surprising, beyond what had occurred to the students. Katz was a teacher who sought to challenge his students.

Other traits that characterized his relation to his students were patience, tolerance, and intellectual integrity. When a student said something silly, Katz was patient and careful not to respond in a way that would insult the student. Instead, he would reformulate the student's words in a constructive manner, so that the student would realize, indirectly, that he had missed the point. Katz was willing to listen to and be tolerant of opinions contrary to his own. His intellectual integrity allowed him to admit an error, even when it was a student who had pointed it out. Benny Kedar reminded me of such instances.

Menachem Friedman, who for several years served as Katz's teaching assistant, sums up this experience: "Katz was a true teacher, who taught his students how to think. To this day I find myself wondering what would Katz think about a certain question." I have heard similar remarks from several of Katz's students.

An occasion everyone remembers with special pleasure was the gathering of all seminar participants in Katz's home at the end of the term—spouses were also invited. Everyone was given the feeling that he or she was not merely a student, but also a member of the family. In the course of those evenings, vehement arguments often arose. I remember one quite well: a strong difference of opinion about which institution was better, the yeshiva or the university. Menachem Friedman, who had spent years in yeshivot, attacked them sharply and showered praises upon the universities. He was countered by Haim Soloveitchik, who, as far as I know, had never attended a yeshiva but, nevertheless, defended the institution of the yeshiva with great enthusiasm, pointing out the weaknesses of the university.

These, then, are a few of the student memories of Jacob Katz's teaching. In his autobiography, Katz expressed his own ideas on the art of teaching:

> There are teachers who find th[e] obligation [of teaching] a burden, either because they lack pedagogic talents or because they begrudge the time away from their research. But such considerations never troubled me. My long years in high schools provided me with pedagogic experience that served me well when standing before university students. Nor does the contention that there is a conflict between teaching and research seem well founded. A teacher of the Hebrew University is given a free hand in choosing the topics of seminars so that he can engage the students in pursuing a subject that he himself is attempting to clarify. I took full advantage of this opportunity. Far from regarding instruction as an impediment to research I viewed it as the perfect opportunity to examine related issues via the free give-and-take with my students. Instruction brought me joy and satisfaction....I knew teachers who reached the professorial chair straight from the benches of the schoolroom, so old age found them totally bored with the routine of teaching. I, who began my academic career only in maturity, preserved my ability to view the duties of teaching as a challenge, new each day, year after year.

The task of the dissertation advisor does not end when the dissertation has been accepted and the student has received the yearned-for degree. Now the young scholar faces the question of his academic future, and the advisor is called upon to help. In this area Katz placed full trust in the selection processes of the academic world. He was pleased to write letters of recommendation whenever asked. However, he, himself, did not intervene behind the scenes. He never tried to pull strings, nor did he throw his entire weight behind his students to ensure their selection. Rather, he suggested that they should be patient, for, as he said, "in the end honor will come." In other words, ultimately the truly qualified people will win the race. This was how he spoke in the 1970s, when the universities in Israel, which were growing rapidly, were crying out for young teachers and when in the home of Shmuel

Ettinger, the strong man of the Department of Jewish History, fates were being decided for teaching appointments in Jerusalem and in the periphery.

Did Katz believe in all innocence that honor would come in the end? Perhaps he applied his own experience to his students: just as he himself had been accepted by the university on the strength of his academic achievements, so, too, his students would find their place by virtue of their academic achievements. Did he believe that a solicited letter of recommendation was preferable to unrequested intervention? Did he take this position because he wished to avoid power struggles whose outcomes could not be foreseen? I have no answer to these questions. In any event, Katz held firm to this approach.

Katz was a mentor of doctoral students for more than twenty-five years. The first two dissertations that he guided were approved in 1958; the last one was approved in 1985. Throughout those years Katz advised twenty doctoral students. In some cases Katz encouraged students to write about a subject related to his own research. Usually the students were attracted to other subjects; Katz would help them define the subject and limit the scope.

Perhaps the greatest tribute to Jacob Katz as a teacher and advisor is the large number of people who regard themselves as his students, although they did not write their dissertations under his guidance. These self-styled disciples include not only those who participated in his seminars or wrote seminar papers for him, but also students who entered the university after Katz had retired as a teacher. The secret of his influence on all these people can be explained, perhaps, by the methodological quality of his scholarship, which introduced to many new ways of thinking and investigation. So, too, Katz's home was always open to young and not-so-young scholars who sought his advice.

I remember Jacob Katz sitting in his regular place, in the corner of the sofa in his living-room. To his right was a small cabinet with several bottles of liquor. He never missed an opportunity to pour a glass of cognac for a guest and for himself, sometimes to toast the publication of a new book or in honor of a promotion, but usually for no special reason. Piled up on the coffee table before him were books, journals, off-prints of articles, and manuscripts. He was always reading something, usually material sent to him for his opinion. He used to invite young scholars whose work he had read, and he shared his impressions with them, commenting, disputing, but mainly encouraging. When the manuscripts or papers seemed worthy to him, he encouraged the authors to publish their work. He showed special interest in the students of his students, whom he fondly would refer to as "my grandchildren."

Katz was never sparing with praise, but it was always measured and balanced. His praise was valued, because he also never hesitated to express criticism. So, too, he would express gratitude to his students for what he had learned from them. The Midrashic saying "[I have learned] more from my students than from anyone" was especially apt when he wrote his book *A House Divided*. In his introduction, Katz mentions three students from whose work he had benefited. In addition to expressing gratitude, he expressed apprehension lest he might be thought of as a trespasser for dealing with a subject that they might treat in the future. The passage from the preface in which he discusses the connections between his students and him is particularly moving:

> I consider myself blessed by the good relationship between myself and my students. Most of them became colleagues and many [have become] close personal friends. God has granted me long years, but with old age comes loneliness, and several of my works in recent years have been dedicated to contemporaries who passed away. I dedicate this book to my students—long may they live—who fill the role of my contemporaries without allowing me to feel the generation gap that separates us.

Many of us now miss that special connection with a teacher who is also a friend and with a friend who is also a teacher.

I conclude with a story I told on another occasion about Jacob Katz's words to me at our last meeting. It was a Friday morning, two days before he entered the hospital for the operation from which he was never to recover. He was very weak from the illness that had been taking a severe toll for months, but, at the same time, he was as lucid as ever. He gave me instructions concerning the printing of his last book, remarking, "It's a good thing for a book when the author is no longer living." After a short pause he added with a wise and mischievous smile, "So that the critics can write without being afraid of praising a man to his face. But I'm not willing to die for that reason. Still, when I'm called, I'll be ready. When they call me, I'll be ready and waiting."

I believe that those last words express not only the sober wisdom of a man who knows that there is an end to all flesh, but also the recognition of having lived a full life, of having fittingly carried out his task in this world. Jacob Katz felt strong satisfaction for having faithfully fulfilled his obligation to his students.